Contemporary urban sociology

This book provides an up-to-date overview of issues and debates in contemporary urban sociology. It reviews critically each of the major theoretical orientations in the field, providing a brief historical introduction to each approach but emphasizing the current theoretical debate.

Classical urbanism and urban community theory, which investigate the effects cities have on the people who live in them, dominated the field during the first half of the twentieth century. The author juxtaposes these approaches and explains their lasting contribution to the field. Developed at the same time but along somewhat different lines, the urban ecology approach is concerned with spatial structure and the underlying patterns of cities. During the 1970s, political economy became the ascendant method in the field. This approach, described in Chapter 3, argues that global capitalism has the prime influence on the structure of cities. The final chapter describes the postmodern approach of the 1980s – which eschews grand theories and looks instead to local studies and the effect of deliberate human action – and its implications for the study of urban sociology.

Adherents of each of these methodologies contribute to the current debates within the field, making an overview volume all the more necessary.

Contemporary urban sociology

William G. Flanagan
Coe College

CAMBRIDGE
UNIVERSITY PRESS

Published by the Press Syndicate of the University of Cambridge
The Pitt Building, Trumpington Street, Cambridge CB2 1RP
40 West 20th Street, New York, NY 10011–4211, USA
10 Stamford Road, Oakleigh, Melbourne 3166, Australia

© Cambridge University Press 1993

First published 1993

Printed in the United States of America

Library of Congress Cataloging-in-Publication Data
Flanagan, William G.
Contemporary urban sociology / William G. Flanagan.
p.   cm.
Includes bibliographical references and index.
ISBN 0-521-36519-8. – ISBN 0-521-36743-3 (pbk.)
1. Sociology, Urban.   I. Title.
HT151.F52   1993   93-6588
307.76 – dc20   CIP

A catalog record for this book is available from the British
Library.

ISBN 0-521-36519-8 hardback
ISBN 0-521-36743-3 paperback

Contents

Acknowledgments

I would like to thank my friend and colleague, Josef Gugler, for the attention he gave earlier drafts of these chapters, and for the good advice he gave me on this and other projects. I am grateful to Lewis A. Coser for his support for the book. I am grateful also to David Diekema, Allen P. Fisher, and Ray Hutchison for their comments. The book has benefited from the critical suggestions of three anonymous reviewers.

The manuscript was much improved by the expert copyediting and production skills of Herbert A. Gilbert. Thanks to Rachael Winfree at Cambridge for her help and support.

I thank Coe College for support during various phases of the writing of the book. Thanks also go to Peggy Knott for coming to my rescue so often when I was tangled in my word processor.

I would also like to thank Michael Crowley, to whom I still owe dinner, for his generous and friendly services in time past.

Introduction

This book is about the study of cities. It deals primarily with ideas, the theoretical issues that characterize contemporary urban sociology, and their roots in the tradition of sociological thought. It is intended as a guide to understanding the conceptual tools social scientists have developed to explain the ways human settlements grow and change, the ways urban conditions affect and are affected by global political and economic developments, and the ways in which urban settings and the extensions of urban settings change people's thinking and modes of interaction.

Urban sociology embraces the most macrological and micrological concerns of sociology. Its subject matter is potentially limitless within the general framework of social science. The recurring challenge for those who identify their work as urban sociology is how to avoid merging with general sociology, while recognizing that the city limits are not a natural boundary for either social processes or sociological analysis. The preservation of a distinct domain of urban social science has become increasingly difficult over the course of the twentieth century. "The city, it seems, is destroyed by its own success. By the time ninety percent of the population are urban . . . the city, one says, has ceased to have any meaning in itself" (Ziolkowski 1986: 5).

Urban social science has never been completely successful in defining its object of study; in fact, there have been few formal efforts to do so. Cities, as enormously complex vortexes of multistranded causes and effects, apparently defy useful definition; there is simply too much to consider. Also, the urban form is a dynamic phenomenon that is constantly in transformation. At the beginning of the twentieth century, Max Weber (1905) chose the medieval town as the basis for his model of the truly urban form. He thus sought to avoid the problem of theoretical obsolescence by purposely selecting an already antiquated urban arrangement, discounting the superficially urban industrial and bureaucratic centers of his own time as regressive. If it had suited his purpose to describe the contemporaneous, expanding industrial metropolis, the

I

generalizations he might have proposed would nevertheless have become outdated.

Cities everywhere in the world have changed dramatically, even within the past three or four decades. Investment capital and population surge back and forth between urban centers, within and between nations, and among regions of the world. In the Third World, cities grow at enormous rates, the largest eclipsing in size the vast world cities of the industrialized West. In wealthy Western nations, metropolitan regions undergo perpetual transformation, simultaneously expanding and contracting as regional populations increase and urban populations within regions decentralize. Where others might choose to focus on the decisive role of investment opportunity and the restlessness of profit-seeking capital, Hall (1986: 138–40) emphasizes the role of technology in the progressive decentralization of urban areas. He notes that the cutting edge of industrial technology tends to locate at or beyond the metropolitan periphery of its day. At the turn of the century the "electro-technical" and motor vehicle industries in the Berlin region were based in satellite locations (in Wedding and Siemensstadt), around Paris (in Suresnes and Argenteuil), or on the periphery of the greater London area (in Hammersmith and Enfield). Today, the process of industrial-metropolitan expansion is extended in the locational tendencies of information-technology industries along Interstate highway 128 in the Boston region, Silicon Valley in California, and the M-4 corridor in southern England. Each of these is an extension of the metropolitan periphery, a continuation of the urban decentralization trend within growing metropolitan regions. The emerging urbanized forms are polycentric units, functional areas with a radius of perhaps 120 kilometers. They test the applicability of old, established categories of reference to settled urban life. They test the imagination as cohesive socio-spatial elements.

Despite the progressive expansion and deconcentration of the urban form from city to metropolis – "urbanized region," "functional urban area," or megalopolis – and despite the fact that urban organization and cultural influence have become ubiquitous features of contemporary society, urbanization remains a nucleated process. In our efforts to understand social change, our attention is invariably drawn to the center of sprawling urban regions where power is concentrated and exercised, even as our efforts to comprehend change at the center is drawn outward by the fact that the most powerful urban agents must react to conditions in a global field of action.

There is thus a centeredness to the spatial dimension of social processes that provides urban sociology with its topical focus. Yet, the behavioral, political, and economic processes we want to deal with are not confined to a given urban arena, or even to urban places in general. Urban soci-

ology has contained a riddle since its inception, a kind of epistemologi-
cal mystery that demands to be addressed the more difficult it becomes
to identify the sprawling "urban" as a "place." The nominal identifying
feature of urban sociology is a geographic rather than sociological object:
Urban sociology is a sociology identified with place rather than with a
unit of social organization. However, in practice, those who study
processes that have urban dimensions are most often examining social
phenomena that are rooted in, but not spatially contained within the
city. Analysis draws the attention of urban sociologists beyond the city
proper. Local events at the neighborhood level need to be understood
as extensions of global events, however they might be modified by specific local histories and agents.

The point is that there is an inherent strain between the nominal identity (urban locality) of the discipline and wider fields of action that must
provide the ultimate context for all sociological analysis (global processes). It may be that the strain is a historical artifact, a product of the
fact that the sociology of the spatial dimension of social organization
emerged at a time when *the city* was the most dramatic and popularly
available spatial manifestation of social change, drawing the attention
of Weber (1905), Simmel (1905), Park (1915), and others. Since that
time, at the turn of the century, we have been stuck with a label that
does not fit the analytic context within which sociologists of space work.
The focus of urban sociology remains anchored or accentuated in important ways in the largest and most densely populated centers. To this
extent the "urban sociology" label remains pertinent. When we search
for ways to characterize the centralized, spatial dimensions of powerful
political and economic forces we sometimes find ourselves using terms
like "Manhattanization" or "Los Angelesization." But when we try to
understand changes taking place in Manhattan, Los Angeles, Aberdeen,
or Houston we refer to the global context. To grasp and become comfortable with this tension between place and wider processes is the first
step in understanding the business of contemporary urban sociology.

Many contemporary urban sociologies

There is a broad array of themes that have drawn the attention of
social philosophers and scientists to the city. Some have been interested in
the experience and behavior of the individual, others in the structural role
of cities in the broad historical sweep of change. Urban study includes all
the implied intermediate subject matters. The field of urban sociology acknowledges that cities are arenas of behavior, dynamic elements of social
ecology, backdrops for the human search for meaningful social ties,

gameboards on which powerful players compete for greater profits while the less powerful struggle to use the same space to make a living and raise families. Urban arenas are the modern battleground for the class struggle, and an incubator for social problems that provide the focus for a range of social movements. Cities constitute a socially defined environment that helps shape the choices that individuals make, choices that in turn continuously create and alter that environment. The questions that engage the attention of urban sociologists are broadly divergent.

As in the case of other specialized fields of sociology, the diverse subject matters of urban sociology have generated further subdivisional specializations. A single, narrow aspect of urban issues is quite enough to provide a lifetime of study for any one individual. Subdivisions within specialized fields develop their own conceptual and methodological traditions. The theme "urban study" has proven sufficiently general to have preserved a good measure of diffuseness and insularity. It is not an exaggeration to state that there are several urban sociologies. Add to this the fact that researchers and theorists in other disciplines – anthropology, geography, history, political economy – are often engaged in work that is indistinguishable from the interests of urban sociologists. Despite recent signs of convergent thinking among some urban scientists, contemporary urban sociology remains a heterogeneous mix of issues and approaches.

In an overview and assessment, such as the one presented in this book, it is necessary to treat all approaches critically and seriously: It would be inappropriate to neglect any widely practiced mode of urban analysis. None of the various paradigms that have emerged since the turn of the century is dead. Although Burgess's (1925) concentric zones and Wirth's (1938) urbanism thesis have been subject to more than a half century of vigorous criticism, the chapters in this book will indicate that these authors' work still provide the basis for contemporary studies. Contemporary urban sociology includes many new conceptual developments that depart in fundamental ways from the earlier body of ideas, but it also embodies an amalgam of extensions, debates, and reexamined issues rooted in the conceptual forms of the early days when the city captured the imagination of the leading students of society.

The objective in the following chapters has been to provide a brief introduction to the historical roots of each of the major approaches to urban sociology, followed by an interpretation and assessment of the most recent developments. Chapter 1 reviews and brings up to date discussions of urbanism and urban community. A surprising amount of contemporary urban sociology implicitly or explicitly addresses the old controversies. Historically, much of what has been done in the name of urban sociology in the United States has been to juxtapose the alleged, socially atomizing influence of urban organization against the unifying experience of neighborhood and community. The implied polar opposition admits to many possible outcomes, and these are explored in the first chapter. The isolating effects that Simmel and Wirth associated with the metropolis and urbanism still provide background assumptions for some current work: the concept of "community," both the uprooted and neighborhood versions, in the community-studies tradition, continues to undergo empirical and theoretical reexamination; the conceptual innovations of subculture (Fischer 1975, 1982) and social network provide new avenues of investigation; the ethnic dimension of urban community has entered a new generation of empirical study, with new waves of ethnic migration, and arguments over assimilation patterns that once again address critically the work of Park (1926a) and Burgess (Park and Burgess 1921). The new questions of community have threads that tie local analysis to structural political economy, relating as they do to the informal economy and global economic change. The empirical emphases of the most recent trends in urban analysis (discussed in Chapter 5) suggest that locality studies, especially those tied to economic change and questions of local political efficacy, will retain a prominent place in urban sociology. In that chapter the same conclusion is suggested by the renewed emphasis on the issue of human agency.

Urban ecology, as a distinctive subdivision of urban studies, has undergone a variety of transformations since Park (1915) suggested the outlines of such an approach. Chapter 2 reviews the development of this self-consciously distinct approach and its logical extensions in the work of contemporary urbanologists. Since the work of Harris and Ullman (1945), ecologists have largely abandoned efforts to discover a general model of urban ecology. Yet, contemporary researchers are still drawn to comment on whether the underlying pattern of the particular city they are studying suggests concentric zones, wedges, or a star-shaped development. There is a weight to classical models that carries over into the contemporary era of ecological study, lending an air of substance to what at times might otherwise be simply descriptive work.

Ecology remains an important component of contemporary urban study. Its division into two branches during the 1950s produced opposite emphases. The empiricist branch culminated in a collection of largely descriptive factorial ecologies. The theoretical branch, embodied in the functionalism of Hawley (1950, 1986), became increasingly remote from urban concerns per se. In the most recent decades, those who refer to their work as ecology have regrouped loosely around borrowed issues of political economy and the reemerging vogue of community studies. Gans (1984: 279–80) has associated the work of neoecologists with the conservative political and intellectual backlash of the late 1970s in the United States, noting that ecologists were heavily concentrated in the expanding universities of the Sunbelt. Their location in regions characterized by expanding, urban-based economies, he reasoned, would give them sufficient reason to harbor positive and optimistic attitudes regarding the benefits of market forces. As Chapter 2 points out, contemporary model building that finds international convergence in patterns of urban expansion and change is essentially equilibrial, and heir to the assumptions of ecology. Whether urban ecology can be tied to the assumptions of political economy and remain ecology is an open question.

Chapter 3 addresses the major, urban-related issues of the political economy of wealthy nations. In Europe and the United States the ongoing restructuring of national and international economies clearly has spatial dimensions, and has produced convulsive episodes of change in local economies. The political economy paradigm, which had a powerful and irreversible impact on urban social theory beginning with the 1970s, has largely been responsible for redirecting the attention of urban analysts away from local arenas of action, and toward a consideration of global economic structure. During the seventies, Marxism briefly flourished as a focused, critical challenge to a sociology that had become caught up in static debates that failed either to predict or address major urban changes occurring during that decade. Marxism questioned the relevance of existing approaches to economically troubled and strife-ridden urban environments. Questions of class struggle and social justice posed by the Marxists are today a more central part of the study of cities than they were prior to the seventies. However, the political economy perspective has become a more diffuse agenda of issues since the decline of declared urban Marxism. Urban political economy today is marked simply by a concern with the larger picture of economic change. Local change remains, in this view, a product of global events. Relatedly, political economy retains a normative concern with economic policy and social policy issues. In practice it continues to be ideologically to the political left, certainly in contrast to urban ecology, maintaining a fundamental mistrust of the way benefits and disadvantages are distributed under market economies.

The urban sociology of the Third World, the focus in Chapter 4, has until recently remained outside of the mainstream of urban sociological concerns. Theoretical developments that have taken place within the past twenty years have begun to draw Third World studies into the mainstream. In the area of Third World development studies, Wallerstein's (1974) world-system paradigm accentuates the dependency argument that links First World and Third World economies within a common system of development and underdevelopment. World-system theory, however, does not interpret the relative status of First and Third World nations as fixed by history, and permits a fluid interpretation of relative First and Third World advantages (as in the area of labor pools). The implications are sufficient to draw the attention of social scientists in the "core" nations to changes in the "periphery." Two decades of discussion of the urban political economy of wealthy nations has drawn attention to global issues where the interests and futures of wealthy and poor nations overlap. The process of restructuring itself, especially in the export of industrial operations to poor nations, has had the effect of making Third World development issues appear a much less exotic topic to urban specialists in wealthy nations.

There are some suggestions that traditional concerns of Third World urban sociology, such as urban primacy, may be productively reconceptualized as international rather than domestic issues. We have learned that it is improper to consider the informal economy a topic of interest only to students of the Third World, and that the informal sectors (unprotected labor) of both First and Third World economic systems are fundamentally the same issue (Castells and Portes 1989). It is suggested that the controversy over the concept "overurbanization," as it has been applied to Third World cities, might be extended to the oversupply of urban labor in deindustrializing economies.

The concluding chapter examines the emphasis on localism and agency that has threatened to overwhelm other issues in the practice of urban sociology during the past decade. Under the influence of Anthony Giddens and others, the 1980s represented a reaction against what was seen as the overdeterminism of either equilibrial or (especially) political economy models that posited the inexorability of global forces, but were unable to predict outcomes in specific localities. To the extent that local conditions vary among cities that are similarly situated with reference to global economic forces, differences in outcome must be the result of historical and cultural circumstances specific to those localities and, as well, due to deliberate human action, or *agency*. The agency thesis reminds us that people, not society or economy, are the actors that move events, that actors must choose, and that choice always means that alternative results are possible.

The focus of debate in urban science is thereby changed again. To what extent are social (urban) actors constrained in their choices by international events that shape local conditions by flooding local real estate development markets with capital, or by withdrawing it? That propel tides of new immigrants to particular cities? That require industrial capital to seek bargain labor in order to remain competitive? To what extent will local elites or common citizens be able to prevail against the forces of the world political economy, and to what extent are those global forces amenable to change by local responses? These are the questions that stand at the center of the debate in contemporary urban sociology. Chapter 5 concludes with a critical discussion of the implications of a movement away from structural principles.

The purpose of this book is to provide an overview of the conceptual debates in contemporary urban sociology, as well as some background to these debates. Descriptions of urban conditions and particular cities are a secondary concern, and they enter the discussion usually as illustrations in the form used by the particular theorist under review. However, a more descriptive excursus can often focus or illuminate the abstracting tendencies of debate. Each chapter concludes with a brief essay entitled "Managing Urban Lives." (This section is placed somewhat earlier in Chapter 5.) These describe a major dimension of the contemporary urban environment. The descriptions focus on a particular problem faced by some element of an urban population, and invite further consideration of conceptual issues raised in the book. The topics that receive attention are, in order, street gangs, gentrification, deindustrialization, the informal economy, and an assessment of the "dual city" hypothesis. Each of these sections focuses on one or more cities and involves an extended discussion of a limited number of studies. Together these illustrations suggest a common underlying theme. Many of the problems found in different cities throughout the world are linked by the common process of worldwide economic change that creates or withdraws opportunities in the formal economy and thus effects the conditions of participation and the life chances in every city.

Trends in urban sociological thought

It is possible to identify two trends that characterize the conceptual movement of urban sociology, one long-term, and the other the most recent phase of the long-term trend. The first involves a sequential alternation between theoretical and empirical emphases that has marked the development of urban sociology from the early decades of the century to the present. The second is the current episode of the long-term trend. In the current phase, the empirical "correction" has set in before the implications of the preceding theoretical movement (the global political economy or world-system model) had been fully explored. The current empirical trend toward locality and agency issues is taking place at the same time that the world-system model and its implications for urban social science are still being aggressively explored and developed. Although many speak of the potential complementarity of the two, the potential for local empirical emphases to contribute to global theory remains to be demonstrated, as the empirical emphases on the locally unique and the theoretical emphasis on the pulverizing forces of the international system pull contemporary work in opposite directions.

For the first four decades of this century urban social thought was dominated by various theoretical strands that argued that urban life produced a profound alienation. The theme culminated in Wirth's (1938) famous "urbanism" thesis. The next several decades saw the publication of many case-study monographs sandwiched between Whyte's (1943) *Street Corner Society* and the republication of Gans's (1962) *The Urban Villagers*. These monographs offered proof that people who lived in cities retained a strong sense of community and social participation. Efforts to model urban life in the abstract and ideal typical sense were thus "corrected" by empirical work that demonstrated strong exceptions to the alienation and "mass society" model. During the 1970s the whole discussion about the true nature of urban culture was overturned by the Marxist accusation that the (North American) issues featured in the argument were at best irrelevant to the political–economic crisis of the cities. The further development of the political economy paradigm demonstrated that theoretical concerns having to do with social space needed to be broadened to the regional or global level in order to address the ultimate sources of change. International capitalism, the economic rationalization of the globe into a single market, was the moving force that created local conditions and provided the necessary starting point for understanding what was going on at the local level. Today there is, once again, a growing emphasis on empiricism and locality that stems from the realization that global levels of analyses will not produce an understanding of locally variable conditions. Past trends have involved the alternation of theoretical and empirical emphases. In this light it appears that the most recent emphases on empirical study and local conditions is a predictable reaction to a brief era dominated by the theoretical generalizations of political economy where remote forces were argued to determine local outcomes. If the empirical documentation of exceptional cases and examples of local autonomy were all that contemporary urban sociology had to offer, the historical significance of the current trend for the development of urban social science would be limited.

However, the present trend represents more than a predictable change in fashion from theory to empiricism within urban sociology. It is linked to a philosophical movement that extends beyond the confines of social science, and raises questions within sociology about the premise upon which much sociological theory is based. The growing emphases on empiricism and localism is a reaction to what are interpreted as overly deterministic theories, theories that emphasize the power of social structure over individual choice. Because we cannot answer, with reference to global political and economic forces, the question of why one community prospers while another, similarly situated with regard to the international economy or world system, stagnates or develops in a different manner, structural interpretations of society fail in application to the local level. In this view it is obvious that local variables can sometimes override the effects of global circumstances, and that we must include among the relevant considerations of how change is determined the choices made by local elites and average citizens.

Although contemporary urban sociology retains its eclectic character, the movement within its various subdivisions toward an empiricist and localist style is clear. At the same time that this movement reflects a frustration with the heavy-handed determinism of formal theory within urban science, it reflects also the popular, postmodern philosophy that represents a retreat from formal, rigid models of interpretation in every academic, artistic, and human service field. Within urban sociology, Hawley's functionalist ecology and the political economy of the world system offer easy targets. Harvey (1987: 262), given his enduring attachment to Marxism and persuasive interpretations of the role of capital accumulation and class conflict, is predictably not wholly swayed by the arguments of postmodernism (he notes that postmodern thought means a retreat from Marxism within the social sciences, for both political and intellectual reasons). Harvey nevertheless offers a useful characterization of the implications of postmodernist movement: It advances the principle of eclecticism (derived directly from the field of architecture where the movement achieves physical expression), the deconstruction of structuralist interpretation, the abandonment of theory for empiricism, and a softening of the edges of science-as-fact – in the appreciation that all that we see and say is subjective ("the impenetrability of the 'other' and the reduction of all meaning to a 'text'").

The greatest tension in urban sociology today is between the theoretical orientations of the global structuralists and the research orientations of the local idealists. It has displaced or subsumed the debates between the culturalists and the structuralists, or between the ecologists and political economists. The movement within urban sociology toward localism and empiricism is consistent with the postmodern impulse toward emphases on the unique, the openness of interpretation, and the application of theory with a light touch. Rather than interpretations that depict elites working together in opposition to other classes, current research emphasizes the conflicts that exist among various categories of elites, and allows for the possibility that they often work in opposition to each other (Gottdiener and Feagin 1988; Logan and Molotch 1987).

The response of citizens at the grassroots is not posed in class terms, but finds average citizens working together in various coalitions in a variety of citizen action groups, neighborhood organizations, and social movements (Castells 1983). Given the assumption of the efficacy of local elites and local citizens, urban political economy becomes an empirical question of pluralistic, popular participation.

But despite the convergence of interest toward the local at the moment, a theoretical counter-trend has over the past two and a half decades inspired a different kind of paradigmatic shift in urban science, and has provided the impetus for the localist backlash. This is the quietly growing acceptance that the global context, the international marketplace, the world system collectively is the ultimate unit of analysis, the context within which all change has come to be understood (Flanagan 1993). This system is the remote, enormously powerful structure that provides localities, elites, citizen coalitions, and ordinary individuals with their agendas and their challenges. The primacy of the global analytic context is widely accepted and has provided the background assumption even for breakaway ecologists who, during the past decade, have attempted to incorporate the concerns of global political economy, shifting from intraurban to intcrurban analysis.

We thus find contemporary urban sociology characterized by two counter-trends. One governs innovations in empirical work, the other operates at the level of theory. The natural impulse is to consider the possibility of synthesis. Synthesis of the localist and globalist orientations is both desirable and very difficult here. In Chapter 5 we examine the contributions of Giddens (1981, 1984, 1985, 1989) to an integration of idealist and structuralist elements; however, Giddens departs sufficiently from the conventional interpretation of structure to leave the potential for synthesis open to question.

The localist movement embraces idealist philosophical principles that are antithetical to the structuralist premise at the root of global theories of change. This means that any integration of findings and theory would tend to be more fundamentally eclectic than synthetic, a problem that is explored in Chapter 5. We are for now left with diverging convergences in urban sociology. Rather than pulling the field of study apart, it appears that the oppositional forces consist of weaker and stronger elements. The stronger trend lies in the growing tacit agreement that the urban environment is primarily a physical manifestation of international capitalism. Even those who emphasize the importance of local history and initiative recognize that what they are describing is the ability of local variables to harness, modify, or withstand political–economic factors that are remote in their origins. The vogue of the empirical case study, on the other hand, appears as the weaker trend. Although such studies are vital to understanding fully the variability of the impact of global market forces on localities, an emphasis on the uniqueness of outcomes misses the point.

Local studies are appealing to the urban sociologist because they reaffirm the importance of the urban environment itself as a unique conditioning agent of social, political, and economic processes. To the extent that local environments demonstrate causal properties, urban sociology has an exclusive domain of study. To the extent localities are the intensified arenas of the world-wide political economy, the domain of urban sociology remains an ambiguous component of aspatial social science. The latter seems to be the more viable interpretation. In the chapters that follow we move from a focus on the urban environment as an exclusive arena that contains and conditions social action, to an interpretation of the urban factor as an element in a global web of political and economic change.

1

Contemporary theories of urbanism and community

Urban sociology emerged at the end of the nineteenth century, at about the same time that sociology itself was achieving a greater measure of distinction among the social sciences. The same features of the changing world provided the impetus for the development of both general sociological principles and for the development of a branch of social science devoted to the study of cities. The social consequences of the industrial revolution raised important philosophical questions about the future condition of humanity: Foremost among these was the question of how the massing of people in cities would affect the social order. It was largely the growth of the eighteenth- and nineteenth-century city, within the wider economic changes that were taking place in the world, that fostered the development of sociology and encouraged the development of urban sociology in particular.

The central question for the precursors of contemporary urban sociology was what would become of the cohesive mechanisms that had maintained the rural social order. In a word, what would become of "community" in a new urban world? What impact would urbanization have on the integrity of preexisting forms of social organization? The tension between city and community has remained a central issue in urban sociology. Although the last two or three decades witnessed a significant expansion of the scope of the discipline, as outlined in the Introduction, there is still a substantial share of urban sociology devoted to the question of how the urban setting modifies the way people think and behave. This is the tradition from which urban sociology has evolved, both in the sense that the tradition has provided a foundation for the development of various interpretations of "urbanism," and in the sense that it provides a target for criticism from various quarters today.

The following several pages briefly introduce the most central classical statements in urban sociological tradition. These provide the basis for the remainder of the chapter which focuses on more recent work, work which builds on the apparent tension between the classical "urbanism" thesis and various urban-community themes. The picture that emerges is that of a multifaceted urban reality, where there is room for a variety of characterizations of the urban environment: alienating, homey, or the city as a richly inviting variety of subcultures.

In recent years urban sociology has moved in the direction of the analysis of broad-scale political and economic analysis. The question of whether cities are best characterized as emotionally alienating or culturally enriching environments is now only one of many issues that compete for attention. Nevertheless, many researchers remain interested in questions of urban alienation and the nature of social ties in the city. In order to understand more fully the nature of urban cultures and behaviors, we need to expand our frame of analysis beyond the neighborhood or city, and address the global economic changes that shape neighborhoods and cities, which in turn shape experience. The underlying theme in this chapter is that the study of urbanism and the various forms of urban community introduced here needs to incorporate more explicitly than in the past the economic basis of urban styles and urban community change. Following the lead of the changing field of urban science, the chapters that follow move progressively away from a focus on the urban experience and the nature of social ties in the city. Yet these are the questions that draw so many students intuitively to the study of cities.

The tension between city and community

During the nineteenth century, rapid change, including the growth of cities, inspired social philosophers to speculate about how the emerging social order would differ from that of the past. Their conclusions have furnished some of sociology's most basic, classic generalizations. Tönnies's ([1887] 1940) well-known observations regarding *Gemeinschaft* and *Gesellschaft* have provided generations of social scientists with a basis for distinguishing between the essences of rural and urban life. Rural life is dominated by group identity, *Gemeinschaft,* the condition of being subordinate to the group. It is a challenge to the imagination of the contemporary student to envision the individual primarily as a fragment of a solidarity. *Gesellschaft,* the opposed condition of being on one's own in the world appears, on the other hand, to be a description of the familiar, the taken for granted. The observations that people operate as individuals, on the basis of self-interest, that each person seeks to profit from interaction, appear today no more than simple descriptive statements, not theoretical speculations. The aspect of Tönnies's thesis that we doubt today is his extrapolation: The dominant motive of self-interest insures that each person is truly alone. Like many that followed him,

Tönnies did not provide individuals with a private sphere in which they might cultivate meaningful and rich social ties.

Durkheim's (1893) classical formulation, contrasting *mechanical* and *organic solidarity,* has for a century reinforced the spirit of Tönnies's bipolar distinction. For Durkheim, rural or peasant life is characterized by a unity of values and vision, as the members of every peasant household experience roughly the same set of circumstances and cycles during the course of their lives. The result of common experience is the unity of ideas expressed in a collective consciousness, in a mechanical solidarity. This social condition cannot obtain in the city. In the city, the density of population demands occupational specialization, hence breaks down the unity formed of common experience, and creates in its place an order based on functional interdependence among people engaged in specialized work. People don't identify with each other, instead they depend on one another to serve the many needs of the populace. In the case of both Tönnies and Durkheim, the moral order of common values in a preurban society is replaced by an instrumental order in an urban society.

Max Weber (1905) is prominent among those who have pointed out that cities are, above all else, marketplaces. Yet, for him, market relations did not undermine social cohesion, but accentuated it. What sets Weber's work apart is that he chose the preindustrial city as most closely approximating the ideal-typical model of urban life and organization. For Weber, what distinguished truly urban life was that all the city's residents were dependent for their very existence on the marketplace and the daily exchange of goods and services. The city was an elaborate system of exchange, residents naturally acquired a sense of allegiance to that economic arena, were prepared to contribute to its defense (literally) against outsiders, and true cities were at least partially autonomous political units. The city, through the consciousness of its citizens (burghers), had a sense of itself, was constituted to regulate and administer on behalf of the interests of its business classes; it was a rational, corporate unity.

Weber thought that such cities captured the potential of human achievement and gave it expression. Yet he saw the promise of the city fading in his own time. The characteristic rationalism of the twentieth century pushed aside the spiritual and cultural essence of the urban promise, as cities became the dense and frantic manifestations of the bureaucratic organization of industrial society. The cities of the Renaissance might be called true urban communities, engines of culture and learning: The industrial city represented the simple massing of populations, human aggregations, where efficient administration according to the bureaucratic model was the goal. All that was left of the ideal city was the unifying self-interest of the marketplace. This idea is at the core of the legacy of classical theory for urban sociology.

Life in the faceless metropolis

The rapid growth of cities during the industrial revolution had intensified the misgivings that social and moral commentators in Western nations had long felt about the impact of living in cities. In both the popular imagination and in social theory, the city was understood to undermine moral values and to weaken social ties.

During the first half of the twentieth century, popular writers and critics were divided over the question of the impact of urbanization on the quality of life. This division of opinion and the changing conditions of the cities themselves contrasted with the best-known commentaries of the last century. The dreary images of nineteenth-century coketowns in Dickens's fiction are more than matched by the descriptions of Manchester from Engels (1845) and Tocqueville (1835). By the turn of the century the image of the city had not improved much. Lincoln Steffens (1904) warned of the moral evils rooted in the political power and economic temptations of the cities in the United States, and Charles Booth (1902) chronicled the desperate conditions of the poor in England. In the decades that followed, there continued to be much critical writing that dwelt on the negative consequences of living in cities, but it was not so single-minded as the social criticisms that had appeared earlier. Despite Weber's indictment of the deadening rationalization of urban life, the evolving cities of the twentieth century had, after all, become more hospitable environments, at least with regard to the material conditions under which most people lived.

The generations of social scientists and social commentators that came of age in the twentieth century were the products of an urban environment. Many had lost the capacity to be awed by that sheer physical presence. Yet the social impact of the city remained an issue for probably just as many others. British writers worried about the potential for political and social revolution, the breathless pace of life, the monotony and the squalor that some associated with cities. George Orwell, for example, commented on the festering, planless chaos of the city, on the one hand, and on what he saw as the prisonlike atmosphere that resulted from planning to control the urban environment and make it more orderly, on the other. For many French writers, Paris in the first decades of the 1900s may have been a modern-day Athens, only on a grander scale; yet others raised the question of whether Paris had grown too large, an arrogant monster that devoured resources that rightfully belonged to the rest of the country. German writers during the 1920s and 1930s regarded favorably the cultural achievements that attached to the great cities, but split along political lines in their concern about the social implications of continued growth. Artists and writers on the political left pointed to injustice, corruption, and the focused excesses of capitalism that were found in cities. Moderates worried about growing congestion and housing shortages. The ascendant National Socialist right was concerned about political drift to the Marxist left in urban areas, remarking ominously about the "biological decline" that they saw resulting from the mixing of "races" in cities (Lees 1985: 259–88).

Sociologists working in the first half of the twentieth century on theories of city life emphasized the alienating aspects of the urban environment. The two outstanding examples of this position were, in Germany, Georg Simmel's (1905) essay "The Metropolis and Mental Life," and, in the United States, Louis Wirth's (1938) essay "Urbanism as a Way of Life."

Simmel is important because he distinguished between the two basic features of urban life that were understood to shape human behavior. First, the crowded and bustling social environment itself caused people to retreat within themselves, to develop a capacity to ignore what went on around them. He argued that it was necessary for people who lived in cities to develop this capacity in order to maintain their sanity. The second compelling feature of the urban environment was the reduction of human motives to a question of cost. In Simmel's view, urban life is a series of exchanges in which each person asks, What will I get out of this? How much will it cost me? The consequences of emotional strain and impersonal interaction are that aversion and calculation are the distinguishing social features of the metropolis. In every sense, people cannot afford to care about one another.

Wirth (1938) incorporated Simmel's point of view as well as those of Tönnies, Durkheim, Weber, and others in his effort to develop a full "theory" of urban life. His much criticized essay on the combined sociological effects of the *size, density*, and *heterogeneity* of urban populations remains an elegant attempt to model the gross consequences of the urban environment. Together, those three factors conditioned the nature of social interaction. An increase in the size of a given population means that relationships become segmented and specialized, and remain superficial. Second, the high population densities that characterize urban life mean that not only people's roles, but also the various physical areas within the city, become specialized. Wirth's teacher, Robert Park (1915; 1929), had described the ecology of urban space as a mosaic of isolated social or moral worlds, each with its own distinctive code of conduct. The principle of heterogeneity was based on the fact that cities contained a wide variety of cultural and class characteristics, and generated or reinforced social differences by promoting occupational specialization. People who lived in cities found it hard to identify with one another and were more than content to allow relationships to remain at the superficial and instrumental level.

Together, Simmel and Wirth, but especially Wirth, set the tone for subsequent sociological interpretations of the consequences of urban life. People in the city are wary, alienated, manipulative, and aversive. Relationships tend to be predominantly superficial and secondary in nature. Urbanites lead isolated existences. This vision squared with much of the popular interpretation of what cities did to people. Contemporary social scientists are largely wary of the one-dimensional character of these early antiurban formulations. Yet, as we will see in the section "Current Trends in Urban Community Research," classical assumptions regarding alienated urbanites both guide and are supported by contemporary investigation. However, they provide only a partial picture of the urban experience.

The urban community studies tradition

The image of the urban way of life reflected in sociological theory was contradicted, almost from the beginning, by the evidence uncovered by researchers doing fieldwork in cities. Wirth (1927) himself had described close ties and a richly communal social life that characterized Chicago's Jewish ghetto in the 1920s. William Foote Whyte's (1943) study of the close-knit Italian-American community in Boston's North End followed close on the heels of Wirth's urbanism essay, and came to enjoy a prominent place in urban sociology roughly equivalent to Wirth's famous essay, their contrary emphases notwithstanding.

Study after study in the emerging tradition of "urban community studies" during the 1950s showed that cities contained neighborhoods where people felt a strong sense of place, where they felt they belonged, and where they were involved with their neighbors, especially with family members who lived close by. These studies focused on working-class areas of the city. Gans's (1962) *The Urban Villagers* depicted second- and third-generation Italians living in a soon-to-be-razed neighborhood, enjoying a set of close social relationships centered on kin. Members of these "peer groups" expressed a strong sense of attachment to other group members and their local place of residence. Kinship also provided the main channel for social life in East London. Young and Willmott (1957) uncovered a matrifocal system of social cohesiveness among this working-class population. Adult daughters with families of their own were closely tied to their mothers. Families tended to remain locally based, generation after generation.

Suttles (1968) has argued that it is the locality, itself, that provides a basis for social cohesion and neighborhood identification in the city. Although the "Addams Area" (a fictitious name) that he studied in Chicago contained a number of different ethnic groups (Blacks, Italians, Mexicans, and Puerto Ricans), and although there were tensions among these groups within the area, a common sense of "turf" or a propri- etary sentiment caused these groups to unite in response to any threat from outside the area.

Hunter and Suttles (1972) have summarized the work of others into a useful fourfold schema for classifying different types of urban "com- munity" according to size and the degree of attachment experienced by their residents. The sense of attachment tends to be inversely related to the size of the space and the size of the population in question: the smaller the size of the unit, the higher the degree of territorial identifi- cation. The "face block" may be as small as a section of street a city block or less in length. Here there is a high degree of mutual recogni- tion among residents. The "defended neighborhood," where residents have come to recognize their common territorial interests in response to some encroaching, threatening force from outside, might extend to several city blocks. The "community of limited liability," an area that is perceived to have some distinguishing characteristic that sets it apart from adjoining areas, may be characterized by more or less uniform property values, a comprise school district, or it may possess some other thematic feature. An even broader area, the "expanding community of limited liability," occurs wherever an extensive area of a city is com- monly referred to, officially or unofficially, by a generally understood label: the Southwest Quadrant, the Lower East Side (Manhattan), the East End (London).

Each of the areas distinguished by Hunter and Suttles is contained within or overlaps each larger spatial unit. Logically, any given indi- vidual may identify with any or all of these territorial units. The useful- ness of these spatial designations is indicated by their common usage in contemporary research.

Is urban space an important sociological variable?

To this point we have reviewed two kinds of argument about the capacity of physical space to affect social life. First, there is the position that environmental factors, such as population size and density, attenu- ate social ties that are characteristic of smaller and more dispersed popu- lations. Second, there is the contrary, empirically derived argument that community ties of various sorts are capable of withstanding the disinte- grating effects of large, dense population centers.

Herbert Gans (1962) suggested a third possibility. This is that the nature of the urban environment is not so important as other, established sociological factors, such as social class, in determining the life experiences of people who happen to live in cities. He maintains that the urbanism proposition is weakened by the fact that there are not one but a number of conditions of urban living. There are a large number of alienated and isolated souls in the city, but the urban population also includes artists and intellectuals who live in the city because they love it, as well as other categories of persons attracted by urban living. The most isolated and alienated people of the city are the poor, the trapped, and the downwardly mobile segments of the urban population. Their alienation and isolation has more to do with their economic place in society than it does with the fact that they live in cities. An analysis of the size, density, and heterogeneity of their surroundings adds little to an understanding of their condition.

A second line of argument that questions whether urban *space* is an important independent variable is directed at the urban community studies contention that urban neighborhoods continue to be an important focus of social life. What basis is there for assuming that residential neighborhood provides the key organizing force for urban social relationships? It is reasonable to assume that people will have some social contact with their neighbors and will also be involved with people outside of the neighborhood with whom they share common interests.

This important assumption is made in Claude Fischer's (1975, 1984) "subcultural theory of urbanism." Fischer finds in the city a vital force for amplifying cultural experience and human creativity, for generating both genius and deviance. It is the sheer size of urban populations, their "critical mass," that provides a fertile soil for the cultivation of ideas. The critical mass hypothesis says that larger populations provide individuals who have a shared interest with a base for establishing rewarding social ties for collectively pursuing, enhancing, and articulating those interests. In large population pools, individuals can find others of like mind with whom to share their ideas, to accompany and encourage them as they indulge their particular (or peculiar) tastes, together to experiment, expand, and innovate their esoteric, unconventional, avant-garde interests.

Fischer's observations reflect an important change in the way students of the city have come to see urban social organization. We may accept that Wirth and the empirical community studies tradition have told us something important about the nature of the urban experience, but it is time to move beyond these limited views of urban life. Recent studies have proceeded in the direction of the "community liberated" model (Wellman and Leighton 1979) of urban social relations, where community is liberated from the confinements of local space. In this view people's social relationships are drawn from the city at large, the total metropolitan area. People sleep in their neighborhood, they identify with it to a greater or lesser extent as being their own special place in the city, but they live their daily social lives within a spatially diffuse and more heterogeneous social network.

Social networks

The conceptual development of the social networks perspective in contemporary sociology is traceable to the work of J. A. Barnes (1954), although some trace recent developments back to Moreno's sociometric studies during the 1930s and 1940s (Rogers 1987: 287). At its simplest level, the network metaphor asks that we visualize individuals as embedded in a set of social relationships that encompass the individual's various group memberships (e.g., family, peers, work, formal group memberships). The social networks imagery urges us to appreciate the fact that an individual lives within no particular group, or even within a set of groups, but that people live within a complex set of social relationships. This complex set of social relationships links individuals, as individuals, with specific other individuals. Thus at any time a given person is subject to influence in his or her thinking and behavior from the full range of his or her contacts with others: These others are people who are personally known to the individual in question. Every person knows some number of other people, and that individual's friends and acquaintances know others, and so on. So, each of us can be pictured as standing at the center of a set of ties that radiate outward from us to and through others. This is our social network.

The imagery of the social network provides a useful metaphor for distinguishing between the structural characteristics of personal ties in urban and rural places. Rural networks tend to be densely structured, which is to say that in relatively small places, like a very small town, everyone knows everyone else. It is appropriate to picture a very highly interconnected web of relationships among residents. In the city, it is rare for all of one person's friends, acquaintances, and other contacts to know and be in regular contact with one another. So, urban networks are said to be loosely structured, or "open." Of course, within the city some individual's networks may be more dense, others more open, as a matter of degree. An urban villager, whose life is circumscribed pretty fully by the territory of the neighborhood, or a woman in London's East End, who is closely attuned to the happenings in her particular street, will have networks more closed than will Gans's cosmopolites. Frankenberg's (1966) edited collection of community studies from

England, Ireland, and Wales remains a very useful illustration of the relevance of the social networks concept for contrasting the difference in social structure between small- and large-scale population centers.

Networks may be seen as resource structures. They provide a reservoir of aid and information that the individual may call upon under particular circumstances. They also link the individual directly or indirectly to well-placed others who can influence outcomes favorable to the person in question. Theoretically, the more open an individual's network, the more varied or heterogeneous that person's set of relationships, the more valuable will be that set of ties under a wide variety of circumstances. This is what is meant by Granovetter's (1973, 1982) wonderfully precise reference to the "strength of weak ties." An urban villager may enjoy the warmth of a small, but close, network of friends and relatives, all of them with roughly the same background and experience, but the resources contained in such a network of strong ties are limited and redundant. This is especially evident if that network is contrasted with the network of an individual who is linked by relatively weak ties to a wide spectrum of others: Weak ties are valuable because they tie an individual to a variety of reference points and thereby potentially link the actor to information that is novel and not otherwise accessible (Campbell, Marsden, and Hurlbert 1986: 98–9).

The social network concept has ultimately contributed in an important way to our ability to create a mental image of the social structure of the city. One begins with a mental image of a single social network, an egocentric structure (based on the relationships and point of view of a single individual). At the center stands that person, surrounded by all the persons with whom he or she can be said to have a relationship. Next, each of the persons in this mental image can be seen to be standing at the center of their own set of relationships, as can each of the individuals they are related to, and so on. Although the diagram soon becomes too intricate to hold in one's mind, it suggests something of the structure of any population, such as that of a particular city. Following the implications of the network image, it can be seen that one important dimension of urban structure is that the city is a network of social networks (Craven and Wellman 1973).

Current trends in urban community research

The imageries of the community lost, community saved, and community liberated perspectives continue to operate side by side in urban sociology. Current research indicates that people who live in cities sometimes suffer the alienating effects of life in the urban arena, sometimes live in urban villages of various types, and inevitably stand at the center of their own social networks. The productive questions that should guide contemporary research are: To what extent and under which circumstances do these features of urban experience and organization operate? Can we determine how important residence is in anchoring the urban network? Under what conditions do people feel comfortably at home in the city, and under what conditions are they stressed by the urban environment?

Consider the example of a particular urbanite – the youthful, street-level, male marijuana dealer in a large city in northern California. His informal-sector, petty-trading utilizes the narrowly circumscribed neighborhood where he grew up. He works a street corner where he can meet the friends and acquaintances he knew before he started dealing; the social space in which he operates resembles most the face block or the defended neighborhood. These are the people he depends on for his all-important repeat sales. Between the dealer and the regulars there is a relationship built on familiarity and trust in the match between price and the quality of the product, important because the illicit transactions are swift and don't allow for haggling, product inspection, and promotion. Yet, the dealer is also a member of a city-wide network of dealers who respect each other's exclusive claim to a particular clientele, who make referrals when they can't fill a particular order, and provide a channel for information about police activity and thus serve as a mutual early warning system in helping one another avoid arrest. There is also an element of aversion and avoidance in the experience of the petty dealer. The city at large remains a dangerous place, and marijuana dealers avoid especially the tougher sections of the city where heroin dealers and their customers operate (Fields 1984: 251–63). Locality, network, subcultural affinity, and aversion to the wider urban environs can all be seen to operate here.

Locality and social ties

During the past two decades, researchers have embraced the idea that "community" is not a place but a set of social ties, that it is an extra-spatial social phenomenon not to be confused with neighborhood. Nevertheless, researchers have also continued to uncover the importance of residence as it influences the spatial distribution of social relationships. Neighborhood continues to play an important role in physically anchoring social networks, especially the networks of those who spend a lot of time in and have a high level of identification with their place of residence (Campbell and Lee 1992).

Greenbaum and Greenbaum (1985: 48–70) studied a modest residential area in Kansas City, Kansas, that was characterized by a high proportion of owner-occupied, single-family dwellings. They asked their respondents (all women) to indicate on a detailed map, showing every residential unit in the area, all acquaintances, friends, and people or families with whom they socialized regularly. The face block – in this case, those dwellings fronting on the same block-length section of street – emerged as a clear focus for friendships and regular socializing relations. With regard to acquaintanceship, there was a clear "distance decay" effect. Residents knew 61 percent of the households within 150 feet of their own, 20 percent of those between 150 to 300 feet away, and significantly fewer at increasing distances.

Greenbaum and Greenbaum's research shows that residential location has an important role in determining who people know and interact with, but (as the investigators readily acknowledge) it cannot show the relative importance of residential influence within people's complete social networks, since it only focused on relationships within the locality. Campbell and Lee's (1992) investigation of a similar Nashville residential area explicitly addresses the question of how important neighborhood ties are within the individual's total set of relationships. Their findings emphasize the importance of demographic features. They found that gender, socioeconomic status, and age all interact with the degree to which individual networks are focused on neighborhood or diffused within wider arenas. The overall picture is complex. Women's acquaintances were slightly more focused within their neighborhood, but the degree of intensity of neighborhood ties or frequency of contact did not differ from those of men. Higher socioeconomic status male and female respondents to the survey knew a slightly greater number of their neighbors, on average, but lower socioeconomic status respondents were on more intimate terms with and depended more for support on those neighbors they identified as part of their network. Age and stage of family cycle interacted with neighborhood focus, but in complex, nonlinear patterns (Campbell and Lee 1992: 1086–92). Overall the study points to the fact that residence is one important focus for acquaintance and friendship.

It is difficult to generalize from Kansas City or Nashville residential areas to other urban settings. How well do neighbors in high-rise buildings in New York know each other and how often do they interact?

One such study shows the classical urban-aversion thesis in operation. Zito (1974) had to give up her strategy for conducting face-to-face interviews because fearful residents in the complex she studied in Manhattan would not open their doors to her. Subsequently mailed questionnaires revealed that only 2 percent of residents could name all of the other fifteen families on their floor, whereas about half thought they could recognize half the other same-floor neighbors on sight. There was a pervasive lack of knowledge about neighbors (e.g., what they did for a living), and residents liked it that way. Zito believed that fellow tenants did not want to get to know each other, and that even a self-introduction could be considered a violation of privacy. Most neither visited nor were visited by any of the 12,000 other residents of the complex on a regular basis.

Low levels of interaction don't necessarily indicate a low level of commitment to place of residence. For a high-rise building in Newark, New Jersey, similar to the site of Zito's Manhattan study, Slovak (1986) found, except for fleeting conversational contacts, that interaction among residents was infrequent. Yet, despite low levels of more intimate forms of socializing (e.g., exchanging favors or advice, visiting), many people were attached to their building, which is equated in this study with "defended neighborhood." Again, many residents simply preferred to be left alone, remained attached to their neighborhood, and were not at all troubled by the lack of neighboring.

The Newark study showed a carryover effect between attachment to defended neighborhood and attachment to the community of limited liability (the city of Newark, itself). People tended to have stronger attachments to the neighborhood than to the wider community: More of them expressed a greater reluctance to leave in response to hypothetical questions to that effect (Slovak 1986: 587). Guest and Lee (1983) report similar findings for Seattle: People were more attached to the more narrowly defined "urban village" than to the broader community of limited liability. Attachment to the wider community tended to reflect a general satisfaction with the area as a nice place to live. The attachment to neighborhood was based more strongly on sentiment, and linked to length of residence. Not all neighborhoods qualified as urban villages, but in those that did residents were more likely to have been recruited to live there by friends and relatives.

What this sampling of studies shows is that many urbanites retain a strong sense of place in the city. They may not interact very much with their neighbors, preferring to be left alone to select social relationships rather than to have them assigned by residential proximity. It is probably true that most people's closest social relations are disproportionately with coworkers and fellow organization members rather than kin and neighbors (Fischer 1982). Even in the classic studies (Gans 1962: 21; Young and Willmott 1957), although people knew many of their neighbors, the privacy of others' apartments was restricted largely to kin. Most nonkin interaction among urban villagers took place in public areas, and was spontaneous. It is difficult to know whether there is less interaction in the urban village today, or whether there is less in high-rise, middle-class apartments than in working-class tenements or British-style terraced housing. Architectural design does appear to be a factor in interaction. In Boston's West End, structural features of tenement housing encouraged interaction between women whose kitchen windows faced each other across narrow alleys (Gans 1962: 75n). In the modern high rise it is more likely that people will know the person or family whose door is directly across the hall than they will be to know their nearest neighbors on either side; more likely still, they will know few of their neighbors. Yet, many are quite attached to the buildings in which they live. Despite having little to do with each other, there is evidence that people perceive other residents on the same floor to be more like themselves, while other-floor residents are perceived as "personally different sorts of people than we are" (Zito 1974: 249). Local residence remains one important source of identification, while the effective arena of interaction is city-wide.

Network studies

Two points need to be made with regard to the acceptance of the network model in current research. First, the network metaphor, that social structure and individual behavior need to be understood as a process and product of nonspatial interconnections among social actors, has become widely accepted. Second, there remain methodological obstacles in the way of fully exploring the nature of social networks.

Survey research, long the favorite approach in empirical investigation within the social sciences, focuses on individuals rather than on sets of relationships. Networks researchers are interested in uncovering "deep structures," complex aspects of social structure that lie far beneath the awareness of those who are affected by them. The conventional survey approach that asks individuals for information about their relationships to others is inappropriate for investigating the relationships *among* those others (Rogers 1987: 291). For one thing, individuals are often mistaken about the nature of ties among other people in their social circles. For another, asking individuals about relationships among their acquaintances is an overwhelmingly cumbersome task, as was discovered by a long-time student of social networks, J. Clyde Mitchell (1987).

Mitchell's research team set out to investigate intimate ties among homeless women in Manchester, England in the interest of understanding the nature of their potential support networks of family and friends. The seemingly modest aim was to ask ten women about their twenty closest relationships, and to ask further about how these twenty were interrelated socially. With regard to each set of relationships, the initial set of respondents were asked about frequency of contact, degree of "closeness," intrinsic gratification of the relationship, emotional support, and practical aid. Because the focus was on the complete set of relationships, the nature of the ties among acquaintances had to be assessed as well as the quality of the relationship between the ten respondents and their contacts. Clearly, what appears at first glance a modest research enterprise sought an enormous amount of information: Each interview sought to elicit 1,900 pieces of information from each of the respondents. Mitchell (1987: 40) writes that the exercise "proved to be onerous and tedious for the respondent and occasionally embarrassingly demanding for the interviewer to complete." In the end, the findings of such research are still limited to the perceptions of third parties about the nature of relationships between other people. A more effective strategy in assessing deep structure would have been to interview each of the persons identified by the original ten respondents. It is easy to see how network questions tend to expand geometrically the numbers of research subjects and the amount of data generated.

In his summary of the state of the art, Rogers (1987: 287, 295) is optimistic that the network method for investigating the structures that influence behavior is on the brink of an important breakthrough. Software developments since the 1970s have facilitated computer-based network analysis, allowing researchers to deal with large blocks of data. But Rogers adds his warning to those raised by others (Burt 1983: 300; Blau 1982: 279), that the focus in network research needs to remain on conceptual development rather than on the elegance of mathematical and computational technique.

The new ethnic groups: Locality and networks

Ethnic groups provide an important opportunity for studying patterns of association in the urban arena (Fischer 1975, 1984). There is a clear and strong interaction between the development and maintenance of a group's ethnic identity and the urban environment. Each helps to shape the other (Flanagan 1990: 100–13). Urban ethnic community studies have become a tradition within a tradition in urban studies.

Major urban centers in the more industrialized nations have, since the 1960s, been the recipients of large influxes of immigrants from the poorer regions of the world. The recent immigrants provide a fresh opportunity for the study of ethnic community in the city, and inform the discussion regarding the relative importance of the neighborhood and the network in framing the social context of urban life. This section of this chapter highlights some of the important issues in recent ethnic urban studies and presents an examination of the Chinese community in New York City, in order to demonstrate the dynamic complexity of the nature of ethnic communities.

Since the 1950s European cities have received hundreds of thousands of immigrants from North Africa, India, Pakistan, the Caribbean, and Southeast Asia. The cities of Canada and the United States have been the immigration targets of hundreds of thousands more from the Caribbean, Central and South America, Asia, and Europe. In the United States, Chicago, Houston, Miami, and San Francisco have received more than their share of the immigration flow, but no city has been more favored by immigrants than New York. In the 1970s and 1980s it is estimated that more than a million people were added to New York City's population through immigration. By 1980 it was already the case that over half the city's registered immigrants had arrived since 1965: The new arrivals made up 13 percent of the city's total population (Foner 1987: 4, 17). In addition, there were perhaps 750,000 undocumented residents (Marshall 1987: 80).

Such large and widespread immigration as New York City has experienced is bound to have a significant impact on an area's economy. While the debate continues over whether that effect is detrimental or beneficial, New York and other cities are demonstrating that the economic impact of large and widespread immigration is a complex issue. Understanding that impact is problematic in terms of the consequences for the local economy and the economic consequences for the immigrants themselves. For example, New York lost an enormous number of manufacturing jobs from the 1960s through the present. During this period, the proportion of the rapidly expanding pool of new-wave, foreign-born workers employed in manual labor remained stable. In fact, there was an increase in the proportion of the most recently arrived immigrants entering manual occupations. In 1980, perhaps 35 percent of New York's total manual labor force was made up of immigrants who had arrived since 1970. The paradox is that native-born U.S. citizens were "abandoning" manufacturing jobs whereas newcomers were being absorbed in expanding numbers into manufacturing in New York. Of course, many new-wave immigrants were also absorbed into low-wage service sector jobs (e.g., in eating and drinking places, personal and household services, and as hospital workers) (Marshall 1987: 81–8).

The question is whether these immigrants are taking jobs away from native-born citizens. The answer appears to be no, at least not directly. Large numbers of new immigrants are absorbed into newly created areas of the economy, into jobs that are unattractive to the native born, or into industrial enterprises that would not be viable without readily available, cheap immigrant labor (i.e., jobs that are created for and perhaps by immigrants themselves). A further question has to do with whether the modal forms of economic adaptation pursued by immigrants – and the economic ethnic enclaves – are on balance more exploitive or more adaptive for the immigrant workers.

In the 1920s, two of the major figures in the history of urban sociology, Robert Park and Ernest Burgess (Park and Burgess 1921; Park 1926b) developed a straightforward assimilationist model of immigrant economic adaptation. The idea is that social mobility requires immigrants to become indistinct from natives in every manner and in as short a time possible; this includes immediately joining the mainstream economy in whatever manner was allowed by the established population of workers and entrepreneurs. In recent years Portes (1981, 1985, 1987) has argued that there may be an intermediate step that facilitates mobility; this involves the establishment of a set of ethnic enterprises that provide a *parallel opportunity structure* for entrepreneurs and workers within the ethnic community. Ethnic enterprise and various forms of ethnic cooperation were an important part of ethnic solidarity in the past, when ethnic enclaves and the cities that contained them were more compact structures. Today's cities are sprawling, diffuse spaces. What may be said today of ethnic community and enclave economies?

Certainly, identifiable ethnic areas persist in major cities. The North End of Boston has the clearly Italian influence it had at the time of Whyte's (1943) *Street Corner Society* study. Recent immigrations have enhanced and expanded the Chinatown districts of New York and San Francisco, fostered a Koreatown in New York, and sponsored the development of a number of Vietnamese and other Southeast Asian communities in various cities. Hispanic barrios and commercial districts have flourished in a number of U.S. cities, perhaps none more strikingly than Little Havana in Miami.

However, given the dynamic and fluid nature of urban space as it is subjected to economic pressures for revision, it is important to raise again the distinction between space and patterns of social involvement with reference to ethnic solidarity. In addition to questions about ethnic residential enclaves, it is necessary to recognize network patterns of ethnic association, especially those with an underlying economic structure. Guldin (1980: 244–5) emphasizes the importance of distinguishing between ethnic neighborhoods and ethnic community: The latter denotes a dispersed but integrated network in the minds of its members. Such a community is city- or society-wide, and presents greater challenges for research and analysis.

One dimension of ethnic cohesiveness is clearly its visibility. Large numbers of coethnics can support an array of services like retail shops, religious institutions, voluntary organizations, communications media, and the like; these reinforce the presence of the community in the minds of insiders and outsiders alike. It is not necessary for members of a particular group to constitute the majority of residents in a neighborhood in order for that area to become identified with a particular ethnic group. Often a relatively small concentration is sufficient to establish such an identity in the minds of the people who live there and those that pass through the area. In fact, the section of a city that has a particular ethnic stamp may not be the area with the highest concentration of that particular group (Guldin 1980: 258–60).

Whether and under what conditions a space is or is not an ethnic territory can be a complicated question. Haitian residents dominate particular apartment blocks in Brooklyn. In Manhattan there are a number of Haitian shops clustered along Amsterdam Avenue. On Saturday nights Haitians patronize Haitian-owned nightclubs in Queens, and on Sunday afternoons they gather in large numbers at soccer matches in Queens and Brooklyn (Laguerre 1984: 52–7). The presence and integration of the Haitian community is thereby manifest, but the issue of its territorial location is problematic.

A second dimension of ethnic integration is the utility of membership to its members. The reason that Haitian residential enclaves are evident in Brooklyn is because new immigrants find apartments by word of mouth. Often an entire building is eventually exclusively occupied by Haitian residents. Coresidence facilitates such cooperative arrangements as childcare, meal sharing, and car pooling. The latter is facilitated by the fact that work is often found for immigrants by friends and relatives, who may also act as translators with the common employer (Laguerre 1984: 89–9). A study of West Indian rotating credit associations shows the importance of visibility within a close-knit network, both in creating a needed institutional arrangement and providing a mechanism of social control that makes the institution work. The credit associations provide sums of money too small to interest formal lending institutions to people often too poor to qualify for a loan. The *Gemeinschaft*-like mechanism of social control that ensures that borrowers will repay their loans is the threat of loss of face in a public "cussing out" of delinquent borrowers (Bonnett 1984: 111–29).

The economic integration of ethnic community extends beyond mutual assistance and self-help arrangements and into the formal economy in a number of ways. Changes in New York's Chinatown district provide a case study in the interactive dynamics of immigration, the economy of the district, and the wider metropolitan economy. The area contains a diverse population that includes long-time settlers (resident since before 1965), second- and third-generation Chinese-Americans, new immigrants, jumped-ship sailors, and refugees from Southeast Asia of Chinese descent. It includes rich and poor, members of youth gangs and corporate executives. Most of the rapidly growing population of the area are immigrants: In 1980, 80 percent were born outside the United States. Rapid growth has meant that the physical area of Chinatown has had to expand beyond the old, six-block area framed by Mott, Mulberry, and Canal streets. New sources of immigration have meant a shift in dialect from Mandarin, Fukinese, and Shanghainese to standard Cantonese (Wong 1987: 243–6).

An influx of capital from Hong Kong, as that territory is scheduled to revert to Chinese control in 1997, has caused the economic nature of Chinatown to undergo a dramatic transformation from what has been called a "precapitalist" service orientation that prevailed in the 1950s (Kwong 1987: 25–7). Any visitor who had been away from Chinatown between 1960 and 1990 would be struck by the increase in people, shops, services (especially bigger and fancier restaurants), and the apparent prosperity of the community as indicated by the construction of office towers. A genuine understanding of the changes taking place requires a deeper examination of the community-wide and city-wide economic integration of the ethnic community.

Postwar legislation that opened the door wider to Asian immigrants attracted a large number of Chinese women to Manhattan's sagging garment industry, an industry characterized by low pay and sporadic layoffs. Despite these liabilities, Chinese women were attracted by the health insurance benefits secured for garment workers by the Ladies' Garment Workers' Union. This was an especially attractive feature to married women with children, because their husbands' jobs often did not offer these benefits. Chinese immigrant men were concentrated in the food industry, overwhelmingly in restaurant work.

During the 1970s, the number of Chinese women employed in the garment industry increased from 8,000 to 20,000. Most worked for Chinese employers in factories that produced garments under contract to larger clothing companies. These intermediate-level factories ran as long as there were orders from the clothing companies: Whenever consumers stopped buying, the clothing companies stopped ordering, and the contractors laid-off workers. Still, the number of such plants increased rapidly. They were easily capitalized: start-up costs were as low as $25,000. In 1980 there were probably eight of these in New York; in 1984 there were 500. Despite poor working conditions and pay, the positive aspects of employment in these factories suited family women. Hours were flexible and facilitated childcare arrangements, some women brought their children to work. The workplaces were conveniently located in and near Chinatown. The employer had the same cultural background. At the same time, the garment industry had acquired a large, low-cost, compliant labor force.

In the 1980s, it is estimated that the two-earner, low-income families in Chinatown added, in the aggregate, $125 million annually to the New York City economy, $25 million of which was spent in Chinatown. The typical ten-hour workday away from home in the garment industry provided partial support for a growing restaurant and rice-shop trade in the district. The expanding restaurants became attractive to other Americans and drew upon a nearby Wall Street clientele. The more affluent patrons, Chinese and non-Chinese alike, looked for more sophisticated dishes and fancier surroundings, favoring the fortunes of the larger restaurants that could import chefs and decorate to higher standards. Uptown Chinese-Americans, more assimilated and affluent as a group than the downtown Chinatown Chinese, were attracted back downtown during the 1970s and 1980s as interest in China and Chinese culture increased in North America (Kwong 1987: 29–35).

The picture of the Chinese community in New York that emerges here is one that invites caution with regard to summary statements and references to underlying cultural cohesiveness. There are cultural (as between old and new immigrants) as well as economic divisions within the Chinese district. Interests are divided between those who favor an upgrading (gentrification) of the area, and those interested in preserving its character. Again, the division has less to do with cultural preservation than economic interests, as the higher rents brought about by upgrading and high-rise construction are driving family-run garment factories and restaurants out of the district to Brooklyn and Queens. The impact on families whose wage earners depend on the convenience of living and working in the same area is easily deduced. Office blocks don't provide jobs for non-English speakers, and this type of building increasingly squeezes the tight housing supply. Organizations such as Asian Americans for Equality and the Asian American Legal Defence Fund have emerged to fight changes that impose economic costs on the local population and to press for improved housing. Meanwhile, the cash flow from Hong Kong and the city government's preference for high-rise construction in the area combine to promote change (Wong 1987: 263–5).

What does New York's Chinatown reveal about ethnic community and urban community? First, regarding ethnic community, there are a number of points to be made. What appears to the outsider as a homogeneous and perhaps static district is in fact heterogeneous in terms of cultural and economic divisions. It is also in a state of change. Not the least of the agents of change is the integration of the community within wider economic arenas (in this case, extending as far as Hong Kong). In addition, there are pressures from within the community that encourage territorial fragmentation, as local housing supplies become inadequate and costs rise, and as businesses that cannot compete as effectively for local space for economic reasons are spun off into other areas of the metropolis.

It is very difficult to evaluate the argument of Park and Burgess that the quickest road to prosperity for new immigrants is through assimilation into the mainstream (nonethnic) economy. This argument begs the question of prejudice and discrimination against Asians, prejudice and discrimination that have contributed to the founding and perpetuation of Chinatowns. Portes's (1981, 1985) point, that ethnic enterprise provides a strategically important intermediate step for many immigrants, remains plausible. But how can the argument be adequately evaluated? Would Manhattan's Asian women garment workers have been better served by seeking a different type of work? Would they have been allowed to immigrate in such numbers if there was no place for them in a dual labor market? Would they have been better off to remain in Shanghai, Hong Kong, North China, or Taiwan? Does raising such questions simply offer a rationale for exploitation and internal colonialism? Clearly, these questions are taking us beyond a discussion of community, but it is the nature of the sociology of community that the questions we raise inevitably draw our attention to a broader frame of analysis. Efforts to evaluate whether immigrant workers and entrepreneurs are better off operating "within" the ethnic community or "outside" of it (e.g., Sanders and Nee 1987), are fraught with methodological difficulty and are open to qualification (Portes and Jensen 1987; Nee and Sanders 1987).

With regard to the lesson of New York's Chinatown for the discussion of community, it is worth reiterating an important point raised above: There are strong economic realities that underlie any community, that give rise to it, that threaten it, that cause it to cohere physically or to become dispersed. Remote political decisions – to change immigration laws, to emancipate a colony, or to embark on an urban renewal project for a section of a city – have an enormous impact on the nature of a particular community, on its very perception as a community, the nature and strength of the sentiments that attach to it, and on its survival. Real estate processes that produce changing land rents and development prospects for an area have an equal and intimately interwoven impact on the nature of community. Decisions and development processes that originate outside of a spatial community can cause it to crystallize as its borders are defended, to be obliterated as its defenders are defeated, to be fragmented as its members are divided, or to be cut free from local space and to float as an aspatial network of economic and social ties and identifications.

Evaluation of the urbanism and community studies tradition

The interests of urban researchers continue to be engaged by questions about the nature and patterns of social interaction in cities. The conceptual approaches we have reviewed in this chapter all suggest possible answers. A Wirthian analysis would predict greater relative isolation and mutual aversion in cities than elsewhere; Gans's treatise on urbanism and suburbanism predicts that whatever the social patterns, certain categories of people are simply delighted to be in the city, while others are stuck where they find themselves. Fischer's work suggests that the city offers the opportunity for specialized social contact, along with the aversion Wirth would predict for public behavior. The community studies tradition leads us to expect to find people identifying with their residential space, while the social networks approach urges us to look for primary ties beyond the residential neighborhood.

It is interesting, and perhaps not so surprising, that contemporary urban research lends support to the predictions that each of these approaches would make about patterns of urban association. It is true that Wirth's famous urbanism thesis is heir to a strong element of antiurbanism in the urban sociological tradition, but its utility as a model, an ideal type, transcends its limitations as social commentary. Although the values implicit in Wirth's essay have long been called into question, it remains a useful exercise to test whether increasing size and density of populations, along with growing differentiation within the population, is associated with a tendency toward more limited interaction.

An anthropological study from a territory within the former Yugoslavia provides a retrospective account of such change (Kremensek 1983: 287–97). At the turn of the century, a small settlement developed on the edge of a city that became the capital (Ljubljana) of the Socialist Republic of Slovenia. Most of the people in the slowly growing little settlement came from the same rural area, and most heads of household were railway workers. Accounts of life in the early 1900s emphasize the types of mutual assistance (borrowing and housebuilding) and sociability that one might associate with a small rural village. There was regular visiting, and families reportedly lived "without any special attempts at privacy" (287). Through 1940, and again after World War II, the size of the population increased dramatically, and the area became incorporated physically within the expanding regional capital.

By stages, the population became occupationally more heterogeneous and stratified, face-to-face familiarity broke down, people kept more to themselves, and mistrust of others increased.

The pattern of change reported here is just what Wirth would have predicted. Yet, there are difficult methodological issues involved in assessing such changes and attributing causality. There were other types of change taking place during the era under study in addition to urban growth. How much of the growing aversion or reserve shown by people toward each other should be attributed to wider political change, and how much to urbanization? This will always be a problem in applying Wirth's thesis. Urbanization is attended by broader changes of which it is a part. In what sense can urbanism be seen as cause? In what sense as effect? This question occupies us in later chapters.

The sociological tradition in which Wirth operated (Tönnies, Simmel, Park), with its emphasis on suspicion and calculation, continues to provide a framework for micrological studies in urban interaction. Many studies that attempt to answer questions about urban modes of interaction begin with the Wirthian premise that urban living attenuates interaction. Although people who live and work in large cities rarely articulate their experiences in the terms that Wirth or Simmel used, they recognize the superficiality of much incidental interaction. It is safe to assume that for the most part superficial contact is perfectly agreeable to most people. It has evolved as the efficient mode of social intercourse in the purely instrumental relationships of the great marketplace. However, people who make their living from selling to the public regularly employ strategies that are designed to overcome anonymity and establish pseudointimacy with customers (Prus 1987: 350–7). The idea is that calling a person by his or her first name (perhaps learned from their credit card) or remembering the surname at a later date, their children's birthdays, or some other detail revealed in casual interaction, promotes the potential for repeat sales in the otherwise featureless and anonymous stream of business contacts. As everyone is aware, such "personal" touches are pointedly instrumental, and do little to warm the heart when seen for what they are. But people recognize and accept the quality of this type of social contact for what it is, and do not feel offended or victimized. Few would be surprised by the words of the salesman who said with reference to his style of interaction with customers, "I'll . . . joke around with them, have a little fun . . . . It's business, but it's more enjoyable for everyone that way" (Prus 1987: 353).

As Gans has pointed out, people accept the city for what it is, prefer it, are "I love New York" cityphiles. A recent study of San Francisco distinguished between general cityphiles ("cosmopolitan urbanists") and those who loved their particular city, though not necessarily cities in general ("local urbanists"). People who like city life like it because of the different kinds of people it contains and the liberalism and tolerance they associate with urban populations. In accordance with Fischer's subcultural theory of urban life, people reported that in the city they felt free to pursue their own interests and were able to find others to share and promote those interests (Hummon 1986: 15–16). Fischer (1984) has pointed out that it is important to distinguish between public and private behavior in the urban setting. People may at the same time feel free to express themselves, yet may be guarded in public places where they are forced into close proximity with large numbers of strangers. It is apparently quite possible to appreciate freedom and diversity, and yet be put off by it.

Simic (1983: 216–17) reports from the former Yugoslav urbanites experience the paradox of private liberation and public guardedness. In contrast to the constraints of village life, "One is liberated in the city to behave in any way that is momentarily rewarding." At the same time, people feel a deep distrust of others in impersonal situations because others' behavior is similarly unpredictable. "It is in this context that the rudeness, obstinance, and indifference that characterizes many instrumental, single-stranded transactions with clerks, waiters, and petty officials becomes understandable." Wirth's words (images) are echoed clearly in Simic's (1983: 216) summation of urban life:

> One requirement of the urban setting is that one must by necessity transact a variety of exchanges with persons he has never seen before and with whom he may never have future dealings. The only expectation that can reasonably be held about these contacts on the basis of prior experience in a traditional village is that they are fraught with danger and the portent of deception and exploitation.

Clearly, the assumptions of Wirth about the negative effects of population size and heterogeneity still guide some interpretations of urban life.

The views of Fischer and Wirth overlap somewhat in their interpretation of the relationship between urbanism and a tolerance of controversial viewpoints and minority lifestyle. In addition to Wirth's opinion that urbanism involved an increase in social distance, he also believed that living in a socially heterogeneous environment made people more tolerant (if not appreciative) of different points of view and lifestyles. Fischer similarly holds that the large number of subcultural differences that cities engender reduces sensitivity or attentiveness to dissimilar others. Thomas C. Wilson (1985, 1986) measured the relationship between population size and tolerance toward controversial and minority viewpoints and lifestyle. Wilson found that city size was positively correlated with more tolerant attitudes toward atheists, racists, militarists, and communists. Residents of larger cities were also less homophobic. His most recent work suggests that a refinement of measurement that takes into account length of urban residence and migration histories of survey respondents enhances the positive correlation between urbanism and political tolerance (Wilson 1991). Thus, Wirth's hypothesis regarding population size and tolerance is supported. The findings also support Fischer's thesis regarding the greater freedom to express oneself and to pursue esoteric interests without attracting disapprobation. However, Wilson (1986: 1,159) also found an inverse relationship between population size and a number of measures of satisfaction with quality of life.

Quality-of-life measures are problematic. How does one establish whether cities are better or worse than other places of residence? The "critical mass" benefits that Fischer describes may or may not be part of the awareness of particular individuals. The richness associated with the choices open to big-city residents may go unrecognized until an individual is transported to a smaller population center. This San Francisco resident loves life in the Bay Area, but his idea of hometown life would likely be very different if he had to pursue his musical interests in a small town: "What is life in San Francisco like? Let me give you an illustration. I belong to this banjo group. Its mostly retired people. They come from all over to play and talk. We get together just to have good times. Its very home town. And there are mandolin groups, too, and newsletters" (Hummon 1986: 21). It takes a lot of retired people, a substantial critical mass, to provide a subset large enough to support a mandolin or banjo newsletter.

In assessing quality-of-life differences between large and small population centers it is necessary to keep in mind that we are addressing not the needs of some monolithic population but of many subgroups, subcultural splinters. The difficulty in making quality-of-life comparisons between large and small population centers is increased with respect to elements of cultural diversity that provoke bias or controversy. Consider gay and lesbian minorities. We have already seen that tolerance is greater for these and other minority positions in large cities. According to Fischer, we would also expect to find greater diversity within a subculture in a larger city. Any moderate-sized city has a gay community with recognized meeting places. A city the size of New York, on the other hand, shows how critical mass offers the opportunity for internal diversity and the potential for establishing a subset of relationships that allow the expression of choice within a more general subculture.

In Jacob Riis Park the gay community limits itself to one section of the beach area. Within that stretch of beach on a sunny day bathers and sunbathers divide into a number of subgroups: Hispanic gays, gay and lesbian parents, deaf gays, and so forth; a wide range of gay styles and orientations are identifiable. Mixed in here and there are heterosexuals who enjoy the company and atmosphere in the dominantly gay part of the beach. These include heterosexual women who sunbathe nude; they reportedly felt less threatened by this crowd in exercising their choice (Canavan 1984: 72–7). Life in the big city is different from life in smaller centers, and to understand that this setting translates into a statement on the manner in which cities enhance the quality of life is to be part of an urban culture.

Research in the 1980s reestablished the importance of locality as a basis for community. This was in response to the network research that had emphasized the elective quality of social ties. Neighborhoods returned to the spotlight. Residential areas were transformed into defended neighborhoods as long-time residents perceived the character of their community to be threatened with change from the outside. New research showed that *formal* neighborhood associations among relative newcomers to an area provided an important basis for the development of *informal* ties among residents. These studies also showed strong identification with and attachment to the local area.

Crenshaw and St. John (1989: 412–15) offer the label "organizationally dependent community" for residential areas where all or most of the residents are recent arrivals and where, therefore, there has been little opportunity for the development of crescive or spontaneous interaction and sociability. Grassroots neighborhood-development or preservation groups are typical of the kind of formal groups that produce more generalized and informal relationships. Members have invested in an area that has been locally promoted and perceived as undergoing upgrading, and so they are keen to maintain and improve housing standards and the image of the location. Their attention is on the shifting fortunes of the locality, and they organize into residents' groups to ensure their collective interests. Crenshaw and St. John (1989: 430) state:

> Because renovators lack social organization in their neighborhood, but do possess organizational skills, they will be more likely than others to respond to piecemeal threats to their neighborhoods by becoming involved in formal organizations formed to deal with them. From collectively seeking to deal with threats through formal organizations, renovators become attached to the entity they are seeking to protect.

It may be that the new form of neighborhood organization fosters the type of weak ties that make the aspatial social network a valuable reservoir of social contacts. The organizationally dependent community would thereby combine the common interest basis of shared residential space with the resource richness of the more heterogeneous social network. Under these conditions neighborhood and network would not coincide, but neighborhood potentially becomes a more important base of identity at the same time that it provides a reservoir of potentially valuable, multipurpose social contacts.

Wireman (1984: 113, 145, writing for the U.S. Department of Housing and Urban Development), also emphasizes the role of formal organizations in fostering informal social relations among community residents. Her work evaluates formal efforts to foster social integration within the racially diverse populations of the new towns of Columbia, Maryland and Reston, Virginia. She believes that organizations like Columbia's city-wide Community Association are instrumental in promoting the development of social networks. Although it should be noted that Wireman's assessment of the creation of a racially integrated social fabric within these cities is more positive than other assessments, she raises a critical point, namely, that it is important in any evaluation of local relationships not to confuse good neighbors with good friends. In her view, the kind of relationships that may be expected to emerge on the basis of common, residentially based interests more approximate "intimate secondary relationships" than they do genuine friendships. This is a point worthy of consideration as we attempt to distinguish the relative content and importance of neighborhoods and networks.

The question of the fate and shape of urban community yields a variety of answers. Contemporary urban sociologists employ a number of perspectives in researching these questions. It is important to ask what each of these points of view contributes to an overall understanding of social cohesion in the city. It is important, as well, to recognize that each of the perspectives has limitations as well as something valuable to say about the manner in which people live urban life, and about the way they believe they and others live in cities. Fundamental to any understanding of the nature of the urban community, local identification, and interaction in the urban arena is the perception and experience of people themselves. At the level of experience, cities are socially constructed images. People use cities in different ways, pursue different routines and interests. Each of us uses only part of the city we live in, experience the urban environment from our own perspectives. These perspectives, in turn, are affected by social class, age, gender, occupation, and many other factors. Because each of us occupies a unique space with respect to all others, our particular image of the city will be unique. In this sense, because each of us has his or her own mental map of the city we use, each of us lives in our own city (Lynch 1960). Yet, the city belongs to no one of us, and we experience it as a world of strangers.

Lofland's (1973) little book, *World of Strangers,* helps to make sense of much that we have reviewed here. Following Lynch, Lofland points out that the city must be seen in part in terms of individual internalizations, as each one of us performs cognitive operations on the urban space, making the parts of it we know our own. The city exists in the individual's experience as a series of places within which that person is to some degree comfortable. The more we use a place, all other things being equal, the more comfortable we are in it, the more we make it ours. It is interesting that Lofland chooses terms that reflect the primarily commercial nature of urban space to describe the three degrees of familiarity found among space users. The "customer" is a person who is in a particular place intermittently, who has firsthand but "casual" knowledge of that particular slice of public space. The "patron" has developed "semipersonal" relationships with the regulars and employees always found there. The "resident" has carved out a "home territory" through regular usage and identification, has developed a proprietary sense.

These labels are intended to convey an impression of gradations of personal mastery of particular settings. Beyond the familiar places still exists the vast remainder of the cityscape that the individual has little knowledge of or personal claim to. That is the world of strangers.

In this chapter we have reviewed the theoretical positions and some of the recent research that characterize the study of urban social relations. Neighborhood and network vie for due recognition. Wirth continues to inform research with the urbanism paradigm he outlined in 1938. Ethnic community undergoes transitions as the ethnicities change and the territorial characteristics of ethnic identity become more fluid. In the following chapters we will be more interested in the structural characteristics of urban growth and change, of the economic and political dimensions of city space. These dimensions have already drawn our attention, just as we will be drawn back in the remaining chapters to the fundamental sociological questions of identity and interaction in the wider urban arena.

In the following section, we turn our attention briefly to one contemporary form of urban solidarity and territoriality that imposes its own order on public space, affecting a much wider population than those immediately caught up in its desperate logic.

MANAGING URBAN LIVES

Southern California street gangs: Solidarity and disorder

Georg Simmel pointed out that conflict between groups produced solidarity within groups. This lesson can be usefully applied to the understanding of various oppositional factions within the urban arena, including the groups of young men and women (and boys and girls) who have taken over many neighborhoods, and whose demeanor is so threatening to the rest of society. Society has not afforded them the safe environment that adolescents need to give them time to learn and mature, instead society's agents of law enforcement are numbered among their antagonists. In poor minority neighborhoods in Southern California, the struggle to create a zone of personal safety has degenerated for young people into a question of vigilance and force, not authority. The familiar fixtures of the national economy and the jobs they provided are withdrawing across former urban industrial landscapes like a retreating glacier. Whether the replacement economy of today's inner cities will eventually provide new opportunities for inner city youth is an academic question. The fact is that for now the restructured economy of the inner city is perceived to offer little chance for meaningful participation. How to create order and livelihood are questions left to those who are being abandoned in their childhood by the legitimate economy and the formal agents of social control.

The disturbances in South Central Los Angeles in 1992 were a reminder of the frustration and anger felt by alienated members of society who see neglect added to the traditions of racism and the multiple dimensions of discrimination. Outsiders, those with good jobs and concerns about law and order, ask why teenaged girls become pregnant and bear children, thus "ruining" their chances for a better life, a life that is assumed to be the default option for those who do not become pregnant. Why do young people turn to socially debilitating drugs? Why do they deal, carry guns, kill each other? The questions betray the mutual insularity of the worlds of questioner and subject, and betray ignorance of the fact that these are the dimensions of a new urban order, the creation of which was left up to economically disadvantaged youth. The young people of the inner cities, left without resources and with dwindling hope, are doing the best they can to make sense of their lives under desperate conditions. True, the arrangements they are working out for earning a living and creating order reflect little of the values of the wider society that fears them.

Moore (1991) interviewed men and women who were members of East Los Angeles gangs during the 1950s and 1960s, and she distinguishes between these earlier gangs and those featured in current studies and news reports. The picture drawn from her respondents differed somewhat from the contemporary corporate gangs that are formed to deal drugs for profit. Moore's gangs have a history dating back to loosely constituted organizations in the 1940s, when they were essentially social clubs that broke with conventions of dress and behavior to a degree sufficient to set their members apart from the wider society. But from the 1950s through the 1970s these organizations had evolved an institutionalized structure of named age grades that incorporated and socialized younger recruits – boys who looked forward to the prestige attached to becoming an accepted insider (31–3). This feature makes the post-1950 gangs described by Moore similar to contemporary gangs in terms of recruitment and structure. These similarities are strongly suggested, for instance, by comparison with the work of Vigil (1988) and reflected in the first-person accounts presented by Bing (1991).

Moore's subjects remembered the powerful sense of belonging and identification that gang membership gave them. Membership elicited a solidarity that is as *Gemeinschaft*-like as any that people in contemporary society are likely to experience: Gang members speak of a territorial allegiance which, in a fragmentary way, calls to mind Weber's effort to characterize the manner in which the true urbanite was tied to the city as a whole. A nostalgic respondent who was a member of an East Los Angeles barrio gang in the 1970s reminisced (Moore 1991: 76–7) "To me it was my way of life, my one and only way. My only mission . . . I felt like it was the only thing going for me. It was my neighborhood. They were like my brothers and sisters." The testimony of members of contemporary southern California street gangs suggests that allegiance is at least as strong today as in the past. Vigil (1988: 3, 27ff) points out that the commitment of individual Chicano youth to their gangs varies, but it is those who have the most problematic lives and street experiences who are the most committed. However, not only those from troubled or broken homes find themselves incorporated into gangs. Bing's (1991) South Central Los Angeles subjects came from a variety of backgrounds: Individuals may have lost a mother to a drug overdose or a father or older brothers to prison. But others had working parents who tried to keep them out of the life of the street, like the teenager whose mother worked for the bank, or another whose father was a police officer.

The behavioral code of the gangs in southern California and elsewhere became more violent during the 1970s and again in the 1980s. Moore notes that the culture of violence and drugs has tended to isolate gang members from the surrounding (Mexican-American) community to a greater extent than in the past. Nevertheless, in various ways the young members remain integrated with the adult culture around them through family and other adult mentors, and Moore observes that "The neighborhood remains a visible – often a coercive – concept" in the lives of young gang members (1991: 131–2). In fact, junior gang members or novices may be warned away by senior members from making purely nuisance-type trouble for residents of their community and thus avoid unnecessary incidents that invite the attention of police (Bing 1991).

According to Moore's study, maturation out of street and gang life and into adult roles in the barrio was a natural process in the old days (the 1950s). Here is a key difference with regard to today's gangs. The maturation process that allowed young adult members to leave the life of the street has been affected by the economic restructuring and deindustrialization that took the "good" jobs out of East Los Angeles and replaced them with unstable, poorly paid, and unsheltered work. This has affected survival strategies, meaning that more and older young adults have turned to transfer payments or remained dependent on illicit sources of income. Absent or intermittent legitimate employment kept some subjects on the streets and undermined the establishment of stable family life (Moore 1991: 133).

Vigil (1988: 16ff) also examined barrio gangs in southern California, and based his analysis, in part, on an interactive urban ecology framework that portrays the emergence of particular youth culture and gang ethos as depending on a combination of local economic constraints and opportunities, in addition to biographical differences of particular group members. The spatial emphasis in his analysis is based on the fact that Mexican-American communities have always been separate, sometimes physically cut off (by rivers, rail lines, highways), from the affluent majority community (20), thus making locational issues a particularly salient feature for understanding Chicano institutions. A history of Anglo xenophobia and discrimination has entrenched the physical separation of Mexican-American communities, and the economic as well as social marginalization of residents. Aside from the fact that this physical separation and isolation from the rest of society means that it is harder to earn a living, it also allows hostility to crystallize between young residents and the outsider enforcers of the law. This contributes to the oppositional sense that young men have of police as the coercive representatives of an outside force, and contributes to feelings of solidarity within the socially and spatially separate community (141ff).

Bing (1991) has produced a useful journalistic account of contemporary African American (primarily) gang life in South Central Los Angeles. It is an account of how rape, murder, torture, and random drive-by shootings are part of an emerging order of the streets, of how for the subculture that controls the streets, life has become cheap. As in the past, allegiance to the group is the primary involvement that gives meaning to existence. What is different about gangs today is the level and routinization of violence among them.

Most of Bing's respondents, interviewed in their neighborhoods or in detention centers, were members of various factions of the Crips and Bloods and were in their early teens. Like their older brothers and cousins, they were hardened by their experiences and the brutal logic of gang

warfare, by the cause of retribution and honor to which these fourteen-
to seventeen-year-olds were committed. They savored the solidarity of
the in-group, the norm of unflinching loyalty, the knowledge that they
were likely to be tested often, given ample opportunity to demonstrate
their commitment. But as younger boys listened to older boys tell their
war stories to Bing, she noted that the younger gang members were at
times visibly shaken by the brutal details. Yet they all proclaimed their
dedication to the principle of doing what they had to do to protect their
interests and the honor of the group: To do less was to invite victimization. For them it wasn't a question of whether they would be able to
kill or not, but only a question of the appropriate style and how much
care you had to give to selecting a target – a question of effectively
communicating your intent and purpose to the various audiences who
learned of the deed.

There are apparent similarities as well as differences between the contemporary gang organization and the traditional barrio gangs described
by Moore, as there are similarities between the emergence of gangs and
neighborhood preservation or Neighborhood Watch groups. All of these
groups have emerged in response to the uncertainties of the contemporary urban arena. Some neighborhood groups have the law on their side,
others number the agents of the law among their enemies or find them
irrelevant to their ends. Anderson (1990: 80) refers to the groups of young
men patrolling the troubled neighborhoods of Philadelphia as "a kind
of informal police force that protects, defends or simply does not bother
those who are deemed deserving of such consideration," while victimiz-
ing those who are not. Gangs are an organ of purpose: That purpose is,
in part, to present a localized, solidary front dedicated to the protection
of group and personal economic interests and personal safety. Obviously,
groups facing different circumstances will need to find different strategies for effectively staking out a claim to their protected quarter. One
urban actor builds a fence or installs a new alarm system, another kills
for the sheer hell of it, but also because he has learned it is useful to
demonstrate to friend and foe that he's capable of anything, not some-
one to be taunted or trifled with. An urban sociology, a spatial sociology, requires us to pay attention to how the urban environment – territoriality and heterogeneity, class and racial differences in close proximity,
changing investment strategies with respect to location – works to give
rise to forms of solidarity, requires us to pay attention to the gross similarities among territorially vigilant groups.

2

Urban ecology and its critics

The obligation of urban social science is twofold. In addition to under-standing the effects produced by the urban environment on social organization, experience, and behavior, it must also form an understanding of the production of the urban environment itself. Besides being a study of social life in urban space, urban sociology is the study of the creation of urban space. In this and the following chapter we turn our attention to the construction and reconstruction of the city, or the structuring of the built environment.

Some social scientists take the view that there are a set of principles generic to settled human space itself which give rise to spatial relation-ships among the constituent elements found in all urban environments. Stated a little less abstractly, there are residences, businesses, various institutions, transportation and communication facilities commonly found in any city, elements of the urban environment which have a certain degree of predictability regarding their respective spatial locations. The relative location of poor people's housing, fancy boutiques, heavy industry, and financial institutions, for example, is not random, but exhibits a certain order. The order of human space follows a logic generated by some combination of the following: competition for the best locations, overall efficiency of the use of that space, mutual compatibility of neighboring uses, evolving changes in population size and composition, patterns of economic expansion and contraction, and the state of communication and transportation technology.

The spatial order of cities in this view is produced by a dynamic mix of factors, but these factors and their interrelationships are knowable, perhaps ultimately predictable, and are intrinsic properties of human settlement itself. That is, settled human space, or the physical urban environment, is the expression of a rational order governed by principles of settled human space, sui generis. One could hardly ask for more felicitous designations for such a viewpoint than the conventional (and, for our purposes, interchangeable) ones, *human ecology* or *urban ecology*.

At the outset of this discussion of the urban ecology paradigm it is important to point out that the current status of this approach to urban analysis is paradoxical. Although it is difficult to overestimate its influence on the study of the city, urban ecology has been for half a century subject to serious criticisms of its most fundamental principles. One may read contemporary comments that its classic works have long been "vilified" by critics (Warf 1990: 73) but, also, that it remains the dominant paradigm in urban science whose practitioners are gatekeepers who exclude alternate approaches from the major sociology journals (Feagin 1986: 531; Gottdiener and Feagin 1988: 166).

It is true that those who take opposing views in large part preface their work with conventionalized criticisms of the inadequacies of the ecological approach. At the same time committed ecologists are attempting to revise (and revive) earlier theory, to incorporate evidence from contemporary urban changes into more dynamic and less linear models of the evolution of human settlement patterns. If it were the case that urban ecology was a dead language in social science, then its importance as a founding set of principles in the conduct of urban studies would still argue for its inclusion in a treatment of contemporary urban sociology. As it is, there are many who call themselves urban ecologists who continue to turn out ecological analyses within what historically has been the mainstream of urban sociology, whereas others are more embraced by the paradigm in the approaches they take to urban analysis than embracing of it.

In the past, as its critics have observed, urban ecology was too often a conservative rationale for the assumption that generalized progress and mutual benefit attended the expansion of the economy. Yet there seems to be no inherent reason that the approach cannot be reconstituted so that it may systematically address social conflict and contradiction as well as consensus and dynamic equilibrium. In any event, the ecological paradigm needs to be examined if we are to understand the state of the art of current urban sociological theory and practice. This would remain true if the ecology were only a critical point of departure for current conceptual developments. A number of contemporary students believe that the approach, including some of its classic principles, hold more promise than that.

One further, introductory point to this discussion of urban ecology: Contemporary urban sociologists are concerned, probably above all else, with urban space and the changing uses to which it is put. They argue over what particular spaces are used for, how agents gain access to them, who benefits from their use. The focus of much contemporary urban sociology, therefore, is on issues of political and economic power. The ecologists were the first urban sociologists to raise these questions in a systematic fashion. From the first, ecology represented a fusion of the fields of economics, geography, and sociology (Gottdiener 1985: 26). The object of study of urban scientists continues to be multidisciplinary (Gottdiener and Feagin 1988: 163), and in the following discussion it has been necessary not to restrict attention to the work of sociologists alone.

The Chicago school and early ecology

If one were to look for a theoretical mentor for urban ecology, Durkheim and his *The Division of Labor in Society* (1893) is probably the most useful referent. His argument that the aggregation of large numbers of people in concentrated settlements required a complex division of labor, his observation that society required the reintegration of special-ized urbanites into a complementary organic whole, provided the principles for a theory of the ecological interdependence of human popu-lations. If we add to this certain social Darwinist understandings of how competition produced patterns of dominance and subordination among the elements of societies, we have the background assumptions of the founding school of urban sociology, the Chicago school, in its approach to the evolution and structure of urban space.

The most prominent members of the school are Robert Park, R. D. McKenzie, and Ernest W. Burgess. It was Park (1926a) who appropri-ated the principles of natural science for the analysis of urban spaces. He observed a correspondence between plant "communities" in the natural environment and the emergence of "natural areas" within cities where similar societal constituents of the urban environment congregated. In addition to the unity of function that identified and set apart these natural areas, there was also a moral unity, a community ethos, that made each area somewhat unique in terms of the values and norms of behavior that prevailed there. In this way, the urban environment was broken down into a mosaic of social worlds that were each in some measure offset, structurally and culturally, from adjacent ones (Park 1915: 612).

McKenzie's work focused on the dynamic nature of the urban arena. He described (1926: 171–82) the simultaneous processes of the central-ization of essential services and the dispersion of nonspecialized ones; there were general tendencies toward residential concentration around commercial and industrial districts, while transportation developments allowed residential deconcentration along major arteries. His most enduring contribution is in the terminology he employed to describe the way in which distinctive populations moved into residential areas, replacing previous residential groups; the process, called *invasion and succession,* typically involved the displacement of higher by lower socioeconomic categories. McKenzie was among the earliest to address theoretically the process of urban sprawl or metropolitanization (McKenzie 1933). Burgess (1925) was also interested in the dynamic interrelationship of distinctive urban areas, and adapted the invasion and succession theme of urban change into a general spatial model of urban growth. It is unfortunate that his effort to diagram what he thought was the general pattern of the major urban regions became the focus of attention for later students and critics of his work. His five concentric zones of urban land use (1925: 51) is perhaps the most indelible and well-known diagram in the social sciences. Burgess intended the diagram, which he based on his knowledge of the aereal morphology of the city of Chicago, as a general, abstract model of urban growth: in fact, he labeled his sketch "The Growth of the City." He was especially interested in the process of invasion and succession through which the central business district expanded into the zone in transition, and in the way successive waves of residential invasion and succession allowed the city to expand outward through succeeding concentric rings (consistent with the biological analogy, like the annular rings of growth in trees).

Although Burgess had proposed a general schema of urban growth, rather than a literal map of any particular city or of cities in general (Hawley 1981: 98–101), the concentric circles of his diagram offered too inviting a target for criticism. It was too easy to demonstrate that the growth pattern of a given city violated the assumption of unbroken concentric rings. The best-known rival scheme was offered by Hoyt in 1939. Based on a time series analysis of 142 cities in the United States, Hoyt concluded that residential growth proceeded outward from center to periphery in a more linear than ringlike fashion, so that residentially homogeneous areas grew outward in wedge-shaped sectors rather than unbroken rings. Neglected and all but forgotten in most debates about whether the outward growth of the city proceeded in wedges or unbroken rings is an early hypothesis (1903) developed by Richard Hurd that some (Hawley 1950; Frisbie and Kasarda 1988: 631; Schwirian, Hankins, and Ventresca 1990: 1,146–7) believe provided a complement or even a synthesis of the later Burgess and Hoyt theses. Hurd observed that cities grew outward from the older center along radial arteries where the leading transportation innovations were overcoming spatial limitations previously imposed on settlement patterns. The interstices sagged against the radial arteries, filling in more slowly, and imparting an overall star shape (with the radial transportation arteries constituting the outermost points of growth) to urban expansion.

The question as to whether Hurd's scheme provided a better way to describe the gradually expanding, nucleated urban pattern was mooted by the explosive territorial expansion of cities during and especially after World War II, as demonstrated by the findings of Harris and Ullman (1945). Where earlier models of urban land use had assumed that cities grew around a single commercial and industrial center, cities had sprawled outward by the mid-1940s and become less focused. Based on their observation of cities in Europe (Harris 1990: 411) and the United States, Harris and Ullman proposed the well-known multiple-nuclei model: The location of commercial and retail sites, light and heavy industry, and residences of different social classes varied widely. Although each city had a "central business district," other elements of the urban landscape no longer located themselves with particular reference to this district. Although, for a given city, there was bound to be an internal patterning of where compatible and incompatible elements were located with regard to one another, it was not possible to predict where the various elements would be found for cities in general. Aside from limited assumptions regarding mutual compatibility, there was no basis for predictive statements about the location of major economic, industrial, and residential districts. Neither rings nor wedges nor stars described the expanding urban landscape: Cities had become an amalgam of districts with many industrial, commercial, and residential zones juxtaposed in a variety of patterns. Harris and Ullman would seem to have marked the end of efforts by ecologists to uncover the grand scheme of urban spatial arrangement. However, the Burgess zonal hypothesis and other elements of classical ecological thought continue to provide a basis for research and debate.

Much of the criticism of early urban ecology has fallen into the trap of debating the shape and arrangement of land-use patterns, even though such criticism is arguably largely misguided (Saunders 1981: 62–3; Hawley 1981: 98–101). However, this leaves ample room to debate the advisability of Burgess's main intention, the effort to explicate a common growth process that produced a functional differentiation and ordering of urban space according to the dominant factors of economic competition. Was the emphasis on the operation of the marketplace overly deterministic? It failed to address the important effects of local culture and sentiments that preserve land uses that contradict profit-maximizing strategies. Critics maintain that individual and collective choices were not governed solely by economic considerations. Firey's (1945) well-known, early critique was based on the city of Boston where the upper-class residents of Beacon Hill long resisted efforts of developers, where the general populace would dismiss as unthinkable any subdivision and development of Boston Common's forty-eight acres, and where ethnic attachments to neighborhoods defied reduction to strictly economic terms.

The counterargument is that Park himself had recognized that natural areas in the city gave rise to local cultures, and that sentimental or "nonrational" values were an overlay on the more universal economic, rational processes of urban development (Gottdiener 1985: 27–9; Saunders 1981: 65). However, this does not adequately address the question of whether Burgess was able to build these into his causal model in a systematic fashion. Alihan (1938) criticized the early ecologists for failing to distinguish sufficiently between model building (creating ideal types) and descriptions of actual urban areas. In this way they emphasized the natural laws of "biotic" determination, translated as economic competition for the most desirable space, over cultural values. Any effect of sentiment, including deliberate policy measures of local government to control or shape growth in ways contrary to those favored by price and demand, was beyond the power of ecological theory to anticipate.

It is remarkable that the early ecological formulations still inspire debate and inform research. It is remarkable because today's cities are so fundamentally different from those that Hurd or Burgess based their observations on. The urban changes they witnessed involved the expansion of very compact patterns of settlement characteristic of North American cities in the previous century. Hurd's star-shaped expansion was a product of the limitations of transportation technology at the turn of the century (which is not to say that transportation technology was causing urban growth). The leading points of the star were the limits of easily commutable distance via mass transit, while the slowly filling areas in between showed the compact nature of urban space with limits set by walkable distances. Burgess's generalizations were based on the city of Chicago during its period of rapid population and economic growth in the teens and twenties. Today's cities are no longer compact, but sprawling. Residential patterns are no longer limited by walking distances or commuter lines. Millions of industrial jobs have been lost, especially in the urban centers. This is as true for European as for North American cities.

Still, the old models and principles have not been put to rest. Among the research conducted within the ecological approach, one still finds reference to elements of the early schemes. Two of these elements draw the greatest interest among contemporary researchers who employ classical ecological concepts: Burgess's concentric zones continue to exert an intuitive appeal, despite urban changes that have taken place since their formulation; the second is McKenzie's process of invasion and succession. Schwirian, Hankins, and Ventresca (1990) argue that the question of the applicability and generalizability of the Burgess zonal hypothesis has yet to be resolved. In their view, the lingering controversy rests in part in the fact that many exceptions may be found to the rule. Their findings indicate that the Burgess zonal hypothesis is *modal* for cities in the United States, although *most* cities do not conform to it. The findings of their survey of residential patterns of 318 cities were consistent with the Burgess hypothesis 45.9 percent of the time: Moreover, they believe that there was a general trend between 1950 and 1980 in the direction predicted by the Burgess model. The authors conclude by raising the question of whether metropolitan residential patterns may be reconverging in a way described by the Burgess model (Schwirian, Hankins, and Ventresca 1990: 1,160–1).

This investigation is typical of those that employ the older Chicago school themes in that it selects only a portion of the total scheme, in this case, residential location, for examination. Another study, by Aldrich, Zimmer, and McEvoy (1989), focuses on another important element of early ecological theory, invasion and succession, in describing the pattern by which businesses change hands in three English cities. The research involves replication of a study of minority business owner ship in three cities in the United States (Aldrich and Reiss 1976) and finds, as did the earlier study, that the transition from predominant majority to minority ownership did not involve panic selling by whites in transitional areas. Asian ownership, in Bradford, Leicester, and London, increased as non-Asians simply did not buy into businesses that were up for sale. Where non-Asian ownership persisted, it was simply a matter of profitability. In sum, Aldrich et al. document orderly episodes of invasion and succession based essentially on economic rather than sentimental (cultural) factors. Critics may recognize the utility of such findings, and yet be impatient with their limitations. Still, viewed from within the ecology paradigm, such findings are apparently sufficient to sustain a theoretical interest in the older patterns and principles.

Post–World War II urban ecology

It is conventional to divide the evolution of thought in urban ecology into prewar and postwar periods. The reasons for the mid-century demarcation include the changing nature of North American cities that was underway during the 1950s, a new direction in empirical studies in ecology, and new theoretical developments.

After the war, the metropolitanization of urban areas proceeded at a rapid rate. In the United States especially, the government-sponsored mobilization of the private housing industry generated an explosive expansion of suburbanization patterns that had been underway (at a more modest pace) for decades. Whereas European policy-making bodies tried with limited success to control the sprawl of urban centers, policy in the United States allowed for the unfettered regionalization of cities. The acceleration of patterns of urban decentralization that characterized the 1950s carried over into the decades that followed, and persists at the present time. It remains all too easy to write the big stories of exurban growth and the collapse of central city economies without a formal ecological theory to guide an understanding of what has been taking place. Furthermore, there was nothing in the Chicago school tradition that anticipated the turn of events that transformed the twentieth-century city.

The newly emerging urban form freed ecologists to embark on new directions in research and theory. Post-1950 urban ecology split into two distinct emphases: detailed, empirical studies of urban areas and populations, on the one hand, and the adaptation of an all-encompassing social philosophy that sought to unify principles of societal and spatial arrangements, on the other.

Detailing the social mosaic: Empirical demography

In 1955 Shevky and Bell offered a refined version of the research technique known as *social area analysis* (also Shevky and Williams 1949). Social area analysis was based on the understanding that there were certain key variables that were sociologically significant in setting certain residential areas apart from others. The idea was that variations among three easily measurable factors – economic status, family status, and ethnic classification – gave insight into the way urban space was patterned, and the manner in which that pattern changed over time. The advent of electronic data processing allowed the number of variables that might be considered in identifying and comparing social areas to be increased. Social area analysis evolved into the computer-assisted technique, *factorial ecology,* which involved factor analysis of multiple social features of urban populations. Clusters of variables associated with specific social areas of the city (typically census tracts) were identified, given thematic labels, mapped onto the surface of the metropolitan area, and tracked from one episode of data collection to the next in order to discern patterns of change.

Although factor analysis typifies the empirical approach of postwar empirical ecology, there are numerous other descriptive techniques that have been applied to the task of tracing the changing map of the metropolis. The criticism of the empirical trend is that it was poorly grounded in theory. The criticism is deserved, but is even more well founded if expressed in terms of empirical ecology's failure to keep up with current theoretical developments within the field of ecology itself. Although there is a great deal of variation, many if not most empirical studies do attempt to address theory. Most often, however, these are elements of theory associated with the old school.

Shevky and Bell (1955: 7–18) originally formulated social area analysis in conjunction with the social fragmentation and "mass society" themes contained in Wirth's (1938) "urbanism" thesis. Although the empirical–theoretical connection may appear tenuous to critics, Shevky and Bell believed that the fragmentation of the urban arena according to their three variables indicated social fragmentation of society in general. Schwirian (1977: 93–5) used social area analysis to describe the differing ecologies of cities of less industrialized Third World societies, where economic status, family status, and ethnic membership vary together. In the cities of industrialized nations, there is more independent variation among the variables. Schwirian's interpretation of the stable and predictable relationship among the social area variables in the Third World is that, there, urban populations reflect a less thorough influence of urbanism over social life: Further, he argues that it is the largest Third World cities that show a trend in the direction followed by the cities of Western industrialized nations.

Yet, the criticism is well founded that, taken as a whole, the empirical orientation of urban ecology has produced a diffuse assortment of ecological findings too closely approximating the abstracted empiricism that Mills (1959) warned against in his classic essays. It is not the case that empirical ecological studies are devoid of conceptual frameworks. The problem, critics argue, is that the framework provided by urban ecology is so unspecified that ecologists have felt free to wander through the city studying anything they encountered (Logan and Molotch 1987: 8–9). Another problem with the empirical emphasis is that data leads theory. The cost of such an approach is that basic assumptions about the principles of social order, the central questions of sociology, become an afterthought. There can be no question as to whether the information and conclusions produced by ecological study of urban populations is useful. The question is whether, in the absence of a guiding paradigm, they lead in any particular direction toward the understanding of the urban environment and change. Of course, for those contemporary sociologists who believe that theory should be applied with a light touch, there is less to criticize here (see Chapter 5).

A sampling of empirical studies suggests the wide range of issues addressed, and some of the practical conclusions that have been produced. Rees's (1979) review of factorial ecologies of North American cities has shown that the original variables identified by Shevky and Bell

(1955) continue to show up regularly as the key factors that distinguish urban residential areas. That is, while the factorial method allows for the inclusion of a large number of variables, in the end these tend to distill down into economic status, family composition (or, alternatively, "life-cycle stage"), and ethnic background. Exceptions tend to prove the rule. In ethnically homogeneous Dublin there is no ethnic factor, leaving only two major factors accounting for variance – income and family status (Hourihan 1978). Knox (1987: 132) observes that this pattern held in most factorial studies of European cities. In those studies, findings indicate a strong socioeconomic (associated with housing type) and family status component, but no ethnic factor. This he speculates is due either to low levels of ethnic diversity, or to insufficient sensitivity of the available, census-tract level data that typically make up the units of analysis for factorial ecologies.

In Tel Aviv (Borukhov, Ginsberg, and Werczberger 1979) in the early 1970s, where the government pursued a vigorous policy of residential integration of immigrants from various geographic origins (at the time 56 percent of the city's population had been born outside Israel), ethnicity did not turn up as one of the three major variance-explaining factors. The study, based largely on 1972 census data did, however, reflect the importance of the ethnic factor: The "ethnic origin" variable (measured as national origin) was a component of each of the three major indices produced by analysis – economic status, family (life-cycle) status, and residential crowding. Incidentally, the authors of the study conclude by noting that socioeconomic differentiation tended to follow a sectoral distribution, while family or life-cycle indicators followed a more concentric one. The data did suggest that ethnic origin was highly correlated with social mobility and, therefore, geographic mobility within the city, indicating that ethnic origin promised to remain an important residential variable.

Summarizing some of the comparative data from Western nations, Knox (1987: 135) argues that, despite differences, it is possible to build a theory around a generalized model of the Western city. As he also observes, however, conceptual debates among researchers have remained focused on nuances of the factorial method, and no general theoretical framework has developed.

The number of specific methodological questions associated with the factor analytic approach suggest that practitioners have plenty to concern them at this level. Problems include reliance on census data that fail to cover a full range of desirable socioeconomic population characteristics; the related problem that the generation of similar factors by different studies (suggesting the convergent evolution of urban areas) may be produced by the similarity in input variables (i.e., an artifact of the method); the possibility that census-tract boundaries (the conventional units of analysis) are heterogeneous, raising the question of whether the use of alternate spatial divisions might produce alternate factors; the fact that most research is forced to take areas within formally defined administrative units (municipalities) as the object of study, rather than functional metropolitan populations; and the related problem that central city and suburban populations are not incorporated in the same analyses. Finally, there is the long recognized problem of attributing areal characteristics to populations and subpopulations, known as the "ecological fallacy," and other errors related to the tendency toward the overinterpretation of findings (Knox 1987: 136–9). A more fundamental criticism, of course, is the question of how any method that is limited to measuring residential patterns can ever give us a full picture of the process of the emergence and changes in patterns of urban land use, including land appropriated for nonresidential uses.

The methodological limitations of statistical approaches in urban ecology are serious, and tendencies toward abstracted empiricism trouble many, ecologists and critics alike. Nevertheless, research in urban ecology has produced a monument of data that contemporary students will continue to sift for what valuable information it may yield about urban spatial dynamics. It is difficult to judge how the finding that snow and cold climate generate denser patterns of urban settlement for cities in northern regions of the United States may contribute to such theory building (Guterbock 1990). However, there is little doubt that such findings constitute worthwhile information for urban planners and administrators, and it is hard to say whether and how such a fact may find its way into social theory in the future. Closer to mainstream sociological concerns are the findings (from Cleveland) that racial discrimination in housing practice tends to be higher in areas adjacent to all-white tracts and tracts undergoing rapid racial conversions (Galster 1987). While the limitations of census-tract level data and other indirect, existing sources do not provide ideally sensitive measures, the evidence from this study is sufficiently suggestive to indicate directions for further research. The study points to a patterned interaction between rational economic motives of the sort emphasized by ecologists, and cultural factors (recognized by ecologists but receiving less emphasis), in the form of racist sentiment, that together determine levels of discrimination in a particular residential area.

A recent study of ethnic invasion and succession in Brooklyn reveals that the frame of analysis for interpreting ecological data has to be expanded to incorporate worldwide social and economic upheavals as well as trends in economic restructuring at the national and regional level. Understanding local housing patterns, therefore, may require reference to the

Irish Potato Famine of the mid-nineteenth century, global inequalities of income and life chances, the mechanization of cotton production in the southern states of the U.S., the impending reabsorption of Hong Kong, or emigration and immigration policies affecting Caribbean populations or Jews in Russia (Warf 1990).

Such global and holistic awareness certainly prescribes a cure for any tendencies toward narrow empiricism. But, it potentially draws into question the future importance of the ecological study of localities. If one ultimately must resort to broad historical, political, and economic frames of analysis for understanding the local, then doesn't it make more sense to begin with the global? If so, investigations of local patterns are case studies verging on the anecdotal, vital to a total understanding, but needing to be placed in a broader context. This seems an important point. If the recent methodological tradition in urban ecology has a role to play in the development of urban theory, it will be as a component of a variety of empirical methodologies. More importantly, the traditional questions raised by empirical ecology, the mapping of the urban (especially residential) surface and documentation of changes in spatial patterns, will give way to deeper questions of how local patterns reflect global influences. Does the ecological approach, in a systematic fashion, lead to an analysis global in scope?

Grand theory: Ecology beyond the city

There has been substantial theoretical movement in ecology in the post-World War II era, but it has had a limited role in guiding empirical work. The major theoretical developments have posited general, abstract schema of social organization and physical space, not easily testable through the type of empirical research on local residential patterns that has attracted so many empirical ecologists. The major theories of ecology today are not based on the urban arena that fascinated the members of the Chicago school. Instead, society has become the ecologist's unit of analysis, and physical space, itself, is only one of many dimensions of human society. At the present time, there is only a tangential relationship between ecological theory and urban sociology, although theoretical development is rooted in the urban tradition.

The major developments in ecological theory date from the 1950s and are attributable to Duncan (1959) and Hawley (1950, 1986). Duncan's work can be characterized more briefly, and his "ecological complex" model illustrates nicely the affinity between postwar ecological theory and Parsons's (1951) structural functionalism which so deeply affected general sociological theory during the middle decades of the twentieth century. The ecological complex consists of the four fundamental conditions whose dynamic interaction produce the state of a given society. The four elements – population, organization, environment, and technology – constitute a feedback system. Duncan adopted the acronym POET to refer to the model. Changes introduced from outside, which effect change in one or more of the constituents of the system, set off a series of adjustments among the constituents, until the system is brought back into some sort of balance.

Such a system is most useful for discussions of the broad sweep of societal changes, such as the transformation of European society between the eighteenth and twentieth centuries. A fairly conventional view would refer to technological innovation and the introduction of new staple foods from outside the region leading to an expanding population and emigration, generating new intranational and international relationships and manners of organizing society, and so on, until some sort of stability was reestablished. Duncan himself recognized the artificiality of applying the analysis to individual communities, except where a community itself approximated a closed system. Instead, the unit of analysis would ultimately be planetary in scope, at least regional.

It is easy to see how this theoretical development tends to limit the applicability of ecological theory for urban analysis because cities are by no means closed "community" systems. Lyon (1987: 48–9) has suggested that the POET system could be used to talk about the process of postwar suburbanization in the United States. The postwar baby boom generated a demand for housing; the tired and unattractive inner city (environment) could not provide for the demand, making suburbanization the logical tendency; government subsidies (organization) were provided through the Veterans Administration and the Federal Housing Administration, while urban renewal reduced the number of units remaining in cities; technology, through the increase in automobile ownership, provided the necessary means for daily commutation.

How useful as a conceptual tool is the ecological complex? In general, it would appear to be most useful as a checklist for functionalist systems theorists interested in broad analyses of social change. Its utility for urban sociologists, in particular, is less clear. As already noted, Duncan's own observations indicate that community-level analyses do not really offer a sufficiently closed system.

The most influential theoretical development in ecology in the past half century has come from Amos Hawley. His work parallels Duncan's in that it moves the focus away from specifically urban analysis, and bears a similar strong affinity for the equilibrial assumptions of structural functionalism. In 1944 Hawley already argued that space was not the central concern of ecology. Instead, the appropriate focus was the functional differentiation and adaptation of human populations (Hawley

1944). Hawley (1950) developed a fourfold framework of what he saw as the essential ecological principles that characterized the adaptation of any society. The four characteristics were interdependence, differentiation, key function, and dominance. He emphasized the *interdependence* that exists among the structural components of society; the functional *differentiation* of social components that supports the preceding assumption; the idea that some components are more centrally important to societal adaptation and must therefore be recognized as possessing the quality of *key function;* and *dominance* which is the natural outcome in any system in which certain societal elements are more vital to the total functioning of society than are others.

Although Hawley later sought to distance his theory from Parsonian functionalism (1986: 29ff), the connection is unmistakable. Social units are integrated according to the ways they are useful to one another, and function in support of the overall adaptive order that characterizes the particular society: According to Hawley, "An ecosystem is an arrangement of mutual dependences in a population by which the whole operates as a unit and thereby maintains a viable environmental relationship." The social elements in the analysis are held together either in symbiotic (differentiated and, therefore, complementary) or commensualistic (similar and, therefore, reenforcing) relationships. It is the institutional arrangements rather than individuals that draw our attention in this analysis because it is the larger, stable units of society ("relatum") that interact and persist, as the human constituents come and go (Hawley 1986: 26–38). Spatial considerations are introduced because such systems do occupy space. System efficiency requires the optimal distribution of social elements whether we are talking about hunters and gatherers or metropolitan regions. The assumption is that the spatial manifestation of the ecosystem is included in the constant equilibrial adjustment.

Hawley's model is liable to the same general objections as those raised against functionalism. Equilibrial models are widely understood to be teleological with respect to their system-needs assumptions, conservatively biased in support of the status quo, and account poorly for the sources of change from within the social–ecosystem. The emphasis on balance and system integration leads away from questions of social class and racism, while introducing what is seen by critics as a tendency toward biological reductionism, not likely to attract much of an audience among contemporary sociologists (Gottdiener 1985: 37–40). Additionally, the emphasis on communications and transportation in that portion of the theory that continues to address the spatial arrangement of society remains subject to the same charge of technological determinism as was leveled at the Chicago school approach.

There is another criticism of functionalist ecology with respect to the traditional standpoint of urban sociology. Until recently, it has seemed important that urban sociologists establish a distinctive domain of study, that any useful general theory would reserve a separate niche for the analysis of localized spatial issues. The work of Duncan and Hawley take us in the opposite direction. As ecology has been appropriately expanded as a framework of analysis to incorporate entire social systems in its scope, it has less to do with urban or spatial questions at the subsystem level. Taking Hawley and Duncan together, Saunders (1981: 79) assesses the situation in the following terms:

> Hawley has been able to resurrect human ecology only by jettisoning its specific relevance to the city, and this development of the ecological approach as an ecological perspective rather than as an urban theory was then taken further by Duncan with the result that the relation between ecological theory and urban theory became purely contingent. Now that ecology has found its niche within the functionalist paradigm, we may debate its validity and its usefulness in that context, but irrespective of the conclusions we draw from such a debate it is clear that human ecology is no longer essentially an urban theory and that it cannot provide a conceptual framework within which a specifically urban theory can be developed.

This is clearly an important point. The following chapters, however, indicate a trend toward globalization with regard to all modes of urban analysis. That is, the paradigmatic movement in urban analysis is toward a broadening of the analytic context of spatial issues to a national or international, systemic frame. On balance, the functionalist biases of contemporary ecological theory appear to be more of a liability than its lack of specificity as an urban theory.

Nevertheless, taken as a whole the criticisms of the ecological approach to urban sociology appear to have considerable weight. Yet paradigms, especially in the social sciences, have a powerful inertial force. Hawley's voice is an influential one among social ecologists, but his theoretical work has split as much as guided the field. The prominent ecologist Brian Berry reacted strongly to Hawley's most recent (1986) extended essay as environmental determinism. "There is no room in this mechanistic logic for cultures to interpose cognitive screens between environment and behavior . . . conservatives take heart: norms, values, laws, are all nature's gifts, not human constructs" (Berry 1988: 139). Zimmer (1988: 135–6), on the other hand, was favorably impressed with Hawley's adaptation of ecology as a general sociological theory, removed from the narrow confines of the urban question; in his view, the work is materialist, yet uncluttered by Marxist ideology.

The assumptions that characterize the equilibrial model and the logical offshoots of those assumptions, have had both a direct and indirect influence on research and policy. Some writers have made the revised ecological theory a formal part of their work, whereas others operate within the paradigm without formal acknowledgement or, perhaps, awareness. In any event, Hawley can be seen to exert an influence over contemporary urban thought.

Although his theory has made settled space a residual consideration, some ecologists have found Hawley's thought all the more useful for the study of cities. Prominent among these is Wilson (1984). He has adapted the guidelines of Hawley's general model to expand the scope of ecological analysis to the relationship among cities, to urban systems. He takes as his point of departure the long-standing urban geographer's observation that cities in advanced industrial nations comprise a hierarchical order. Each city's place within the order is determined by the "key functions" it contains relative to the entire system: "The most influential places tend to have much higher concentrations of wholesale activities; transportation and commercial facilities; and decision-making units that regulate production activities, thereby controlling capital flows, credit, and the dissemination of information, and employment." It is important to recognize, as "most ecologists" do, that these cities are not like corporations with a formally organized structure, vying with one another for dominance. "Thus, such terms as key function and dominance are simply composites of the totality of influences exerted by the decision units within the boundaries of urban communities" (1984: 287–9).

Ecologists have integrated neoorthodox ecological concepts with complementary concepts taken from economics and geography to explain urban expansion and patterns of intercity dominance and subordination. The results indicate that formal models have a modest utility if historical factors associated with wider patterns of regional growth and decline are taken into account. The results also indicate the limitations in the nature of the enormous, existing data bases upon which ecologists must rely for evaluating the sweeping postulates of contemporary theory.

LaGory and Nelson (1978), for example, explored the proposition that cities with specialized functions grew more rapidly than others because they provided a scarce (i.e., basic) service to the system as a whole. However, their analysis of patterns of growth of major cities in the United States between 1900 and 1940 revealed that regional location (whether the city was located in the North or the South) had a major impact on growth prospects. Also, they found that the nature of specialization is crucial: Cities whose relative importance was invested in the provision of goods or services for which demand is falling within the system as a whole will obviously not be experiencing higher rates of growth than the rest of the system. LaGory and Nelson did find a strong correlation between population growth and transportation technology, especially railroads, which led them to conclude that ecologists had not placed a sufficiently strong emphasis on this variable.

Once again, the implications of research are limited by the shortcomings of the kind of data available. Aside from raising empirical questions, LaGory and Nelson's findings do not defeat the key function–dominance hypothesis of ecological theory. Instead, research simply points out the dynamic nature of environment, where regional decline or economic misfortune articulates with the spatial aspects of the system. For ecologists, the message is that specialization and key function are not the same thing, a distinction already made by Hawley. In a dynamic equilibrium one expects change. Also, from this perspective, the correlation between rail transportation and urban growth does not introduce a grounds for modifying the model. The period of the study, 1910 to 1940, should reflect the importance of the railroads. But changes in transportation technology since that time would make such a finding surprising in the 1990s.

In a similar multidisciplinary approach to that of the LaGory and Nelson study, Eberstein, Wrigley, and Serow (1985) employ mutually compatible postulates from economics (the same basic versus nonbasic services concept employed by LaGory and Nelson), geography (central place theory), and sociology (metropolitan dominance: Cities in a region will be subject to the dominating influence of the one at the functional center). Among the 117 urban regions of the United States that were studied, it was found that big cities with specialized and important functions that provide a geographic focus for a given region tend to be dominant within that region. That is, similar theoretical predictions from economics, geography, and sociology–ecology having to do with regional intercity dominance are generally supported. However, this study also indicated the need to consider both the shift in regional fortunes between the North and South, and the transformation of the economy from an industrial to a service base in order to account for anomalies in the general pattern. The major implication, once again, is that static assumptions about the stability of dominance patterns within urban systems are in error. Dynamic economies produce changes in key functions and dominance, and changes the spatial manifestations of social systems ecosystems.

Although equilibrial models have an inherent difficulty explaining the sources of the changes that in turn require adjustments within the system, Hawley (1986) recognizes this, and devotes two chapters to the topic. For him, the ultimate origin of changes introduced to the system is straightforward: The source of change must be external. Changes that appear to be internal result mainly from continued repercussions of earlier-induced exogenous changes (49–60). The balance between territory and populations is subject to economic and technological factors. Although Hawley's discussion on this account is apparently meant for application to various types of human populations, the example he chooses to illustrate the point is pertinent: "Many an early town has lost its eminence in production and trade as technological changes and new industries have favored other locations" (64). The point here is that Hawley has constructed a dynamic model. Equilibrium is an ongoing tendency, not a steady state. One cannot assume stasis either with regard to leading sectors or patterns of dominance among urban centers.

One further point in Hawley's ecosystem theory needs to be noted if the influence of his mode of thinking on current urban sociology is to be appreciated. This is his perception of the tendency toward convergence in form and function among systems: "Although the various ecosystems of humanity were formed in widely different circumstances and have in each instance been exposed to different historical experiences, the ecosystems have tended to become more alike as their interactions have increased because communication requires a standardization of terms of reference, operating procedures, and forms of organization" (Hawley 1986: 84). He notes that critics who have faulted convergence assumptions on the basis of tendencies toward linear evolutionism and technological determinism in those assumptions, and who have found contradiction in the fact that differences persist among ecosystems after long periods of system interactions, have not made their point. He recommends that researchers look for the process of convergence, not its consummation. Today, a number of urban researchers are taking heed of this advice.

Wilson (1984: 290–1) says there is evidence that ecologists are swayed by the convergence hypothesis. Recognizing that the convergence thesis follows upon Hawley's assumptions of dynamic equilibrium, and citing communication and transportation technologies as leading modifiers, Wilson focuses his attention on the pattern of population deconcentration taking place in Western industrialized nations: "In the case of advanced industrial systems, the process of population deconcentration can be viewed as the product of a society's increased ability to spread the benefits of urbanism throughout its entire territory; no area is left isolated and all become integrated into one collective enterprise." The movement is toward an equilibrium state of population deconcentration resulting from technological innovation.

Perhaps the best measure of the persuasiveness of the convergence assumption may be derived from the analyses of those who do not explicitly acknowledge the influence of the ecological paradigm on their work. The kinship between neoorthodox ecology and the currently emerging staged or cyclical urban growth hypotheses is unmistakable. Both bodies of concepts rest on the equilibrial assumption relating to the importance of technological innovation. During the 1980s several studies purported to show universal tendencies in the process of metropolitan concentration, deconcentration and/or reconcentration (Hall and Hay 1980; Van den Berg et al. 1982; Cheshire and Hay 1986; Van den Berg 1987).

Cheshire and Hay (1986) present an eight-stage schema modified from an earlier six-stage (Hall and Hay 1980) schema, which they say reflects "empirical regularities which theory must seek to explain rather than constituting a specific theory of urban change" (151). Cheshire and Hay focus on the functional urban regions of the United Kingdom, West Germany, and Italy to show that Western European cities are following a pattern of deconcentration, but at somewhat different rates. During the 1950s, half the cities of the U.K. were already showing clear signs of deconcentration, Italy's cities were still undergoing concentration, and the cities of West Germany provided an intermediate case. By the late 1970s, the cities in each of the countries had moved further in the direction of deconcentration while maintaining their position in the evolutionary scheme relative to one another.

Van den Berg's (1987) account is bolder in that it attempts to explain patterns of deconcentration by positing an interactive causal process involving three major sets of actors: families, businesses, and government. The four stages of concentration–deconcentration adhere to the following pattern. The first stage is characterized by the rapid growth of the core, followed second by the growth of suburbs, which, together with the core, comprise the functional urban region (fur), or metropolis; next is the stage of disurbanization in which the population of the entire urban region declines due to out-migration; in the final stage reurbanization occurs with the core population growing once again. Van den Berg draws our attention to studies from Japan (Kawashima 1987) and Australia (Connor 1986) that show that the deconcentration stage is in progress in those countries. A contrast of Eastern and Western European population centers between 1950 and 1975 shows that cities in Eastern Europe lagged behind somewhat in the pattern of deconcentration. The largest Western European cities showed signs of having reached the earliest stages of reconcentration: The urban cores of large centers in Switzerland, Denmark, and the Netherlands had shown a marked decline in rates of population loss, whereas the center of Copenhagen was showing signs of growth by the mid-1980s.

According to Van den Berg, the pattern of decline and resurgence is based on a simple costs–benefits equation affecting the choices of individual families, employment-providing businesses, and governments.

Settlement and resettlement patterns within the metropolis reflect the aggregate decisions of families, employers, and policy makers:

> Families, companies and government are confronted with discrepancies between the actual welfare or profitability levels and those they would want. . . . the reactions of one actor are determined also by those of the other actors. When families decide to move to another place of residence, they change the spatial distribution of the population and hence the spatial functioning of market potentials, which in turn may induce companies to adjust their spatial behavior. (Van den Berg 1987: 32–4)

Although these observations appear to assign remarkable autonomy and power to consumers in leading the reorganization of the built environment, Van den Berg notes that it is only in the deconcentration or suburbanization stage that "the spatial behaviour of families is the dominating factor" (114). Private investment is the leading factor during the stage of concentration. Government's role is at times to serve as a catalyst within the market-based system, at times to adjust welfare discrepancies that are the consequence of spontaneous growth patterns, but always to influence the respective potentials of the productive and consumer sectors in the positive sense.

The importance of Van den Berg's interpretation lies in the allegation of inevitability. Although he is unwilling to predict the future, he has presented a highly structural model that affords actors the ability to reason, but not to resist. The structure is provided, once again, by the related assumptions of equilibrium and convergence. The path along which the future lies is that of least resistance. The beacon is the marketplace, the means and restrictions set by technology. The equilibrium assumption, based as it is in belief in the collective nature of social welfare (all classes are in this together) and on consensus, imparts an inexorable quality to the process of evolution. It has the potential for immobilizing social policy.

In a discipline whose subject matter is to understand the largest and most complex social unit, short of the state, ever known to humankind, there is an inviting security in predicting a future in which equilibrium, convergence, and common interest capture the essence of social reality. Yet, the hazards that have always attended entertaining such a model of society remain. Consider the implications for social policy.

We might begin by assuming, along with the ecologists, that technology is the leading edge of change, and that knowledge will replace industry as the key function in social space (Knight 1986). In the emerging urban system, the creation of wealth and power is determined by where technology is produced and advanced, not where a thing is made. The relative importance of an area will be measured in its knowledge "exports" rather than its manufactured exports. The dominant, productive hub of a metropolitan region will no longer be its industries, but its knowledge centers – including magnets of convention tourism related to key technologies such as Boston's Harvard and MIT, Berlin's International Conference Center, and the Mayo and Cleveland medical centers.

The dynamics of the fundamental shift in the base of the metropolitan economy is likely to be lost on local populations, unions, and governments, whose initial reaction will be to resist the changes and attempt to preserve the past, only to insure that their cities will be left behind. "The community's reactions, the unions' reactions, the local residents' reactions are usually counterproductive and, in the long run, dysfunctional because the changes are not understood." Workers, especially, caught up in "the old industrial mind lock," will continue to be concerned with issues of exploitation and see the preservation of their jobs as the responsibility of mill owners. They will fail to grasp the shift to the world of the knowledge worker (Knight 1986: 397–431).

The policy implications of the equilibrium, convergence, and collective welfare assumptions are straightforward. Government's duty is primarily to anticipate and facilitate future arrangements, rather than to ameliorate the social costs of collapsing systems. For example, Kasarda and Friedrichs (1986: 223) point out that they don't mean to argue that "aid to people and places in distress is unnecessary." In this view the reactive policy of targeting areas of the greatest economic distress to receive increased shares of public housing, community nutritional and health care, and other federal welfare assistance is not in the best interests of the recipients. Instead, reactive measures have had the effect of "anchoring disadvantaged persons in localities of continued blue-collar job loss. . . . The outcome is that increasing numbers of potentially productive minorities find themselves socially, economically, and spatially isolated in segregated areas of social decline where they subsist, in the absence of job opportunities, on a combination of welfare programs and their own informal economies . . ." (Kasarda and Friedrichs 1986: 223).

This point of view has not been lost on federal policy makers in the United States. In 1980 the Carter administration's Commission for a National Agenda for the Eighties issued a report that in part addressed urban economic change: The subreport was later embraced as a centerpiece of urban policy by the Reagan administration. It acknowledged the proposition that the dynamics of national development often meant that local populations would suffer the pangs of economic displacement. Although it is a responsibility of government to provide a certain amount of aid to obsolete localities, the government's primary responsibility is to retrain and relocate workers left behind (Ledebur 1982; Hicks 1982). According to its critics, the neoorthodoxy of ecological thought has its policy counterpart the neoconservativism of the 1980s and early 1990s. Feagin (1986: 532) argues that the component of the Commision for a National Agenda for the Eighties report that recommended the hands-off policy for the federal government regarding the economic and industrial shift from the North to the South drew directly on the conservative bias of leading urban ecologists.

The continuing influence of the ecology paradigm

Urban ecology as an orienting conceptual methodology has been under attack for more than a half century. It has been faulted, in its original form, as biologically and technologically determinist, and in its most recent functionalist incarnation, as technologically determinist, conservative, and empirically uninformed. Critics argue that it cannot address the major economic, political, and racial divisions that demand the attention of even the most casual observer of the city. What is its status in contemporary sociology?

The answer is a complicated one. First, in the social sciences we are well aware that criticism does not dissolve existing paradigms. As new paradigms emerge in response to the failure of existing ones, they do so alongside rather than as the successors to previous models. (Invasion, yes; succession, no.) At one level, it is possible to agree with Warf (1990: 73), that after a half century of "vilification," Chicago school "social ecology is remembered largely as a colorful anachronism," fatally flawed by its central Darwinist and Spencerian qualities. However, Gottdiener (1985: 36–40), a leading student and critic of the ecological approach, observes that current ecology, especially Hawley's theory, is rooted in and bears an affinity to important elements of Chicago school ecology. Hawley builds upon the more cooperative and functional components of McKenzie and Park, and defends the intent of the Burgess zonal hypothesis, pointing to its continued utility as a general schema. It may be that the basic distinction to be made between functionalist ecology and the early ecological schemes is the minimization of competitive struggle in the more recent work. Although the assumption of convergence in the earlier theory does imply that progress and mutual benefit are the result of economic competition for space, the empirical work attended to impoverished, conflicted, and otherwise troubled elements of the urban population. Empirically, Chicago remained the great laboratory, and its students were drawn to the lessons of strife and disorganization. Yet, the early ecologists, especially Park, appear to have been interested in the development of a totalizing theoretical perspective, such as that developed by Hawley, where the division of urban space was a secondary concern (Matthews 1977: 132–47). The theoretical, as opposed to the descriptive, earlier work laid greater stress on social progress and equilibrating tendencies. Functionalist ecology builds on these themes. Helmes-Hayes's (1987: 387) characterization of early urban ecology might be applied without modification to Hawley's functionalism: "Society was described by ecologists as an ever-changing, symbiotic, organic whole comprised of a large number of different 'types' and 'levels' of interrelated systems and subsystems." If ecology in general remains a viable body of theory in contemporary sociology, with Hawley's work as the centerpiece, then we need to recognize important thematic linkages with early ecology.

Quite apart from the question of establishing such theoretical linkages, there is the question of whether recent research has used what might be termed the low-brow, descriptive heritage of the Chicago school approach. Do ecologists still look for sectors and zones a la Burt, Burgess, Hoyt, and Harris and Ullman? As we have seen, here the answer is simple: Yes.

Human ecology remains an influential paradigm in contemporary urban sociology. Feagin complained in 1986 that the paradigm dominated the sociology journals, with mainstream ecologists serving as gatekeepers, stifling the discussion of more critical approaches (Feagin: 1986: 531). Problems of quantification make it difficult but not impossible to determine the relative influence of ecology in the relevant professional journals. Not surprisingly, not much of this has been done. The results of a survey of articles published in *Urban Affairs Quarterly* is inconclusive (Schmandt and Wendell 1988). The authors indicate a dramatic increase in the number of articles published within the rival political economy paradigm in recent years, but their evidence shows a concomitant rise in the number of urban ecology articles (the review does not include theoretical and policy-oriented articles that we might recognize as inspired by the assumptions of one or the other paradigm).

In fact, the influence of neoorthodox ecology should be viewed more in terms of a hidden than a recognized or formally expressed influence. As such its power over urban sociology is akin to the influence of structural functionalism over mainstream sociology in general. It is the influence of popular ideology elevated to social theory, that assumes that cities are coproduced by market forces and communication and transportation technologies working together in a natural evolution of the settled environment. If it makes any sense to raise questions of the social costs induced by social change, and policy-related issues having to do with questions of social justice for groups hurt by the direction of change, then these are philosophical issues. To the extent that equilibrium and convergence are together the essence of unfolding social arrangements and the window on the future, then urban science simply involves an accommodation to present and future arrangements.

It does not appear that most urban sociologists subscribe to such a view. It is doubtful that many who consider themselves urban ecologists would be willing to embrace it. Yet equilibrium and convergence remain powerful, unexamined, and often unarticulated background assumptions in much urban analysis. One needs to remain alert to the assumptions that underlie functionalist ecology in order to recognize it in others' as well as one's own work.

MANAGING URBAN SPACE

Gentrification: The competition for residential space

The well-established pattern in the United States of affluent classes fleeing the cities for the suburbs was unexpectedly modified during the 1970s and 1980s. Although suburbanization was a more long-standing trend in North America than elsewhere in the West, a modest alteration, which became evident by the end of the 1970s, appears to have occurred more or less simultaneously in a number of Western nations. Rather than leaving for the suburbs, some affluent urbanites were leaving established middle-class enclaves within the city for other inner-city neighborhoods occupied by poor or less affluent populations. The pattern, by now as well-known as suburbanization itself, came to be termed gentrification. Studies during the late 1970s showed that the gentrification ("revitalization" is an equivalent term) of neighborhoods in cities in Australia, Canada, and England (where studies focused mostly on London) was well underway (Gale 1984: 109–19). Amsterdam, Copenhagen, Munich, Paris, and Amsterdam were by 1981 showing distinct signs (Gale 1981). In the United States, gentrification has affected cities of every size and in every region. Although there has been a tendency on the part of interested parties (city officials, developers, real estate brokers and investors, area home buyers eager to be imitated) to oversell the generality of the trend (K. Nelson 1988: 16), there can be no doubt that the impact on large tracts within particular cities has been dramatic.

The phenomenon has revived interest in the process of invasion and succession described by McKenzie (1926). But until the 1970s invasion and succession were concepts that nearly always described the residential turnover from more to less affluent populations as neighborhoods physically aged. Now, a segment of the affluent classes chose to take up residence in formerly declining neighborhoods in inner cities. This was invasion and succession in reverse (Hudson 1980).

Ambiguities regarding the benefits and liabilities of gentrification for different segments of urban populations were immediately apparent. On the positive side gentrification meant, at the very least, that some number of affluent people were committed to remaining in the city, and they demanded that government officials devote part of their attention to questions of housing and neighborhood enhancement (Teaford 1990: 241, 282). The message was that the decline of urban neighborhoods was not an inevitability, that it was a mistake to neglect sections of the city where people lived, and some neighborhoods were adding a new cross section of affluent residents whose demands for sponsorship of neighborhood preservation and upgrading resonated more effectively within the halls of local government. On the negative side, these changes raised questions about what happened to the individuals and families who were displaced by the invasion. A 1979 U.S. Department of Housing and Urban Development report devoted to the subject minimized the problem of displacement. However, Legates and Hartman (1986) estimated that during the mid-1980s gentrification was displacing an estimated 2.5 million people a year in the United States.

Anderson (1990) has done much to illuminate the nature of the process and the experience of various actors involved in gentrification in his ethnographic account, *Streetwise*. Through several years of participation as a resident observer of a gentrifying neighborhood in Philadelphia, Anderson pieced together a portrait of the transition, not only of the revitalizing "Village" community, but of the adjacent African-American neighborhood of Northton to which it was tied in unequal partnership. The increasing affluence of the Village was not altogether beneficial to the residents of Northton. Most importantly, the "edge" that comprises the boundary between the two communities is advancing into Northton, as the Village expands by incorporating more and more housing units for renovation and rent increases, driving out the poor. The growing affluent community provides the opportunity for work for Northton residents, but this is mostly in the form of the informal, temporary, unskilled labor involved in cleaning up and maintaining renovated properties. Meanwhile, a second type of invasion and succession is taking place in Northton, as upwardly mobile blacks leave the area to an increasingly socially and economically troubled, and increasingly homogeneous lower-class population. Whereas the Village becomes more affluent, adjacent Northton becomes more poor and desperate.

The most striking image of the gentrifying neighborhood that is transmitted by Anderson's book is that of racial animosity across class and neighborhood boundaries. The daily lives of Village residents are dominated by questions of safety and security. The title of the work, *Street-wise,* refers to a quality of alertness and in-depth understanding that all residents of the two neighborhoods need to acquire in order to live successfully in these communities. The atmosphere of the street is dominated by tensions provoked by young black males, whose routinely uncivil and menacing behavior is motivated by two factors. First, it is a requisite for avoiding victimization by not appearing soft or vulnerable to other young black men. Second, for many it is a way to strike back at the invaders, at what appears as a monolithically affluent, white society that has nestled into tempting proximity. Anderson's intended message to the would-be streetwise is to remain vigilant but to avoid becoming rigid or categorical in one's thinking and, especially, to avoid the racism inherent in viewing every group of aggressive young black men encountered in public places as a danger to person and property. Many affluent white – and black – residents don't persevere long enough to learn that lesson.

Anderson's analysis of gentrification and its consequences reaches beyond the classical constructs of urban ecology. Invasion and succession are useful descriptive terms, but they provide only limited insight into the nature of the transformation of the two neighborhoods. Thousands of independent decisions by individuals and families about where to live are a fundamental part of the process that produces a gentrified neighborhood like the Village, so also are the efforts of the city Redevelopment Commission and the city's decision to condemn and remove pockets of residential structures occupied by low-income blacks. That is, government is not a disinterested bystander in the conversion of neighborhoods. It has an ability to command change, to intervene in any purely ecological working out of the use of local spaces. Also, local space provides an insufficient analytical arena. Anderson indicates the importance of deindustrialization in understanding the internal dynamics of Northton. The withdrawal of the solid industrial employment opportunities that had provided previous generations of Northton residents with the opportunities to buy homes and establish stable family lives, robbed the next generation, today's generation, of potential mentors and role models.

The conversion currently taking place in many cities, especially New York, of former industrial lofts into residences presents a special case of gentrification. In general, the competition for residential space eventually leads us to broaden our perspective beyond the confines of the city in order to give meaning to the trends we observe. Williams and Smith (1986) argue that we stand on the edge of an era in which residential space is becoming rationalized into a single world market. This has already taken place in the premier world cities, as exemplified by the Manhattan real estate market, where prices are bid up in the realty section of the Sunday edition of *The New York Times*. Buyers from around the world have sent prices soaring, and this "Manhattanization" of residential realty is gradually working its way through other less centrally placed cities.

It is precisely with regard to Manhattan, in particular the invasion and succession involving loft conversions, that Hudson (1987) finds Hawley's ecological framework (supplemented by other perspectives) most useful. The conversions involve an orderly revitalization of useful space. As the manufacturing and warehousing industry of SoHo declined and lofts became vacant, artists experimenting with new materials, technologies, and more large-scale forms of expression became attracted to the area by the nature of the spaces that were being abandoned. SoHo provided cheap, large spaces for work and living that attracted no competing users, and the invasion extended the life of architectural structures that had antique value and structural integrity. The area's new, colorful reputation attracted tourists who contributed to a change in atmosphere that lent itself to the process of succession. Hudson sees the loft movement as a matter of individual needs and decisions coalescing into a group awareness, something of a movement focused on a protection of group interests (neighborhood residents' organizations), eventually spreading to other areas of lower Manhattan.

Zukin's (1982) analysis of loft living in Manhattan is based on her own experiences as a Greenwich Village loft dweller, and on a critique of the gradualist ecological interpretation of how change took place. Her neighborhood underwent a conversion within the space of two years from buildings that featured a mixed use base (including residential, artist's studio, and manufacturing rentals), to cooperative (condominiumized) buildings with professional tenants who could afford the purchase prices that drove out the manufacturers and many others. The invasion–succession sequence was orchestrated by building owners, realtors, and others interested in promoting the escalating cost of local properties. The strategy could not work independent of aesthetic values and popular taste, but these cultural phenomena do not exist independent of wider structural change. "A close examination of loft living warns us not to take for granted any style for what it superficially appears to be" (173). Where an ecological analysis would account for the spiraling costs and changes in tenure in loft living in terms of competition and the natural power of those with the ability to pay to have their way, Zukin finds a different explanation for the upscaling conversion to purely residential uses.

She discovered that there really is a question of displacement here, the displacement of the original small businesses still occupying positions of many of the buildings when the area was discovered by pioneering risk takers, the artists and artisans who made up a first wave of invaders. Together, these groups turned out to be relatively powerless to withstand a second wave of "in-movers," professional and other affluent parties who were interested in investing in buildings that were uniformly residential. The interests of the second wave of invaders were served by local government, financial, and corporate institutions whose design it was to stabilize the residential class character of the area. In Zukin's view, the loft-living trend became a preferred outcome by the most powerful private interests (banking, realty, and companies that had invested in land and buildings in the area), acting in concert with policy makers and public officials, to preserve or enhance the value of land and buildings.

The fact that displacement occurs along with gentrification, even to the point of generating homelessness and the loss of jobs, need not undermine the functionalist model of society. Their point is not that conflict and suffering does not occur, but that concerns about such matters need to be subordinated to a general understanding of the way in which societies change and progress. The focus is on the end product, not the strife involved in producing it. What stands between the functionalist interpretation of social (urban) change and alternative views is the assumption of the dynamic permanence and internal rationality of the system and the generality of the benefits it ultimately produces. The political economists do not share the act of faith, and it is their perspective that we turn to next.

3

Urban political economy and its critics

Robert Park was a newspaper writer when he determined, early in this century, that the "big story" of the city was going to be written by social scientists. He studied social science and laid the foundation for the science of urban ecology. Ironically, urban ecologists are criticized today for having missed the big stories of the city. As we have seen, the ecological paradigm has featured the careful empirical investigation of the physical order of cities, on the one hand, and equilibrial assumptions about the spatial structure of society, on the other. It has been argued that such a discipline is poorly oriented to anticipate or explain conflict and change. Historically and at present, conflict and change are the features that draw our attention to the urban arena.

At mid century, urban housing, economic revitalization, and transportation policies led critics in Europe and the United States to raise questions about whose interests these policies served. There was a growing awareness that plans that served business interests did not necessarily serve the interests of the urban population in general, and the poor and near-poor in particular. Urban riots in the United States in the 1960s increasingly drew attention to conditions of urban poor and minority populations. The eruption of student and worker riots in Paris in 1968 led to a national investigation of urban unrest. At the same time, housing shortages and conditions in cities in England continued to draw international attention. During the 1970s and 1980s, foreign workers confronted native-born Europeans over jobs and housing in major urban areas. The acceleration of the suburbanization of middle-class and affluent working-class elements of the urban population of the United States, along with the suburban drift of industry, employment, and retail trade raised serious questions about the viability of the urban center.

By the 1970s, it was clear that urban populations were to bear the brunt of the impact of what came to be called the "restructuring" of the international and national economies. City administrations in the industrialized nations faced massive devaluation of fixed capital investments and the erosion of their tax base. By the end of the decade, local governments in the United States had received the news that the federal government would curtail the redistribution of taxes that localities had come to depend on to provide services and pay their municipal employees. Major cities, notably New York, teetered on the edge of default and bankruptcy. Western European cities in the 1980s became the arenas of confrontation between squatters and police, while cities in Eastern Europe at the end of the decade provided the backdrop for dramatic collective expressions of the demand for political and economic change.

The drama and urgency of the major social upheavals taking place in the urban arena remained out of focus for urban ecology. Data gatherers, without the firm guidance of a social theory to indicate what it was they should be looking for, suffered from empirical myopia. The grand theory of functional ecology and convergence models of staged metropolitan growth were too remote to spend much time on any social consequences that might result from the hypothesized equilibrium-seeking behavior of the system. A new paradigm was needed to satisfy the call for an urban science relevant to the hour. The call was answered by the emergence of a school of urban studies that drew on a body of theory based on the assumption that conflict, not equilibrium, lay at the heart of the social order.

For the most part the new approach focused on the role of capitalism, the international economic order, the accumulation and concentration of wealth and power, the relations of social classes, and the role of the state in administering a stable social order ultimately hospitable to economic interests. Cities symbolized the inequalities of wealth and power generated by a profit system, as they represented the arenas where capital accumulation and class conflict were concentrated and given spatial expression. The new approach that emerged in the 1970s included a diversity of ideological constituents and theoretical viewpoints. What its proponents shared was a critical view of the marriage of public policy and private interest, and they more or less consistently raised the question of whose interests were being served. Collectively, the approach became known as *political economy*.

The following section reviews the urban issues that demanded the attention of a conflict-oriented body of social theory. This is followed by a more detailed characterization of the political economy approach, and then a review of the criticisms regarding the limitations of political economy.

Economic restructuring and the new urban reality

Cities have always been the creatures of the expanding world, reflecting the political and economic conditions that characterize that world.

This is as true today as it was in ancient Sumeria, Mesoamerica, and China. Cities have reflected the critical placement of the local territory within colonial empires, the industrial revolution, and the present international economic order. Just as the world order is dynamic and subject to continuous restructuring, cities, as components of that order, grow, shrink, change functions, and otherwise adapt to wider changes. The period of restructuring and adaptation since World War II is the era of immediate relevance to an understanding of the current phase of urban adjustment.

"Restructuring," as the term is used here, refers to widespread economic changes with profound sociological consequences. Although the term might be applied to any age that witnessed major change, such as the extinction of the feudal order or the spread of European colonialism, it has come to refer more specifically to the present age of industrial reorganization. The most prominent features of restructuring include the relocation of industrial investments, the internationalization of markets, the transnationalization of corporate competition, the withdrawal of capital from manufacture in favor of diversified investment, the continued movement in manufacturing industries to capital-intensive production, the shift for a large segment of the labor force from industrial to service employment, and the active competition among agents of local economic growth for mobile investment capital. The consequences of this trend are of vital importance to contemporary urban sociology.

The refocusing of the urban economy

In the United States the postwar 1950s were a period that featured a high level of housing demand (following decades of the market's failure to replenish urban housing stocks at anything like adequate rates) and a modest prosperity. Federal housing and highway construction policies encouraged the demand for suburban, single-family dwellings – the market did the rest. The story of the dramatic exodus of the middle class (and more affluent elements of the working class) to the suburbs is well known. Retail and service trades, and eventually the construction of new industry, followed the consumer dollar along the improving motor transport routes, out of town. As residential, commercial, and industrial development snaked along highways and intertwined with the exurban developments of neighboring urban centers, the effective population of "the city" became blurred, as expanding metropolitan areas merged into "conurbations," and ultimately into the sprawling urban region that Gottman (1961) called "megalopolis."

European nations struggled more vigorously to prevent the "Los Angelesization" of their major centers – so named for the North American metropolis that grew most rapidly and shapelessly in open accommodation to private transportation. Britain built greenbelts and satellite towns to contain urban sprawl, only to have it leap these development-free zones and designated satellites and devour the areas beyond. The planners of Paris and the Netherlands experimented with urban corridor schemes to contain growth (Hall 1984). As was the case in the United States, however, it quickly became evident that the task of urban planners was not one simply of containing the growth of over-large cities, but of preventing the decentralization that caused these cities to go dead at their hearts. For the urban center, sprawl meant the end of locally available taxes, shrinking retail trade, and the loss of jobs. In the United States, between 1963 and 1977 the central cities of the twenty-five largest metropolitan areas lost 700,000 manufacturing jobs, whereas their suburbs added 1.2 million (Logan and Golden 1986: 430).

Employment shifts have been taking place on a wider scale as well. First in the United States, then later in Europe, urban growth shifted away from older industrial cities to urban growth poles in regions that traditionally had experienced lower levels of urbanization. Sunbelt cities in the United States had already shown signs of potential growth early in the century. However, strategic considerations involving the dispersal of defense production plants, especially those producing aircraft, away from older industrial centers during World War II, provided the basis for continued growth in the South and Southwest in the decades to come. Although it is not clear that the cities that have most recently experienced rapid growth have actually taken existing jobs away from established industrial centers, they have provided for a disproportionate number of new jobs and, more importantly, they have been the locus of the most rapidly growing new industries. In the United States, between 1958 and 1972 northern metropolitan areas lost between 14 and 18 percent of their manufacturing jobs, whereas the Sunbelt cities experienced an increase of between 60 and 100 percent of the same types of positions (Checkoway and Patton 1985: 6).

During the course of the 1970s, the rate of manufacturing job losses were also highest in the most urbanized regions of European Community countries. The twenty-one most highly urbanized regions, including large nineteenth-century industrial cities, lost 17.9 percent, whereas the next most urbanized areas of Europe lost 9.7 percent. Together, these categories represent the loss of over two million jobs from the largest and best-established urban regions of Europe. The regions experiencing the least percentage loss were the least urbanized (Keeble 1986: 171–2). The pattern within European Economic Community countries is complex. Although the shift of jobs to the southeast of England has been well-noted, the city and region of London have experienced losses of high-potential growth industries. These are the same kinds of industries that have moved to Sunbelt cities in the United States. By the mid-1980s London retained less than half the industrial capacity it had in 1961 (Leigh, North, and Steinberg 1986). Cross-sectional analysis of the data on the locational preferences of high-technology industries in Britain shows that, more than city size, new industries favor sites that are not associated with an older industrial "image" (Begg and Cameron 1988). Similarly, the cities of Randstad (Holland) are in general experiencing a loss of their traditional industrial hegemony within the Netherlands. The older central areas are losing industrial employment to their suburbs and exurbs, the larger metropolitan regions themselves are losing industrial employment to less urbanized regions, and there has been a shift away from the Randstad (some areas in the northern rim of the urban ring are doing somewhat better than areas in the south) toward the east, a "half-way zone" between the western region and the more economically remote north (Jobse and Needham 1988).

Certainly, the older centers of the industrial world have not all become vacant lots and car parks as a result of their economic decline. Construction of high-rise office towers and convention centers that continuously revise the skylines of every older city center would seem to deny the whole notion of economic decline. The new architecture clearly reflects a change in the nature of inner-city employment opportunities. Heralded at various recent junctures as a possible "turnaround" in central-city fortunes, the office building boom from Chicago to Frankfort to Tokyo replaces housing and related round-the-clock land use patterns with a city center that lives only during working hours (Burns 1986: 256–7). Very often, periods of rapid expansion of space in a given city have represented overinvestment and overbuilding, and the impressive skyline may point to high vacancy and insolvency rates rather than to general prosperity.

Although it is not possible in this book to do much more than sample general trends, the patterns of urban changes indicated so far have gained the concerned attention of governments and social scientists throughout the industrialized world. The suggested pattern of concentration, followed by deconcentration, followed by the transformation of the economic and residential functions of the urban center, has given rise to the kinds of convergence models proposed by Van den Berg (1987; reviewed in the previous chapter). Where ecologists speculate that the changes simply indicate the progression of the metropolitan form through a similar sequence of stages along the path to greater functional efficiency, political economy focuses attention on the negative consequences and social costs.

The wider context of urban change

The restructuring of employment goes beyond the redistribution of work opportunities within and between metropolitan regions. It further includes the internationalization of labor markets, the division of domestic labor markets into the well-paid primary and poorly paid secondary (largely immigrant worker) sectors, technological (labor-saving) changes in industrial production, and the transformation from a manufacturing to a service-based economy. Each of these have had the effect of withdrawing relatively well-compensated industrial positions from the most highly industrialized nations. The factors are so generally known as to warrant only minimal reiteration here.

The globalization of labor markets that puts First World and poor Third World workers in direct competition for many of the same jobs easily translates into the accusation that the former are "unproductive" and "spoiled." The mobility of the employment-creating capital of the multinational firm follows the easy solution: Jobs are moved "off-shore" to the cheaper labor supply. Critics believe that the argument that the routine manufacturing jobs that have been transferred abroad will come back, "like karma," in the form of better paying headquarters and product-development jobs is a myth. "Instead, the evidence suggests that investment abroad causes U.S. labor to lose wages and inequality to grow, just as long-standing research indicates that inequality and deprivation often increase in the Third World as a result of the *receipt* of such investment" (Logan and Molotch 1987: 284).

Domestic European and U.S. labor markets have been further internationalized with the immigration of workers from poorer world regions. These may be invited "guest workers" in the terminology of European policies of the 1960s and 1970s, or illegal/legalized/legal immigrants to the United States. The consequences for the labor market are the same, as many of the new workers assume minimum wage and insecure positions at the bottom of the domestic labor hierarchy, and struggle to survive the high costs of living in metropolitan areas. The argument over whether foreign labor depresses the wages and employment opportunities of the native-born workforce is pointless. These jobs have been lost for the well-paid workforce in the international restructuring of the labor market, whether they are filled off-shore or at home.

Restructuring includes the transformation of manufacturing technology in leading industries to more capital-intensive methods. The shift involves the loss of jobs. Prime examples are the automobile industry, where "robotization" has eliminated large numbers of the best-paying industrial jobs, and steel manufacturing, where disinvestment and the scaling down and closure of plants has likewise led to the permanent loss of employment on a massive scale. Displaced workers and those seeking their first jobs today are expected to look primarily to service rather than industrial employment. Although the nature and compensation levels of service work are varied, taken as a whole the pool of new jobs is highly weighted toward the lower end of the scale in terms of skills, wages, benefits, and security. For most, the service sector promises a future quite different from that expected by the first-time industrial job seeker in the 1950s: Remuneration is so low that many service positions go unfilled, even in periods and areas of high unemployment.

In sum, economic restructuring has not been kind to industrial workers. Yet, like any society-wide economic trend, the decline in industry has not fallen evenly across the shoulders of all elements of the working class. Some regions, such as those favored by the location of cutting-edge electronic industries or oil exploration and refining have boomed while others, burdened with the gritty image of heavy manufacture, have declined. But, restructuring is a dynamic process, and as such it produces no final end product. As conditions of international competition and supply fluctuate, so do the fortunes of temporarily well-placed industries and the local populations associated with them. New sites of prosperity are as subject to cycles of boom and bust as were the old centers of industry during the early phases of the industrial revolution. Cities as different in their origins and place in the international economy as Boston and Denver, Pittsburgh and Houston, move back and forth, out of the shadows of economic decline and into the light of growth or recovery. Local business and government leaders, and their consultants hired specifically for the purpose, compete vigorously with the representatives of other cities in an effort to promote the growth potential of their city and attract or retain investment capital. In the words of Logan and Molotch (1987: 290):

> The world's cities today are engaged in a self-defeating struggle for advantage. . . . This is, at best, a zero-sum game in which victories for some limit the possibilities for others. Those places at the bottom of the hierarchy compete for waste dumps, and on the poorest terms, because otherwise they will get not even waste dumps. The growth dynamic in this system of cities informally puts into practice the philosophy of the enterprise zone [see below]: [the objective is] to reduce to a bare minimum the place constraints on the organization of capital. This philosophy drives all places down.

In the mounting conservative mood of the 1970s and 1980s, both at the local and national levels, government continued to look to the market and to count on growth to remedy any shortcomings of the market-based society.

At the same time, there are glaring reminders that market-guided growth produces liabilities in areas that have prospered most. The legacy of success in the Sunbelt has often been fraught with problems. Houston is a prime example, but other Sunbelt success stories might do as well. By the early 1980s, the reported three to five million tons of toxic waste produced annually in the Houston area posed serious disposal problems. In addition, there were sewage disposal problems due to overtaxed facilities, poor oversight of new development, and the dubious strategy of making (subsidized) private developers responsible for the construction and maintenance of "temporary," on-site sewage treatment facilities for their projects. Solid waste presented a problem due to the shortage of disposal sites and led to accusations that minority residential areas were being targeted for a disproportionate share of newly proposed sites. Like all large cities in the southwest, Houston has water supply problems. Some estimates projected an adequate supply only through 1992. In addition, growth brought problems of subsidence (sinking) of developed land due to the pumping out of ground water, traffic problems resulted from the proliferation of automobiles which outstripped human population growth, and the Environmental Protection Agency in 1983 issued warnings about the quality of the city's air. Since the 1970s, the people of Houston have been airing their criticism of the problems that face the city, and the results of a 1983 poll showed that 71 percent either thought rapid growth was a bad thing or had mixed feelings about it. Business leaders responded with a campaign to improve the city's image (Feagin 1985: 168–81).

The market, social policy, social welfare

The official economic optimism that characterized the politics of the 1980s, and the persistence and deepening of social problems, eventually led social scientists to renew their criticisms of the idea that the workings of the market automatically promoted the general social welfare. Many workers in those older cities of the United States that were experiencing recovery found that they were priced out of their housing by rising costs: The restructuring of local employment found many members of the working class commuting long distances to work because the local housing markets were inflated by affluent newcomers employed in the new corporate office towers. Even the expanding economies of cities in the Sunbelt did not automatically produce a living wage or substantially improve housing for local populations, and those who were not directly employed by new industries were relatively worse off than before. Many of those who did find employment in the new industries did not prosper. In California's Silicon Valley and in New York City, the nature of many of the jobs being created has been marginal, nonunion, nonsecure, and low-wage (Logan and Molotch 1987: 282).

Throughout the more industrialized nations inadequate urban housing supplies have helped to drive up the cost of shelter. The housing shortage has been aggravated by the "revitalization" or "gentrification" trend, whereby particular older, modestly priced rental housing, because of its attractive architectural style or convenience of location, has been converted to serve elements of the affluent urban class who reject suburban living. The most recent phases of restructuring have included growth in the population of homeless people. At one time explained away as comprised largely of the emotionally disturbed (deinstitutionalized) or chemically dependent, the fact has become inescapable that the homeless population includes large numbers of people who have been priced out of a home. In addition to homeless individuals, city administrations and homeless shelters are faced with providing services for families with children, many with working-poor heads of household, who have been squeezed out of even the shabbiest and most inadequate housing by cost. Of course, the problem of "homelessness" might be expanded to include the segment of the population just above those actually on the street – those who make do with dangerous, vermin-infested dwellings that lack adequate heat, plumbing, and other services.

Critics believe that the faith that governments place in the capacity of the market to correct the problems of the city is misplaced. The problems, instead, are market-induced. Just two decades ago Western European governments were still bent on carrying out national market-taming policies designed to match, in their vigor, the robustness of the centripetal locational tendencies of international investment that favored the largest existing centers of population and industry. The stagnation of the international economy since that period has led gradually to a market-facilitating posture in urban policy. In the 1980s, the United States, which has never had a clear urban policy or the jurisdictional apparatus to implement one, moderated its already minimal urban policy goals, and pursued a pure philosophy of market accommodation. The earmarks of this philosophy, which are indicative of the desperate faith the federal government has placed in market mechanisms to cure social ills, are evident with regard to both housing and employment needs. Since the late 1970s, efforts to provide public housing have been greatly curtailed, restricted primarily to the provision of shelter for the elderly. The primary features of housing policy in the eighties and nineties has been to subsidize the rent payments of poor families for private rental housing (which has had the effect of inflating rents); sell-off, at minimal cost, government held housing units which have proven otherwise unmarketable (few poor families – certainly not those in greatest need – qualify as safe prospects for home mortgages); and to propose the sale of public housing to those who qualify to become owner-occupants (raising questions of who will be the future owners of these units).

Similarly, in the area of creating employment in the declining inner city, recent administrations have been attracted to the "enterprise zone" idea originated in Britain. Under the well-known features of this scheme, depressed areas are designated in which investors in job-creating enterprises are relieved of standard tax rates and code restrictions, while they become eligible for employee training and other government subsidies that underwrite the cost of job creation. Critics charge that the low wages and poor working conditions that result make the enterprise competitive with other locations in the international labor market by emulating Third World conditions in the workplace.

Just as conservative government policies that accept market mechanisms as the vectors of change can be faulted for their timidity, conventional ecological approaches are faulted by critics for their lack of critical imagination. Gottdiener (1985: 39) charges that the important, concrete issues "of everyday life," which arise from the unequal distribution of resources, are obscured by "the use of mystifying abstraction and an emphasis on a noncontentious process of functional integration" in contemporary ecological theory. According to the remote and insensitive (to the social costs involved) perspective of the ecological paradigm, restructuring is a reflection of the growing functional complexity of the metropolitan region. This can be described coldly as a changing mix of population and businesses at the center, a change that features a growing proportion of white collar jobs (Gottdiener and Feagin 1988: 175).

From the ecological perspective, the essential features of the story of contemporary economic change are the same as those emphasized by critical political economists: The difference between the two approaches lies in their contrasting assumptions. The ecologists assume the market-based system generates net benefits; political economists emphasize the costs. Ecologists emphasize the changes in transportation and communication technology as causal factors in suburbanization and metropolitan decentralization. In their critical analysis of the same processes, political economists feature the role of government policies, industrial strategies directed at isolating factory workforces and controlling labor organization, and the active intervention of real estate and other development interests. Although ecologists see the shift to Sunbelt growth as a natural equilibrating phenomenon related to relatively lower taxes, a more pliable labor force, and friendly government, political economic analysis is more sharply focused on direct use of public funds to subsidize business, the role of military spending contracts awarded to southern firms, and pointedly antilabor policies of southern states (Gottdiener and Feagin 1988: 177–9).

Do the differences that divide the ecologists and political economists merely reflect an ideological division that leads them to emphasize different levels of reality regarding the same process? Is it desirable or possible to devise some theoretical middle ground, a synthesis, a new paradigm that permits social science to rise above the political debate? These questions need to be put off until the final chapter, where it becomes clear that the question of synthesis or eclecticism is not so simple. For now, it is clear that there is a debate over the central issues addressed by contemporary urban science. If one wants to write the big story of urban life, it is critical whether one adopts the assumptions of urban ecology or political economy.

Urban sociology as political economy

The point that is conveyed most clearly in the foregoing account of restructuring is that locally manifested change is not local in origin. In other words, the big story of the city is bigger than the city itself. This presents at least two methodological issues to would-be urban scientists. First, if one is to do an urban analysis, one needs to relate what is going on in cities to wider changes in the world. The second issue is even more fundamental. Is an urban science at all necessary? That is, if we study within the urban arena phenomena that have their origins in wider structures of societal organization, then what is the substance of urban analysis? During the 1970s, a new perspective emerged in urban studies that has come to be recognized generally as political economy. A diversity of practitioners attempted to deal with these questions.

Although the term political economy may have its origins in structural Marxism, it has come to have a much broader application. With some qualification, it is appropriate to say that there has been a certain amount of mainstreaming of the perspective during the 1980s. Many premises that have their origins in Marxist critiques of capitalism have become the mainstay of works by scholars who do not consider themselves Marxists. At the same time, many of those who in the 1970s operated within the Marxist paradigm have moved away from it during the 1980s, their work becoming a broadly derived mix of Marxist and non-Marxist elements. Political economy continues to refer to the work of Marxists as well. This has led to some confusion, especially for critics, as to precisely what is and what is not political economy and how it relates to Marxism.

The assumption that unites political economists in their approach to urban studies is the idea that the urban arena is a physical extension of market factors supplemented by government policy (the state). Political economy often also extends to consideration of other political forces in the city, including coalitions of influential elites, and the collective actions of other citizens. Although it is difficult, given the diversity contained within the perspective, to briefly summarize it, the following early statements (Ilchman and Uphoff 1969: 26–9) may shed some light:

> Political economy may be described as the analysis of the consequences of political choices that statesmen and other persons make involving the polity's scarce resources . . . the political economist wants to know: 'Given the resources of the regime, now or potentially, what political choices are possible and what might be their cumulative effects.'

> The study of political economy is as relevant to the choices made by revolutionaries as it is to those made by authorities, as relevant to the choices made by various sectors of the population as it is to those made by the government itself, as relevant to choices aiming at political chaos as it is to those that seek to achieve political stability.

Applied to urban studies, political economy guides researchers to ask questions about the ways in which policy has articulated with economic forces to produce particular kinds of urban environments, with particular costs and benefits for different elements of the urban population, eliciting particular popular reactions from citizens. In general, it is an invitation to extend broader sociological theory to the analysis of space, more particularly urban space. We do not look for a monolithic body of ideas here, except that the dominant political and economic structures of society have a spatial dimension that may provide a domain for urban social science.

Although it is clear that political economy has not displaced the ecological paradigm as the mainstream approach, its influence increased substantially during the 1970s and 1980s. A review of one of the major American journals, *Urban Affairs Quarterly,* over its first twenty-two years of publication, revealed that the increase in the number of articles that could be classified (rather loosely) as political economy constituted the greatest single change in the journal's content (Schmandt and Wendel 1988: 8). Other periodicals (*Comparative Urban Research, International Journal of Urban and Regional Research, Urban Geography*) which emerged in the 1970s, gave the perspective a more prominent place. In addition, a modest number of important anthologies during the 1980s clearly carried the stamp of political economy (as cited by Abu-Lughod 1991: 242). Although the body of work that may be included within the political economy perspective is today undergoing challenges and revision, it has come to constitute a major alternative to urban ecology, even as its content continues to be negotiated.

The following sections present an overview of the development of the political economy paradigm within urban sociology. The review is roughly chronological, beginning with adaptations of Marxist theory, followed by an account of the movement away from Marxist ideas that has characterized the more recent work.

The emergence of urban political economy

By the early 1970s urban sociology faced a crisis of legitimacy. As students turned to the study of cities, the focal arena of much of the dramatic political and cultural expression of the era, they were met with ecological theory and decades-old discussions of "urbanism." The social conflicts and confrontations between popular movements and the elements of force available to state authorities in the late 1960s had the effect of liberating social criticism within the social sciences. Radical criticisms, criticisms that challenged the legitimacy of the status quo, naturally turned to the legacy of Marxist thought. Marxism also provided a plausible framework for the analysis of the relationship between rich and poor countries, and an explanation for persistent underdevelopment in the Third World. During the 1970s, the gathering strength of the Marxist criticism of conventional sociological approaches raised fundamental questions about the legitimacy of urban sociology.

The urban geographer David Harvey explains his drift toward Marx:

> The emergence of Marx's analysis as a guide to enquiry (by which token I suppose I am likely to be categorized as a "Marxist" of sorts) requires some further comment. I do not turn to it out of some *a priori* sense of its inherent superiority (although I find myself naturally in tune with its general presupposition of and commitment to change), but because I can find no other way of accomplishing what I set out to do or of understanding what has to be understood. (Harvey 1973: 17)

Among those who approach urban analysis or the question of space within the framework of Marxism there has been serious disagreement (see especially Gottdiener 1985: Chapter 4). Some feel that the emphasis on formal, structuralist elements of orthodox Marxism leads to a sterile, at least fragmentary, understanding of the urban arena. In turn, these critics (heirs of the Frankfurt School) are viewed from the perspective of the structuralist Marxists themselves as engaging in a kind of neo-Hegelianism, wherein ideas are assumed to have considerable independence of material conditions of existence. Structuralists, as the term implies, believe that the future of economic (and, therefore, social and spatial) relationships will be determined, not by new ideas, but by past and present economic (and, therefore, social and spatial) relationships, i.e., structure. From the structuralist point of view the alternative Marxism reduces to a type of social psychology. Antistructuralists acknowledge the importance of capitalism as a fundamental feature of society, but believe that culture and the state are features that exert an autonomous and reactive influence over the course of history. The proponents of this approach believe that differences in local histories and even the autonomy of individual reflection and action deserve attention as potential influences on the future, since popular sentiments can either intervene to support the system or to attack it. The humanist bent of such ideas holds out the promise of praxis, of social responsibility and action, of deliberate revolutionary change. The structuralists see such ideas as a fundamental abandonment of Marxism.

We cannot be detained, for the purposes of this brief book, by a detailed discussion of important debates internal to neo-Marxism. It is important, however, to note this basic split because it is reflected in the development of urban political economy. In what follows, the structuralist Marxists are represented by Castells and other early 1970s proponents of political economy. Castells, especially, is indebted to the structuralist interpretations of Louis Althusser (1970; Althusser and Balibar 1970). More recent developments in political economy, which have come to place a greater emphasis on the fractionalized nature of class interests, the negotiation of meanings relating to space and its use, and the flexibility of pathways into the future, build on the work of the antistructuralist Henri Lefebvre (1970, 1972, 1973, 1974).

It is widely accepted that the effective introduction of Marxist analysis into contemporary urban sociology was accomplished with the 1972 publication of Manuel Castells's *The Urban Question,* and its English translation (1977). In this book Castells set out to issue a challenge to the legitimacy of existing urban thought and to offer a structural Marxist analysis as a viable alternative. Although he is more widely acknowledged to have accomplished the former than the latter goal, he did help to set off a revolution in urban theory, and created an intellectual environment in which each theoretical statement at least implicitly addresses the "ghost" of Marx.

Castells stands within the structuralist Marxist tradition that has a closer affinity to orthodox Marxism, and the Althusserian emphasis on the value of the scientific independence of Marxist methodology. In this view, Marxism offers a departure from conventional scientific approaches, approaches that are bound to be enmeshed in prevailing intellectual conventions, categories of thought, or simply "ideology."

In Castells's estimation, the conventions of urban social science have been trapped in bourgeois modes of thinking, "bourgeois ideology," because its practitioners have accepted the idea that the city itself produced ways of thinking, behaving, and associated forms of social organization. They failed to penetrate the appearances of the urban form, they failed to ask what it was that produced "the urban." The Chicago school of urban sociology and its intellectual heirs neglected the basic responsibility of an urban science, namely to establish the city as a discrete structure worthy of specialized study. And, their neglect of these issues stemmed from the fact that they had never been successful in defining what it was that constituted the object of study; that is, they had failed to devise a theoretical definition of the object of their study.

Castells (1976a: 60–1) notes that Marx, Durkheim, and Weber's analyses of industrialization took the existence of cities into account, but it was the Chicago school that first sought to formulate a theory of the city. Following on the work of Park and Burgess, it was Wirth who came closest to formulating a complete urban theory of the city (Castells 1977: 77). The effort failed because it was based on the ill-advised attempt to attach to cities, as "urbanism," a set of cultural phenomena that at a more fundamental level correspond to "mass society," which is a manifestation of industrialization under capitalism. That is, "everything described by Wirth as 'urbanism' is in fact the cultural expression of capitalist industrialization, the emergence of the market economy and the process of rationalization of modern society" (Castells 1976b: 38). The problem with the "culturalist" approach is that it assumes that a distinctive cultural system emerges from a particular ecological form (the city), but that same cultural system has been described by others as "modernization" or "Westernization." The historical origin of the confusion is easily understood, since the most characteristic features of modern society were embodied by the city (1976a: 66–9). Presently, as the setting of social life has become almost entirely urban, "the subject matter of urban sociology becomes limitless, and urban sociology becomes general sociology" (1976b: 56). Castells (1976a: 70) concludes, "Urbanism is not a concept. It is a myth in the strictest sense since it recounts, ideologically, the history of mankind. An urban sociology founded on urbanism is an ideology of modernity ethnocentrically identified with the crystallization of the social forms of liberal capitalism."

Having thus disposed of the mainstream culturalist approach to the study of cities, Castells offers in its place his assessment of the significance of urban space. It is the arena within which the reproduction of labor is concentrated; that is, the urban consists, among other things, of a system within which individuals reproduce their labor power (rest, recreate, procreate, learn, etc.) through private (self-provided) and collective (state-mediated) consumption. "The urban units seem to be to the process of reproduction what the companies are to the production process" (Castells 1977: 237). Urban space is the built environment, a subsystem produced by the structural system – the larger, societal order constituted by a matrix of economic, political, and ideological conventions. In this manner, Castells does not end up in a rejection of urban analysis, merely a rejection of the ideological focus on urbanism. For Castells, the urban is a distinctive spatial aggregation of the economic arrangements of wider society, and the modern city is the physical expression of capitalism in particular. The urban remains an analytically distinct framework on the basis of its distinctive spatial features.

Castells's early work interests us here because of his effective criticism of the conventional approach, his challenge to urban sociologists to establish a theoretical object of study, and his initial efforts to establish a Marxist analysis of the urban arena. Others have more fully articulated the details of the production of urban space within a neo-Marxist framework.

From this perspective, urban space is an arena in which two related and vital aspects of the economic underpinnings of the social order are worked out: the accumulation of capital and class conflict. These represent the two basic features of the process of the expansion of capitalism. It is perhaps appropriate that a geographer rather than a sociologist has taken on the responsibility of extending Marx's historical materialism to the question of spatial analysis, a dimension largely neglected by Marx, himself. David Harvey's work spans two decades and represents the development of an unflinching Marxist analysis during a time when many believe that the utility of Marxist urban analyses had risen, flowered briefly, and withered under the criticism of the post-Marxist 1980s. Harvey has treated the full range of urban processes more completely than any of the other neo-Marxists, devoting special attention to the problem of the concentration and circulation of capital.

The central theme in Harvey's work is that:

> Capitalist society must of necessity create a physical landscape – a mass of humanly constructed physical resources – in its own image, broadly appropriate to the purposes of production and reproduction. But I shall also argue that this process of creating space is full of contradictions and tensions

and that the class relations in capitalist society inevitably
spawn strong cross-currents of conflict. (1985a: 3)

Harvey thus attempts to address all of the complexity of the contemporary metropolis, but retains a single coordinating theme: The built environment is the rational product of the process of capital accumulation.
This theme is supported by a number of corollary observations. First,
the supply of capital invested in urban property, construction, and
financing is created by overaccumulation in the primary circuit of capital. This is the tendency (indicated by Marx in Volume 3 of *Capital*)
whereby the production of commodities produces "too much" capital
(through profits) relative to the opportunities for reinvestment in
commodity production. The idle capital seeks investment opportunities, and
finds them in the (less lucrative) secondary circuit of capital, the built
environment. This includes fixed capital investments in both productive
(offices, factories) and consumption (e.g., housing) sectors (1985b: 3–7).

A second element of Harvey's schema has to do with the creation of
a physical environment that serves to accelerate the circulation of capital. Capital takes time to circulate, to create profit. Under capitalism,
the building and rebuilding of urban space is like the creation and modification of a machine that makes the work of capital (the creation of
profit) more efficient (1985a: 27–9). Because it is investment that deter-
mines land use in the city, why would any other principle be assumed
to operate? However, individual capitalists would find real estate
development projects unfamiliar and difficult, and would anyway be predisposed to continue investment in more familiar productive enterprises,
thus exacerbating the overaccumulation problem within the primary
circuit. Here, Harvey presents a third condition, observing that financial institutions have been created that pool reserves of capital for investment in the secondary circuit; also, the state intervenes with policies that
facilitate circulation (e.g., in guaranteeing mortgages, and creating municipal debt through the investment of public funds) (1985b: 7). Finally,
Harvey shows how the articulation of surplus capital and government
policy have worked together to modify the built environment, creating
suburbanization and metropolitanization.

Harvey argues that there has been a long-standing recognition on both
sides of the Atlantic that the central city comprises a potentially volatile
environment, as a vehicle of class consciousness, in contrast to what has
been called the "moralizing influence" of the suburbs (1985b: 28–9).
Pointing to the rapid growth of private home ownership in the United
States, he emphasizes the effective social control function this exerts over
workers who own such property. It provides a means of unifying the

perceived interests of homeowners with the rights of private property in general, and divides workers' interests between those who do and those who do not own homes (1985a: 42–3). The extension of private property to workers also meant the expansion of the built environment into suburban locations, enormous public expenditures on roads that facilitated the marketability of suburban homes, an enormous increase in automobile dependency, and the transformation of the city into the metropolis.

One further element of Harvey's work reflects a refinement that critics lose sight of when they attempt to homogenize the urban Marxists into an easy target. Harvey recognizes a division of interests within the bourgeoisie as well as within the working class. In his many writings, he has pointed out that construction and landlord interests may be at odds with each other and with other capitalists in pursuing their goals in the construction and reconstruction of the urban machine. Ultimately, he does, however, posit an abstraction – "capitalism in general" – a force administered by the state that regulates intraclass conflict for the general benefit of capitalism. In so doing, he is criticized for having embarked on a "terminally functionalist path" assuming an objective confluence of the interests of the ownership class, and he has identified the state as a simple agent of this capitalist omnipresence, drawing his work closer to orthodox Marxism (Gottdiener 1985: 90–2).

Class struggle is an endemic part of the accumulation process. The focus of the struggle is contained in whatever contemporary setting corresponds to the "factory floor" of Marx's day. Yet, there are displaced components of that struggle that spill beyond the workplace, and the competition for the use of urban space is a part of the class war. To the ownership class, the uses of the city represents dividends, rent, interest, and capital gains. Workers, on the other hand, are essentially consumers of urban space. In the factory, or its equivalent, owners attempt to maximize profits to stay ahead of their competition, to stay in business. What workers gain from owners represents a loss of profit ("competitiveness"). The competition for urban space is the same. "Owners as a class must seek to organize society and, more specifically, urban space in order to enhance profit maximization. Workers' interests, however, are in organizing society and urban space in a way that permits a humane and rational ordering of consumption" (Sawers 1984: 6).

Class conflict may be manifest in battles over rent control, traffic safety, health, and other issues. If one begins with the assumption that class conflict underlies most of the struggles we witness in the metropolis, just as it does elsewhere, then much of what we witness begins to make sense. The fact that the subsidies paid to wealthy homeowners and landlords is many times greater than all of the government's subsidies to low income housing makes sense because the ownership class controls the policy-making apparatus of state. The urban renewal program of the 1950s and 1960s was in part fueled by an act of Congress that pledged decent housing to all American families. If one begins with an assumption of class conflict and bourgeois control of the political process, then one is not surprised by the fact that urban renewal destroyed the housing of the poor, eradicated their communities, and raised the costs of similar housing elsewhere in the city. Municipal transportation subsidies draw critical attention only so long as they are seen as primarily benefitting the poor, rather than affluent commuters who are the primary beneficiaries of public subsidy (Sawers 1984: 9–10).

Certainly, the most dramatic example of class conflict that manifests itself today involves the mobility of capital and the relative lack of mobility of labor. The millions of manufacturing jobs that have been lost to inner city residents in North America and Europe reflect the internationalization of the labor market. Wherever local labor forces have been most successful in wresting higher wages and benefits from employers, placing these workers at some advantage relative to labor elsewhere, their employers are induced to calculate the long-term costs of relocation against future raises. At a more subtle level, Harvey (1985b: 25–31) argues that capitalism has attempted to reach into many phases of "the living process." In the same way that suburban housing can be viewed as a tool of political control, it can be argued that bourgeois values have reached into the school curricula to foster good work habits among those who will not receive a living wage in the future. In this view even the idea of "community" can be manipulated as an element of social control.

Scholars who have applied Marxism to urban analysis have advanced the cause of urban social science by focusing attention on the economic underpinnings of urban social arrangements. They have suggested a framework for the reinterpretation of urban history, for example, as in Gordon's (1984) history of the North American metropolis: The three phases of development (the commercial city, the industrial city, the corporate city) that he suggests correspond to stages in the evolution of American capitalism. Marxism has provided a paradigm that has guided the work of some, offered a point of departure for others, and provided a critical target for others who, operating from within the old mainstream, have been set the task of exercising more rigorous theoretical discipline. Not surprisingly, an avowedly Marxist body of theory that emerged to challenge an existing tradition has drawn considerable criticism. Although some (especially Harvey) have continued to hold up the urban process to the light of historical materialism, others have moved away from the Marxist framework. However, the counter-Marxist movement has not, for the most part, led back to the eclectic, ecological mainstream. In the following section we review the "new" political economy, or as some prefer to call it, simply the "new urban sociology." The Marxists have left their mark.

Recent developments in critical theory

Since the early 1980s there has been a growing impatience with the narrowly Marxist structuralist tradition in urban sociology. Analyses in political economy have expanded to incorporate an ever greater emphasis on the role of the state and public policy, the various features of local history and other circumstances that require us to recognize the uniqueness of each city as a case history (with a greater emphasis on close empirical work in the "case study" tradition), and attention to the operation of elites or even coalitions of common citizens in shaping the future of the locality. The objective is to reflect the variety of influences, in addition to international capitalism, that operate to produce particular outcomes, local variants.

Gottdiener's (1985) extensive critique of the existing (including Marxist) approaches to urban analysis argues for the need to incorporate economic, political, and cultural forces in understanding the way urban space is produced. In part he argues that no single political-economic model can account for the present-day form of the metropolitan complex. He is especially critical of the stages-of-capitalism argument, such as that undertaken by Gordon (1984), which links urban morphology and function to discrete categories of market evolution. Efforts to understand the urban complex, which are based on the effects of the international division of labor or the influence of multinational corporations, are bound to fail because they consider only part of the picture. They focus on the vertical axis of integration while ignoring the myriad horizontal linkages that draw local groups and interests together in cooperation and conflict. Constructed and reconstructed urban spaces are not the "pure manifestations of deep-level social forces." They are social productions that owe some part of their form and use to the mediation of local interests who have their own, culturally shaped tastes and agendas (Gottdiener 1985: 196–9). The course for future research is clear. Studies of locality will reveal the ways in which public and private agents modify the influences of international capitalism.

In this vein, Feagin (1987) set out to test Harvey's thesis that investment in the built environment is the result of overaccumulation in the primary (goods-production) circuit of capital. Feagin begins by reiterating Gottdiener's (1985: 98–9) criticism that Harvey fails to consider the fact that real estate development follows its own logic and rhythms that are in some measure independent of primary sector patterns. Feagin's analysis of the sources of real estate capital for financing office space development in Houston showed that the origins of capital were international in scope and difficult to trace. He notes that, although it is reasonable to expect a direct connection between locally accumulated petro-dollar profits and real estate development, his interviews with prominent elites failed to confirm such a simple pattern.

By the early 1970s, Houston had become part of a world market of real estate investment. Local real estate ventures attracted investment capital from European, Middle Eastern, and South American firms and individuals. At the same time the profits of locally based petroleum industry corporations went primarily to executive salaries, shareholders, acquisition of nonoil firms, corporate mergers, and loans to Third World countries (182–3). Feagin notes that it is not possible to trace the ultimate origins of international capital, but believes it is logical to conclude that money that came to be invested in Houston real estate development had a diversity of immediate origins, including profits from real estate investments in other urban centers around the world.

Feagin also argues that an exclusive focus on the primary circuit fails to consider the important role of government as well as what must be called emotional factors within the international pool of real estate investors in deciding where investments will be made. First, government subsidies provided an important incentive to continued office space investment. Direct investment of federal funds paid most of the costs for the development of an extensive highway system that allowed Houston's weakly zoned urban region to sprawl to cover 600 square miles. This has provided the city with a distinctively decentralized nature, including the dispersion of business districts. Decentralization, with its multiple points of potential commercial growth, has indirectly provided a rationale for the development of a much higher level of office space than is the case for other North American cities with more centralized business districts (163.5 million square feet in 1986), in contrast to cities of similar size like Boston (54.4 million square feet) or Philadelphia (41.8 million square feet). Feagin also points to federal tax policies that invite real estate owners and investors to make what are often unreasonable claims about property depreciation (up to 10 percent per year), which allow them to reduce their tax liability for those properties, thus lowering their tax liability for other properties as well (185).

According to Feagin, we must also recognize that there is a social psychological dimension to real estate investment that does not necessarily have anything to do with the primary circuit of capital accumulation, in particular, or sound economic strategy, in general. He refers to a herd mentality that causes a pool of international real estate investors to follow smart money to emerging development hot spots. This ensures that the current hot spots will experience overdevelopment, shoddy design and construction as architects and construction companies try their hand at unfamiliar structural challenges, and, following the building boom, a period of high vacancy rates that plunges the local market into postboom crisis.

Clearly, Feagin's focused knowledge of the Houston case adds to our understanding of the patterns and processes of urban development in general. He demonstrates that other factors are involved in urban real estate development besides leftover capital. The agents of growth have established and courted a social policy structure that facilitates their current interests; the agents of growth are diverse and global; and their investment behaviors are not as sophisticated as outsiders might suppose. However, has he been able to demonstrate that the connection proposed by Harvey between primary and secondary circuits does not exist? At most, he is able to show that the nature of any linkage is obscured by time, distance, and complexity. Although there appears to be little left of Houston's petro-profits to fuel local growth, we are left with questions of the ultimate origins of the European and Middle Eastern capital that flowed into Houston's office boom and the ultimate destination of the local dollars that flow elsewhere. With regard to the question of local agents of change, it remains clear, in this analysis, that although elites maneuver in the spaces created by economic opportunity and government policy, the common people have little influence. It is not our purpose here to try to draw conclusions in this debate, but it is necessary to highlight remaining questions, even though the answers to these questions are clearly very difficult to come by.

Together, Gottdiener and Feagin (1988: 176–7) have continued to try to put distance between the older political economy approach and what they refer to as the "new urban sociology." Their work is important, distinct from (especially) neo-Marxist approaches, but it still falls within the framework of political economy as it has come to be more broadly defined and as it is used here. The main features of their viewpoint are the familiar ones shared by political economists in general: The global economy, with its powerful multinational corporations, is the ascendant force. Recent urban economic change is characterized by the flight of manufacturing from the central cities, and has led to abandonment and blight. Labor-intensive industries using cheap immigrant labor have moved selectively into central cities and have revived the role of downtowns as manufacturing sites – but now as centers of low-wage sweatshops. Alternatively, or in parallel, parts of many downtowns have been dramatically renovated with federal aid. Although they point to the same global influences, the departure for Gottdiener and Feagin is that they advocate greater attention to the local influences that set the experience of one city apart from others. They want urban sociologists to be especially attentive to social policy and local political movements.

The new urban sociology of Gottdiener and Feagin requires a new research agenda. The implication of formal, orthodox Marxism is taken by critics to imply a uniform evolution of spatial development consistent with the processes of capital accumulation and class conflict. In its stead, the new sociology posits a number of contingent forces of urban change that alters the ways in which specific localities experience and respond to the global forces of restructuring. Gottdiener and Feagin begin with the assumption that global factors are the ultimate source of changes in the local area, and they acknowledge the enormous impact that these factors have had on the way people live. However, in addition to the operation of expanding corporate monoliths, there are policies of municipal and other units of government to be considered, as well as other distinctively local characteristics. These include the motives and strategies of local and international investors and financiers, local histories and existing land-use patterns and the conditions and sentiments surrounding them, and, at least potentially, popular reactions that may deflect or help to mold emergent development strategies. Given the welter of contingent factors and the multiple ways they may interact, it follows that a fuller understanding of the process of urban development and change will depend heavily on empirical work. That is, we may assume that the contingent factors will interact differently in different cities at different times to provide different outcomes.

This is the whole point of the new urban sociology, and case studies, with their characteristic emphasis on the uniqueness of the case under consideration, provide insight into the process of urban development on a case-by-case basis. With guarded, comparative interpretations of other case studies, findings may lend insights into the general case. Thus, Feagin's close attention to Houston provides a detailed understanding of change in that city, and raises questions about the circulation of capital in general. When he turns his attention to a careful contrast of Houston and Aberdeen, Scotland (Feagin 1990), two cities whose place in the world economy has been determined primarily by their proximity to oil and gas fields, he is able to show how a difference in timing in exploration and development has led to fundamentally different outcomes in their international roles. That is, similar factors that suggest a superficial similarity between the two cases have not led these cities to hold the same kinds of positions in the international economy. Aberdeen's later emergence as the administrative center of North Sea oil exploitation meant that it would remain largely an outpost of the international oil industry, a "field-office management city" where oil company profits were generated, while decisions regarding their strategic deployment were made elsewhere. In contrast, Houston lacks the stature of a corporate headquarters city for most of the oil majors, but it does provide the technology, tools, and headquarters function of an "international operations subsidiary city." The point here is that while these oil cities have much in common, the ways in which the fortunes of each articulates within the world economy are fundamentally different. Case study and comparison, as opposed to grand theory, are the keys to understanding.

Similarly, a recent study of Los Angeles indicates how local factors interact with general, societal patterns. In this case, regional seismic uncertainties and high levels of immigration interact with economic restructuring to exacerbate the problem of homelessness. Again, there is something to be learned here about the general linkages between restructuring and homelessness, but with the implicit qualification that each city may have its own variation of the story. The case study (Law and Wolch 1991) has the added advantage of illustrating the unevenness of the impact of economic change in the Sunbelt.

Downtown Los Angeles bears the characteristic imprint of restructuring: It has undergone a heightened integration into the world economy as an important hub of the Pacific Rim trade, and this is reflected in the expansion of downtown office towers, luxury hotels, cultural facilities, high-income housing, and in the growth of service jobs. However, the city center also remains a dominant locus of low-skill industrial employment. The typical inner-city, bi-modal job distribution prevails – a concentration of high- and low-skill jobs, with relatively sparse opportunities in-between. The spatial concentration of low-income jobs within the urban center coincides with the concentration of low-income housing. Further, this area is historically the locus of well-established minority communities, which both newly arrived and long-time minority residents are assumed to prefer. Not surprisingly, many of the low-income, inner-city jobs are filled by minority workers. Law and Wolch also observe that women, especially single mothers who are disproportionately represented among the poor, prefer locating close to work. In fact, their study shows a residential concentration of low-skill workers downtown, clearly a "major reproduction space" for the area's low-skill labor needs.

Up to this point, Los Angeles would appear to offer a Sunbelt version of the restructuring effects that have been experienced by many of the older industrial cities. However, added to the usual picture are features that make Los Angeles a somewhat unique case. The inner-city population increased rapidly between 1976 and 1984, mostly due to immigration from Southeast Asia and Central America. Almost half the local population is foreign-born (other cities, like New York, have also been targeted by the new waves of immigrants during the 1980s, and these also have favored the inner city). At the same time, there has been an increase in the high-skill–high-wage population. This has led to a substantial increase in the demand for inner-city housing. Again, the increase in the office and management workforce includes women who tend to prefer to reside closer to work.

The housing supply has not kept up with demand. During the period of study, housing demand in the city of Los Angeles grew at the rate of 25,000 units per year, whereas the supply grew by only 14,000 units per year. The annual shortfall is, of course, cumulative. Most of the modest growth in housing has been in higher priced units; Law and Wolch also report "some gentrification" of existing housing. There has also been a vigorous program of housing demolition, in part due to the city's Earthquake Hazard Reduction Ordinance. This affected mostly older units, which means that most of the demolished housing was low- to moderate-income. The competition between high-income and low-income in-movers has been especially acute in the inner city: Here there was an 80 percent increase in the population and a 3 percent decrease in the number of units. Demand drove the cost of housing up. During the decade of the study the median value of owner-occupied housing in the city increased by 260 percent, whereas rents increased by 122 percent.

The causes of the increase in crowding are inescapable. The consequences are dramatic. An estimated 200,000 people in Los Angeles County reside in garages, most illegally, lacking in cooking and sanitation facilities. An additional 35,000 to 50,000 are homeless. Law and Wolch are unable to demonstrate the step-by-step or case-by-case relationship between restructuring and the homelessness of individuals and families. They instead simply point to the logical connection, observing that there are many living in makeshift housing, and/or paying over half their income in rent: These are the "protohomeless" who stand on the brink of homelessness. It would appear that the causes of the local housing crisis have for the most part been imposed from outside of the Los Angeles metropolitan area. We can assume with certainty, even if we cannot identify them with any precision, that new changes presently taking shape outside the local area will unfold gradually in the lives of the metropolitan population. Presently, only the most ambitious local measures could effectively improve the quality of shelter for substantial numbers of people most in need. Still, the source of change and the direction it will take remains beyond the control of local policymakers. Do common citizens have the power to resist such changes, to shape their own futures?

Bringing the people back in

In recent years, there has been considerable concern with overly deterministic models of society and change, and this concern has come to be reflected in new developments in urban theory. It is thought that the emphasis on the deep and hidden structures that organize life and mould behavior deny the efficacy of human reflection and deliberate action. There is a growing movement toward a more humanistic theory of social change where the ideas of individuals, collective sentiments, and deliberate action play a greater role. Certainly, structural Marxism offers itself as a ready target of such a movement. A fuller discussion of "human agency," the term attached to the more idealist models of society, is undertaken in Chapter 5. Yet, the issue connects with the present discussion of the political economy paradigm, especially in its more recent expressions.

According to the emerging paradigm, we must acknowledge the lessons of local histories, that people do make a difference, that ideas and meanings are not perfectly subject to the dominant economic and political forces, and to the material conditions that these forces produce. People are free to reflect, to react, to effect. As Lefebvre has pointed out, the very fact that the economy and the state have such enormous power to pulverize and rework space causes a popular reaction in which people take back and rename space, give it new definitions and meaning. This has generated an "explosion of spaces" with reference to meanings and the way people are prepared to act on these meanings (Lefebvre 1979: 289–90). Utopian vision and strategic action are for Lefebvre within the scope of imagination (Gottdiener 1985: 150–1).

When human actors reenter the picture as deliberate agents of social change, it is at two levels. For present purposes we will divide society into elites, on the one hand, and everyone else, on the other. Elites are agents of change by virtue of their strategic placement in positions of power. The remainder of the population wields influence through their numbers. With regard to elites, the most important current recognition is that they are not so unified in their interests as a simple division of society into two social classes would imply. Harvey (e.g., 1985b: 152–5) acknowledges this point, but the emerging literature on "growth elites" makes the intraelite division a centerpiece, and thus reemphasizes the importance of the case-by-case empirical approach to understanding local change. We will put off consideration of elites until our discussion of human agency in Chapter 5.

Although theorists have at times acknowledged the relevance of popular action to a comprehensive political economy, there had been, until recently, relatively little explicit attention devoted to the "grassroots." Broad treatments of urban change most often focused on the actions of powerful institutional agents, with some reference to the costs involved for various elements of the population at large. The masses have been depicted as the recipients of change and, in various measure, its victims.

There has been, however, during the course of the 1980s, the emergence of a literature devoted explicitly to the question of popular reaction and action. A most significant feature of this literature is that its most prominent proponent was the leading figure in the Marxist onslaught against classic urban sociology, Manuel Castells.

With *The City and the Grassroots* (1983), Castells "candidly renounced" his former Marxist view that the class struggle was the prime mover of social change (Lowe 1986: 3). In his recent work, social class is just one of the bases for urban coalition, along with many other bases for the formation of interest groups that struggle to impart a particular "meaning" to a given city or part thereof. The meaning or symbolic significance that a particular urban area takes on is in part the outcome of a struggle among different interest groups that compete to control urban space (Castells 1983: 303). Castells's political interests have broadened from support of vanguard political and workers' movements in Europe to include alternative and counter-culture movements in the United States that are not based on class (Lowe 1986: 192). Whereas social class may be one of the major social divisions along which interests are aligned, Castells (1983: 291) states that "The autonomous role of the state, the gender relationships, the ethnic and national movements and movements that define themselves as citizen, are among other alternative forces of urban social change."

Castells introduces a strong qualification with regard to the power of urban social movements to effect wider change. Although urban social movements may provide the spark for social change, they cannot themselves achieve and institutionalize changes. For this to happen, they need to articulate with established political structures at the societal level, such as the party structure. The urban base alone is too limited in scope and constituency to modify the effects of world-wide processes of power. Urban movements may stand as a "symptom of a social limit" that may in turn be effective in "transforming the meaning of the city without being able to transform society. They are a reaction, not an alternative" (Castells 1983: 327). Castells seems to have discovered a political mechanism that involves, at most, a set of veto groups that are based on some common spatial interests. In order to be more widely effective their causes must resonate with broader, more well-established organizations (feminism, labor, etc.). In sum, "Urban (social) movements are totally dependent upon the success of other social movements to create the conditions in which changes of 'urban meaning' can be carried through" (Lowe 1986: 191–2). This reduces considerably both the importance of urban space as an arena for generating change, and the efficacy of movements based therein.

Some found hope in the early 1980s in the promise of an activist age arising from the institutionalization of the idealism and community organization tactics of the 1970s. For reformers it was possible to look to the movements based on values surrounding family, institutionalized religion, ethnic traditions, or the code of the locale, as meaningful and powerful symbols of that popular revolt. It was argued (Boyte 1980) that democratic consciousness would emerge out of democratic experience, a dividend of the political education that people were receiving as active members of tens of thousands of grassroots movements that had emerged in the United States.

However, the social movements emphasis leaves two troubling questions for those who hope that the city will prove to be the crucible for change in the name of social justice. The first is that during the 1980s the cities of England and the United States have with few exceptions remained strangely quiet as conservative administrations sabotaged social programs that had been effective in improving the conditions of poor people and minorities. Disturbances in Miami in 1980–1, and in England in Brixton, Handsworth, Toxteth, and elsewhere through the mid-1980s did not signal the beginning of widespread movements for social or economic reform. Neighborhood activism remained strong, but it did not blossom into anything like a mass movement, nor was it effectively mobilized by society-wide political institutions. The second question regarding the efficacy of urban movements is the largely unspecified nature of the manner in which urban movements affect and are affected by policies of the state (Cox 1988). The literature on urban social movements and the literature on the state remain segregated, and the theorists of human agency are impatient for conceptual articulation of the way structure and movements modify each other. The social movements literature has at best posited an area of study that suggests a potential linkage between global structures and human responses.

In the meantime, one of the side effects of dramatic political changes taking place in the world at the beginning of the 1990s is bound to be a renewed interest of the role of urban space in political upheaval. Although it may be true that through the 1980s there was much less intensity of the more dramatic social movements in Britain and the United States than during the previous decade, the imagery of citizens taking to the streets has in the past few years reentered the consciousness and vocabulary of social change in the most forceful sense. Beijing and Berlin, along with the national and provincial capitals of eastern and southern Europe, have provided more than a dramatic backdrop for demonstrations of political sentiment that have been revolutionary in their impact. In addition to the demands for democratic reform there have been rallies and confrontations in the cities of former East Germany as unemployment rates rose and factories closed. The cities of Western Europe have witnessed similar demonstrations for housing. Widespread demonstrations against the poll tax in Britain led to its eventual modification and contributed to the downfall of the Thatcher government. The riots in Los Angeles and other U.S. cities in 1992 appear to have been a response to racial bias and economic despair systemic to society and not to any city in particular, although the efforts of local agents in Los Angeles must be acknowledged in making that city the flashpoint for the first widespread disturbances of the 1990s in the United States. The point is that the city itself does not always give rise to the issues that bring the people into the streets, but under the right conditions it provides such numbers that the popular voice may draw the attention of the stewards of the state, and it may affect policy.

Criticism

There are at least three levels of criticism of the treatment of the city by political economists. Within the Marxist perspective there is the criticism of the more economic determinist theories of social change. (This debate goes beyond the scope of this book, because it deals with far broader issues of social change than those limited to urban analysis, so no more will be added to the distinction noted earlier regarding this philosophical division.) Second, there is the criticism that has been leveled at political economists by mainstream sociologists, many of whom equate political economy with orthodox Marxism. Third, there are the concerns raised by both traditional urban sociologists and those political economists who wonder what the implications of the perspective are for the future of urban sociology.

Gottdiener and Feagin (1988: 164–7) in their essay on shifting paradigms in the field of urban sociology have provided a succinct and accurate summary of conventional criticisms that have come from within the mainstream on political economy. Their statement serves as a critique of the critics. First, Gottdiener and Feagin point out that textbooks on urban sociology either neglect the political economy paradigm or give it a summary, distorted treatment. Second, they cite Hawley's (1984) misrepresentation that political economy constitutes the Marxist side of the debate between contemporary ecologists and nineteenth-century Marxism, employing Marxism "as a convenient, politically loaded label." Other ecologists also have used the tactic to undermine the opposition. Finally, they cite the inclusion of the Frisbie and Kasarda piece as the only article on urban sociology in the most recent *Handbook of Sociology* (1988) as evidence of the institutional control of ecologists over the field of urban sociology. In the following criticism of the *Handbook* entry, Gottdiener and Feagin (1988: 166–7) refer to political economy as the "new urban sociology."

> Instead of providing a serious consideration of the significance of the critical urban work in the United States and Europe, they [Frisbie and Kasarda] provide a brief summary of the work of a few critical analysts, with the goal of showing parallels to ecological research. The attempt to make the new urban sociology safe for, and compatible with, urban ecology runs roughshod over the former's theoretical premises and blatantly ignores what is most salient about the new approach, namely, its direct challenge to the theory and method of ecology. Instead, the authors pick and choose from some of the new literature to point out areas of compatibility, thereby turning the new approach into a mere footnote of the old.

From those more attuned to the significance of urban political economy, Marx, Marxism, and Marxian leanings are being put back in the closet. Logan and Molotch (1987: 10–12), whose important book focuses on the diversity of powerful agents of urban change, criticize the one-dimensionality of Marxism. "Residents" cannot be reduced to "labor" whose urban role is to be "reproduced." It is simplistic to assume that "Whatever exists in the urban realm, as in any other, serves the exploitation of workers by capitalists," etc. Cadwallader (1988: 231–2) enumerates the possible criticisms that may be leveled against a purely Marxist analysis of the urban. These include the point that economic determinism ignores the relevance of cultural diversity as an independent variable, that it borders on a functionalist interpretation that explains observed relationships as serving the "needs" of the system, that it implies convergence in the direction of change, and that it casts all social conflicts in terms of social class, ignoring conflicts such as those based on race and gender. Finally, and the most important with regard to the new, humanistic direction of scientific and popular philosophy, "Structural Marxism, in particular, has tended to generate a passive model of men and women that underestimates the processes by which human beings change their economic and social environments" (Cadwallader 1988: 233). Gans (1984: 283–4) adds the criticism that "the framers and users of economic paradigms," in general, pay insufficient attention to the "social consequences" of economic phenomena (in his view, the ecologists are equally guilty in this regard). In their discussions of the economic forces that produce and modify central cities or suburbs, those who employ the new approach lose sight of the human dimension: "dwelling units and communities are fundamentally shelters for the family, according to Gans."

These are all important criticisms from the mainstream of a Marxist approach to the city. As such, they are also all misguided as criticisms of urban political economy. Contemporary urban political economy is simply not synonymous with Marxist urban analysis. Szelenyi's (1986) review of Harvey's (1985a, 1985b) two-volume summation of Marxism and the city is intended as a postmortem. Titled "The Last of the Marxist Urban Sociologists?", Szelenyi writes that while he is sympathetic to Harvey's enterprise, he is not at all convinced that the ghost of Marx has been raised, noting that even Castells is writing in a post-Marxist vein. The fact that Harvey remains true to the cause does not diminish the fact that the field of political economy, as a whole, has moved beyond, and continues a deliberate drift away from Marxism. While elements of Marx's thought may still be found in *all* of the work in political economy, this has to do with assumptions regarding the preeminence of international capitalism in fostering change, and in the assumption that class interests are divided. This leaves broad latitude to search for the degree of Marx's influence in all works, offering the prospect of unproductive speculation about what constitutes the "threshold" of Marxist work.

More important than the question of whether urban political economy is Marxism is whether it is sufficiently urban. That is, does this paradigm that leads us, as students of the city, to an analysis of the international economic order, restructuring, and social movements, lead us back to the urban arena? Does it leave room for a specialized study of urban sociology? Or does urban sociology become a marginally distinguishable fraction of the sociology of things in general? Gans (1984: 282) points out that an emphasis on economic processes may involve just such a problem for the student of the city, in that "it becomes difficult to put boundaries on the analysis, which moves quickly from urban to national and world levels. To be sure, what American firms do in Taiwan's low-wage factories is directly related to the fate of American cities, but once analysis turns to the world economy, it is sometimes difficult to return to the American city."

This remains the open challenge to the preservation of an urban sociology, but, at the same time, all specialty sociologies are challenged in the same way to maintain a balance between the holistic and the particular. The study of religion, industry, aging, minority groups, the family draws our attention beyond the confines of the institution or the thematically defined process. In fact, the new urban sociologists have taken it as their goal to link the particular and the local with the major forces of change in the wide world. The following section reflects on the impact of deindustrialization on two industrial cities in the United States. This process is a prominent component of economic restructuring, a process global in scope, but where the resulting social consequences are most clearly evident in communities that have long been dependent on industrial employment.

MANAGING URBAN LIVES

The deindustrialization of northern U.S. cities

In their classic analysis of the deindustrialization of the U.S. economy, Bluestone and Harrison (1982) point to the "contradiction between capital and community." The historical accommodation between industrial capital and organized labor in the United States, which lasted roughly from 1945 to 1971, dissolved when annual profits in heavy manufacturing drifted below 13 percent during the 1970s. Although there is plenty of room for argument as to the reasons industrial investments lost some of their attractiveness, the decline in profitability was ultimately reducible to the gains of international competitors.

More and more industrial concerns followed a policy of disinvestment during the decades of the 1970s and 1980s. They ran their plants and equipment into the ground while diversifying capital investments, especially outside of manufacturing, often planning at the same time to move their remaining manufacturing interests out of town and away from expensive labor (and land, tax, and utility) costs. It is this mobility of capital that produces the contradiction noted by Bluestone and Harrison: Capital must be mobile in order to compete successfully for customers (by reducing the costs of production and the price to consumers) and for investors (by returning satisfactory value to stockholders in the form of stable or rising share prices and dividends). Sometimes prudent business practice means moving investments out of town, out of the region, or out of industrial enterprise altogether. Governments, whether in smaller cities (Portz 1990) or world urban centers (Savitch 1990), are not helpless to respond to the threat that industry will move. But an effective response requires that local leadership have an appropriately vigorous view of the role of government, and effectiveness is facilitated by the existence of government jurisdictions that are regional in scope. The declining numbers of industrial jobs located in cities indicate that a great deal of the time government is not successful in persuading industry to stay put.

Bensman and Lynch (1987) have presented an account of a classic case of deindustrialization: the closing of steel plants in an industry-dependent community within a northern metropolitan area in the United States.

International Harvester learned in 1973 that a substantial investment would be required to keep its subsidiary Wisconsin Steel mill in East Chicago (South Deering) competitive, compliant with environmental regulations, and open. The corporation quietly searched for a buyer while allowing equipment to run down and while executives denied rumors of an impending sale of the mill. After a search that lasted four years, with few alternative prospects and equipment deteriorating to the point of endangering workers' lives, the steel operation was sold to an enthusiastic but inexperienced corporate purchaser with little in the way of steel-making expertise or cash reserves. Less than three years later workers showing up for the three o'clock shift were told abruptly that the plant was closed. It had closed for good.

The problems that had closed Wisconsin Steel reverberated throughout the region and across North America. The outdated manufacturing technologies, so often cited as the root cause of the competitive disadvantage of American steel makers in the 1970s and 1980s, were only part of the problem. Another of the steel plants located in the Southeast Chicago Region, United States Steel's South Works plant, had adopted the new, more efficient technologies used by their more innovative overseas competitors. The company had also begun massive layoffs in response to reduced demand occurring at about the same time as Wisconsin Steel closed down. Monetary policies in the late seventies, which inflated both the value of the dollar and interest rates, made imported steel a bargain in the United States. At the same time, these policies constricted domestic building and automobile industries, both heavy users of steel. The result in the Southeast Chicago area was the collapse of the region's economy, as tens of thousands of steel-related jobs evaporated. Dozens of related firms in the metropolitan region that included nearby northern Indiana closed down (Bensman and Lynch 1987: 73–4, 92–3).

The stories of personal tragedy resulting from plant closings and the loss of union jobs are by now familiar. One displaced worker in his mid-fifties reported that he was living on a pension of $300 a month. Because he owned a house, he could not receive Medicaid support for an operation he needed, so he lied to the hospital when he was admitted for treatment, telling them that he had insurance. He didn't qualify for food stamps. A skilled electrician, plumber and pipefitter, he had been turned down for employment at McDonalds, Burger King, and K-Mart. At the time, he was eating one meal a day, ashamed to seek further help, and uncertain of where to look for it (93).

Bensman and Lynch report the ways in which displaced workers fought back. Such workers were unwilling to believe that the life they had built with companies that seemed so solid, and an industry that had seemed so essential, could simply have disappeared, could not be called back. They organized around church leaders and the remnants of their independent labor organization, but they faced enormous difficulties in confronting the powerful and remote force of a changing economy. They sued for lost pension funds that had vanished when the mills closed, lobbied for an extension of unemployment benefits, and got the state unemployment board to staff a local office closer to the community for one day a week. Coalitions of the unemployed also worked for improved local schools, the provision of a local mental health clinic, and a reduction of transportation fares, all measures related to long-term adjustment to the new reality of the deindustrialized community. Bensman and Lynch deliberately and sensitively avoid creating the impression that these local efforts amounted to a quixotic tilting at windmills. They conclude, however, that effective policies designed to prevent disinvestment, deindustrialization, and the abandonment of communities of hardworking, committed individuals must be formulated and carried out at the national level. The authors comment that one useful function of local efforts is that they give people a vehicle for applying angry energies awakened by a sense of having been abandoned, "to keep up a sense of possibility" (Bensman and Lynch 1987: 184).

In Milwaukee, the closing of the Joseph Schlitz Brewing Company – "the beer that made Milwaukee famous" – and the conversion of the plant into a massive welfare bureaucracy, symbolizes the economic crisis of the deindustrializing city. The study by Hagedorn (1988) focuses on Milwaukee street gangs. He contrasts the reality faced by today's young minority group members with that confronting the subjects of classic gang studies of the past (Cohen 1955; Thrasher 1963; Miller 1969).

Hagedorn's analysis echoes Moore's interpretation (summarized in the "Managing Urban Lives" section at the end of Chapter 1 in this book) regarding urban economic change and the persistence of individual affiliation with the gang. Like Moore, Hagedorn proposes that deindustrialization prevents the natural process by which individuals have in previous decades "matured out" of gangs as they reached young adulthood. This is the key feature that makes the reality of today's gangs different, especially from the early Chicago school interpretation which saw gang membership as an immigrant and transitional phenomenon. Hagedorn's understanding also closely parallels W. J. Wilson's (1987) argument that just as the long-standing tradition of racial discrimination weakened in the 1960s and 1970s, the availability of the kinds of industrial jobs that had paved the way to the suburbs for other groups declined sharply. The consequence was that blacks and Hispanics who had been denied upward mobility historically by overt racism are now denied access to good industrial jobs by technologically induced reductions in labor demand and regional and international shifts in the locations of those jobs. Although the 1980s were generally a disastrous decade for African Americans, this was especially so in Milwaukee. The city had the second highest unemployment rate for blacks among the larger cities in the nation, and was second to none in the black to white unemployment ratio.

As a direct result of deindustrialization in Milwaukee, there is no longer a ladder for many older gang members to climb out of the hustling life on the streets, to mature out of the gang. Instead, there is the "institutionalization of gangs as a means for young adults to cope with economic distress and social isolation" (111). Today, the senior members of Milwaukee's gangs are a manifestation of the underclass, a segment of society excluded from the kind of participation in the formal economy that would allow them to escape poverty. Where Wilson has spoken of the excluded as a permanent underclass in the postindustrial city, others have observed that the restructuring of the international economy divides the population of each city in two. The "dual city" has a well-educated and appropriately skilled affluent population that profits from the kinds of opportunities provided by emerging economic arrangements, and a struggling underclass that is further and further removed from the opportunity for meaningful and rewarding employment. We evaluate the dual-city hypothesis as it applies to the city of New York in the "Managing Urban Lives" section of Chapter 5.

In the next chapter we turn to the subject of the Third World city in the international economic system.

4

The Third World and the world system

The conceptual controversies that characterize contemporary urban sociology, are accentuated in the study of urban growth and change in the Third World. For the most part, Third World urban study has traditionally been a specialized branch of urban study. As such, it has applied the sociology of place to particular places, setting aside the Third World city as a special case. Although there are sound reasons, both historical and contemporary, for separating the study of Third World urban processes from the study of urban processes elsewhere, the conventional division is presently undermined by ongoing theoretical developments.

The trend today is to draw the analysis of Third World patterns back into the mainstream of urban sociology as the scope of urban analysis takes on global dimensions. The objective in this chapter is to review some of the major issues that have marked the separate study of urbanization in underdeveloped nations, and to recognize conceptual linkages through which Third World urban sociology may be drawn into global urban analysis. The chapter is not intended to provide a complete introduction to Third World urban studies, but rather to provide a sense of the trend toward the globalization of urban analysis with particular reference to the Third World.

It is widely recognized that Third World cities are not replications of cities in the economically advanced economies, either with regard to their origins or present circumstances. Discussions of economic change, community, networks, urbanism, and so forth, that assume such parallels lose sight of the important historical, political, and economic differences that underlie urban growth and change in Third World regions, in contrast to the circumstances that produced and have modified cities in Europe and the United States. Among the reasons that the urban sociology of underdeveloped regions must be conceptualized differently from that of the advanced economies are the lingering effects of colonialism, the international division of labor expressed in terms of the nature of exports and imports, and the enormous difference in population size that separate the experiences of currently rapidly urbanizing nations from those of the industrial revolution in its various phases.

However, there is at the same time a growing recognition that it is a mistake to cut off and isolate the discussion of Third World urbanization. It is a mistake to isolate the analysis of Third World urban growth and change because these are component processes of a single world system that influences patterns of settlement and other features of spatial organization everywhere on the globe. The recognition is consistent with the trend in the urban analysis of advanced industrial economies that emphasizes the contingent nature of local conditions and global events. The organization of space throughout the world is the physical manifestation of international relations of political and economic forces. It is appropriate to view Third World cities as different, but their study cannot be separate from the study of cities in general.

The size and rate of growth of cities in the Third World demand the attention of urban social science. Although the heterogeneity of Third World regions has often been commented on, these regions have in common recent or current rates of urban growth that have produced rapidly expanding urban centers. Many of the largest, and certainly the most rapidly growing, urban areas in the world are in less developed countries. By the end of the twentieth century most of the largest conurbations will be in the Third World, including Seoul, Cairo, Madras, Manila, Buenos Aires, Bangkok, Karachi, Delhi, and Bogotá, all with above ten million people; Bombay, Calcutta, and Djakarta will have above fifteen million; São Paulo, Beijing, and Rio de Janeiro near or above twenty million; and the world's largest city, Mexico City, is expected to have more than thirty million.

Although some Third World countries are highly urbanized, such as Chile, Argentina, and Venezuela, where over 80 percent of the population live in urban areas, others have enormous rural reserves of population. In most states in Africa and Asia, only between one-fifth and two-fifths of the national populations live in urban places. These are countries with rapidly growing populations, and high annual rates of urban population increase (often compounded at between 4 and 8 percent per year). A substantial part – 40 percent in many areas – of urban population growth comes from rural-to-urban migration. Historically, as today, migrants for the most part have been young adults in a position to make their presence felt: They have an immediate impact on the employment market (Gugler 1986) and they are in their peak reproductive years (Todaro 1979; 1984: 16). Recently there has been an increase in the number of nuclear family units joining the urban migration stream, as well as a gradual trend toward more balanced sex ratios in Third World cities (Gugler 1992a: 79, 84).

The dimensions of urban growth in the Third World make it more dramatic than the growth of cities during any other era, including that of the industrial revolution in northern Europe. Urbanization in the poorer regions of the world is not typically driven by the expanding need for industrial workers, even though the displacement of industrial jobs from the First to the Third World is having a major impact on urban workforces in the more advanced (sending) economies. Although many in the urban populations of Seoul, Taiwan, and Hong Kong do find industrial work, the urban populations of every Third World city suffer high rates of unemployment and underemployment. The industrial roots of Third World urban growth are more remote to today's most rapidly growing urban populations than during the industrial revolution, as the poorest economies continue to rely heavily on the export of agricultural products and raw materials. Machinery and other manufactured goods are imported. The international division of labor among nations was established during the colonial era, and has persisted as Third World nations gained their formal independence. The picture had become more complex and generalization more difficult by the mid-1980s, as oil exports and transplanted manufacturing enterprises from wealthier nations began to diversify the economies of the somewhat better-off Third World states. Yet, expanding foreign debt, lack of effective domestic and regional markets, and limited levels of popular participation in economic growth cast doubt on any prognosis of a second industrial revolution for the Third World. The different international context of Third World urbanization sets it apart from the circumstances under which the cities of the industrialized West grew and prospered. Third World economies and the populations of Third World cities are considered to be at a disadvantage within the single web of economic expansion, competition, and change that links the world regions together.

Major issues in urbanization and underdevelopment

The discussion of Third World urban issues is intimately bound up in the wider discussion of economic underdevelopment. This is natural, of course, because, whether we are predisposed to the ecologist's or political economist's approaches, we understand the city to be the physical and spatial expression of economic arrangements and conditions. Although the operational details of what the term underdevelopment means may invite endless debate, having to do with definitional criteria and the ideology of social justice, the concept is widely understood to refer to the following circumstances: Underdevelopment means the protracted relative poverty of large segments of a given a population who, because of stagnant economic conditions or the unfavorable consequences of economic policy, have little prospect for all but marginal participation in an expanding economic mainstream and little likelihood of substantially improved life chances.

The cold, aggregate indicators of underdevelopment include high infant mortality rates, low life expectancy, limited access to health care, low levels of literacy and limited years of schooling, and insufficient diet. Averaged national figures do not tell the whole story of the way in which limited economic resources and economic benefits are actually distributed within the population of an underdeveloped nation. Differences in life chances that result from differential access to the benefits of economic growth are obviously subject to class, frequently racial or ethnic division, but often also show a spatial or regional bias. Regional bias exhibits a rural–urban dimension, as the benefits of economic growth accrue largely to urban centers (Gugler and Flanagan 1976).

There are three major theoretical approaches to the problem of underdevelopment, and each sees the process of urbanization as a major factor. These are modernization theory, dependency theory, and world-system theory. The three theoretical approaches are based on two paradigms that provide the foundations for arguments over the causes of underdevelopment in general and the particular role played by cities. These are the modernization and political economy paradigms. The modernization paradigm provides the basic assumptions of modernization theory, while the political economy approach provides a broad theoretical orientation for dependency and world-system theories.

Modernization theorists see cities as the potential engines of economic growth, while political economists emphasize the parasitic effects that urban concentrations have on the territories that they dominate. The debate between the proponents of these views has strong ideological overtones. In the section that follows, we explore the manner in which the debate has softened, somewhat, as the emphasis of political economists shifted from dependency theory to world-system theory. Some recent interpretations attempt to reconcile the generative and parasitic effects of cities. At present, there is a healthy volatility surrounding conceptual development, with broad implications for reconceptualizing the international structure of urban change.

The study of Third World urban processes today is characterized by simultaneous trends toward the internationalization of analytic perspectives and a localization or particularization of understanding at the level of case study. This is an extension of the debate, introduced in the last chapter and addressed further in the next, as to whether global theories are adequate to the task of producing a useful guide to understanding local conditions. On the one hand, it is recognized that certain common features of Third World urbanization must be produced by common historical and contemporary factors faced by many or all underdeveloped regions. At the same time, the local manifestation of common patterns must be seen as unique or peculiar to some degree, subject to the influence of local histories, local economic potential, and present and past policies and strategies in that particular place. Uncovering the particular is the job of the empiricist. Although no theory can withstand the discovery of unlimited exceptions to the general rule, it is the function of theory to address the general pattern.

The general patterns attached to Third World urbanization tend to have an urgent or "problem" nature that stems from the limited assets of governments, the desperate poverty of elements of the populations concerned, and the enormity of the dimensions of urban growth. Each of the theoretical approaches reviewed in this chapter – modernization, dependency, and world system – has implications for the way the major issues are understood. The focus of attention in urbanization studies are divided into two broad areas. The first concerns the consequences of market-driven patterns of growth. The second relates to the informal sector. Both raise questions of policy.

Perhaps the most heated debate in the study of Third World urbanization involves the implication of the rate and pattern of uncontrolled urban growth. There are two related issues here. One has to do with the sheer aggregate growth of the proportion of a national population living in cities, the other with the concentration of the population in a particular city.

It is possible to establish, theoretically, an ideal distribution of population among cities and rural areas. The ideal distribution would be established according to demographic and economic principles. Under optimal conditions, a national labor pool would be distributed in such a manner that a balance would be achieved between the numbers of workers present and the potential contribution of their combined efforts to some scale of national labor productivity. Needless to say, such a functionalist ideal is present nowhere in the world. However, the misallocation of labor, according to this model, has taken on special significance in the Third World, where migration has produced a pattern referred to as "overurbanization" (Gugler [1982] 1988). In addition to the redundancy of labor in the urban sector, the misallocation produces an increase in the cost of providing services for a country's growing population.

Under the condition of overurbanization, the misallocation of labor is manifest in a pattern whereby labor may be employed full-time eking out a living, but where the task performed contributes little to the general social welfare or to national productivity.

Much misemployment focuses on getting crumbs from the
table of the rich. The member of the local elite or middle-
class, the foreign technical advisor, or the tourist who is
begged for a morsel, or made to maintain a company of
sycophants, or has his wallet snatched away. The relationship
is vividly portrayed in three activities: the army of domestics
that cleans and beautifies the environment of the privileged;
the prostitutes who submit to the demands of those able to
pay, and who in the bargain become outcasts; and the
scavengers who subsist on what the more affluent have
discarded, and who literally live on the crumbs from the rich
man's table. (Gugler 1988 [1982]: 78)

The waste is that the labor is so cheap, its cost related to oversupply –
to the misallocation of labor. Overurbanization assumes that these units
of labor could be more productively applied elsewhere, perhaps in agriculture. But labor is not moved by national interest. Instead it is allo-
cated according to the perceptions and locational choices of individuals
who are interested in improving their own circumstance. This is the key
to understanding the tide of migration sweeping into Third World
cities. There is misery, poverty, and overcrowding, but cities are where
the limited supply of jobs are concentrated.

Analytically separate, but closely related to concerns about the overall rates of urban growth, are the issues of urban primacy and urban
policy. The pattern of urban primacy, in which the largest city in a nation
is several times the size of the next largest, is understood to violate the
"rank-size rule" which is understood to prevail in most economically
advanced nations. According to the rule, there is at least a tendency for
cities to follow a rank order whereby the second largest city is roughly
half the size of the first largest, the third largest one-third the size of
the largest, and so on. In this way a city's size is predicted by its rank
with respect to the largest city. The scheme is purely descriptive, but
has been observed to broadly distinguish newly developing urban systems from those of older, more established industrial nations.

Certainly, the Third World contains some of the most pronounced
examples of primacy. Among the well-known examples are Buenos Aires,
twelve times the size of the next largest city; and Bangkok, with forty
times more people than the next in rank. The question of whether such
concentrated growth best serves the national interest has been answered
both in the most positive (Richardson 1984: 134–5) and negative (London 1980, 1985) terms.

The urban primacy issue highlights a general concern with the nature
of social and economic policies in Third World nations. Development

policy typically involves an "urban bias." Lipton (1977 [1988]: 40–5) who was among the first to identify the problem, in the 1960s, expresses the bias in class terms:

> The most important conflict in the poor countries of the world today is not between labor and capital. Nor is it between foreign and national interests. It is between the rural classes and the urban classes. The rural sector contains most of the poverty, and most of the low-cost sources of potential [national economic] advance; but the urban sector contains most of the articulateness, organization, and power. . . . Resource allocations, within the city and the village as well as between them, reflect urban priorities rather than equity or efficiency.

According to Lipton, a growing awareness on the part of national governments, that a reallocation of investments and development schemes to rural areas is both politically prudent and a sound economic strategy, has not been enough to reverse the urban bias. As in the case of urban primacy, the tendency to favor schemes that concentrate the benefits of the investment of public funds does not require a conspiracy assumption: It is the result of a convergence of interests among urban-based elites who control or influence policy decisions. We return to the discussion of overurbanization, primacy, and policy bias at various points in the chapter.

Another general area of concern in urbanization and underdevelopment studies addresses the measures undertaken by individuals to house and employ themselves. Taken together, these constitute an *informal sector* of the economy, to the extent that the activities fall outside of the efforts of formal authority to regulate and tax. The typical Third World city is dotted and ringed by the makeshift housing of people who have constructed dwellings on property they do not hold title to (the question of property title is quite complex in Third World cities; see Gilbert's [1992: 121–4] summary discussion). The so-called spontaneous or self-help housing occupies vast tracts of urban and suburban real estate, and in many areas the permanence and systematic upgrading of these squatter settlements, including the provision of utilities and social services, represent the tacit acceptance by urban authorities of a fait accompli. Some who can afford to do otherwise choose to reduce housing costs by attempting to establish squatter's rights. For most, however, the sprawling illegal settlement stands as a monument to the desperation of those without any other option but to shelter themselves, an understatement of the potential power of the poor to act in concert, diffused for the time being by the immediate problem of personal shelter.

The economic arrangement of the Third World city involves a complex overlay of activities. The settings in which the parts are acted out range from the boardrooms of banks and multinational corporate branches to the streets where the gifted hustler or pickpocket lays in wait for the unwary tourist or other careless mark. Layered in-between the ostensibly legal and the clearly extralegal activities, and overlapping both, is a grey area of employment referred to as the *informal economy*. The informal economy is neither coterminous with the population of the self-employed, nor with that of the poor (Castells and Portes 1989). Instead, it refers to both the self-employed and those who work for others, to the extent that they are not counted on official employment rolls available to government, where activities and contributions are not accessible to official censuses of employment and economic productivity, and where the activity remains unlicensed and untaxed by any official authority. The informal economy may be impossible to broadly delineate, to identify in terms of the sum of activities that go into making it up (Gugler 1992b: 97). Some self-employed street vendors are duly licensed and taxed, whereas multinational companies often subcontract to firms that evade the scrutiny of government. The best guide to ascertaining involvement in the informal economy is offered by Castells and Portes (1989): Informal workers are not known so much by the fact that their labor is unreported and unregulated as by the fact that they are unprotected. They are the superfluous members of the labor force who have taken refuge in jobs that are subject neither to government oversight nor union intervention.

This sector of the urban economy throughout the Third World has absorbed a large segment of the increased urban population in the decades since World War II. Of course estimates vary as to the relative proportion of the workforce employed in the informal sector. It is estimated that informal enterprise provides employment for between 35 and 65 percent of the labor force in most developing countries, and anywhere from 20 to 40 percent of the gross domestic product (Chickering and Salahdine 1991: 3). A rough estimate of the proportion of the urban workforce employed in informal trades in the typical Third World city is between 40 and 50 percent of the working population (Sethuraman 1981: 188–200). The contribution of the informal sector to urban employment for particular urban populations can be much higher: For example, in 1982, 85 percent of Morocco's urban service workers and 73 percent of artisans were in the informal sector, which had been growing in the previous decade at an annual rate twice that of the formal sector (Salahdine 1991: 16). In sum, the informal sector is an important generator of employment and income for urban populations.

Although many informal sector workers find higher incomes and greater freedoms than they would in the regulated sector (Peattie 1975: 115; Peil 1981: 109), the informal sector also constitutes a last resort for the desperate and redundant who barely subsist among the throngs of newspaper sellers and scavengers on the fringe of the urban economy. Entry into the more viable ranks of the informally self-employed may not be easy or automatic for those who cannot find other employment (Peattie 1975: 113–18). Nevertheless, the unregulated sector has in the long view provided the shock absorber for overflow urban growth. We thus may recognize a systemic link between the elastic capacity of the informal sector to house and employ and thereby to sustain high rates of growth, and so-called overurbanization.

Overurbanization, primacy, urban bias, squatter settlement, and informal employment are the issues that receive the most attention from those concerned with urbanization and underdevelopment. Their implications have been viewed somewhat differently as the fields of development studies has evolved differing theoretical emphases over the past several decades.

From modernization to the world system

The large urban centers of underdeveloped nations have been characterized both as the engines of positive change and parasites that suck the potential for growth out of the economy. The metaphors more than hint at the deep ideological division that has separated the proponents of each point of view. The politics of the debate are not relegated to ivory tower disagreements, but find profoundly important real-world expression in the way that relations between rich and poor nations are perceived, and the ways in which domestic and foreign policies are formulated.

This is the issue: The economies of rich and poor nations are linked in trade, technological exchange, and investments carried on by private interests, and through national policy. In what measure are the linkages beneficial, and in what measure are they exploitative, especially with regard to the general welfare of the populations of the states concerned? Third World cities energize the international exchange process, by concentrating the resources for growth, or for exploitation.

Theoretical development concerning the role of urbanization in underdevelopment has been rapid. As elsewhere in the social sciences, sequential theoretical developments have not led so much to the replacement of older ideas as to their contemporaneous opposition.

Modernization theorists have emphasized the inherent backwardness and dysfunction of indigenous culture, organization and technology in underdeveloped regions, and the need to adopt the values and political and economic strategies of the industrialized nations (Inkeles 1966; Parsons 1951; Rostow 1960). The assumption is that developing nations will converge toward a common economic and political system that features the operation of the marketplace, individualism, and multiparty political democracy. This paradigm was promoted as an intellectual component of the United States-dominated effort to confront the threat of the growing influence of socialist states in the Third World, and combined naturally with the tenets of Parsonian functionalism (So 1990: 17–23). A fundamental assumption of the approach is that the relationship between rich and poor countries is essentially a beneficial one, with an emphasis on the benefits that accrue to poor nations as a result of the diffusion of the habits and conventions of the richer nations.

The theoretical link between modernization theory and urban sociology reaches as far back as Tönnies and the transformation from *Gemeinschaft* to *Gesellschaft*, and Durkheim's postulate of the reintegration of society through organic solidarity. Modernization was operationalized to mean differentiation, specialization, and functional interdependency. The lack of those features in underdeveloped societies was precisely the cause of their underdevelopment.

From this perspective, it is easy to appreciate that rapid urbanization is no problem, but a solution to a problem. Likewise, the case of primacy. Whether any Third World country is overurbanized remains an open question (Wilson 1984: 302). Cities are seen as the most efficient instruments of change in an international system of cultural diffusion, and the larger the city is the higher the rate of transfer. It follows that many Third World primate cities may be too small rather than too large (Richardson 1984: 134–5). Also, the question of urban bias on the part of policy makers loses much of its urgency.

Such a single-minded view of the beneficence of the world market system and its political and economic agents presented an inviting a target to critics. The critical response to modernization theory dates roughly from Andre Gunder Frank's (1967) essay which posited a causal relationship between underdevelopment and the degree to which a Third World economy was tied to the economies of wealthy nations. Further, he emphasized the instrumental role of the international system of cities in perpetuating the disadvantage of poor nations: The profits extracted from poorer regions grew in size as commodities moved from city to city, up the urban hierarchy, away from the producer and toward the consumer.

During the 1960s and 1970s the criticism of the modernization approach cohered into dependency theory, and the new perspective quickly attracted a large following, especially among Third World social scientists (So 1990: 91–5). The dependency perspective emphasized the systematic disadvantage of the underdeveloped economies in their relationship with rich nations. The disadvantaged position of those who exchange raw materials for the products of advanced manufacturing technologies is exacerbated by the imbalance that exists in political as well as economic power between poor and rich economies. The terms of trade are dictated by international politics, powerful multinational corporations that are the vectors of exchange, and the weight of history. The poor nation is struggling to overcome a colonial past, and the rich nation remains entrenched in the advantaged position of the colonial master state. Under such neocolonial arrangements, the economy of the poor partner remains "extraverted" (Amin 1976), organized to serve an international system in which its paradoxical advantage is that it supplies labor and materials at bargain rates that insure its continued disadvantage.

Like modernization theorists, dependency theorists also saw urbanization as an important component of the spreading influence of the industrialized West. However, the tradition that dependency theory drew on was Marxism, and that cast Western influence in a much different light. Although the influence of Marxism increased during the 1970s with regard to urban studies in general, its influence in the study of urbanization and underdevelopment was, if anything, more pronounced. Where modernization theorists had paid little attention to the imperial past during which the regions of the Third World were drawn under Western influence, the Marxists focused on it.

> The impact of the Marxian and dependency critiques has been to move the study of Third World urbanization beyond the stage at which passing mention is made of the importance of taking into account the colonial history of the countries in question . . . Proponents of these perspectives have argued persuasively that urbanization must be studied holistically – part of the logic of a larger process of socioeconomic development that encompasses it, and that entails systematic unevenness across regions of the world. (Timberlake 1985: 10)

Recognition of the historical importance of the colonial era has been an important first step in reintegrating the study of Third World urbanization to that of the rest of the world. King (1990, 1985) observes that colonial cities were the vital link that held together empires in the age of formal imperialism, global "pivots of change" that were "instrumental in creating the space in which today's capitalist world economy operates" (1990: 7). King believes that all cities, and the process of urbanization itself, can be conceptualized in terms of colonial expansion and domination. The observation holds, according to King, for both local circumstances and for the international network of economic relationships that integrates the cities of the world. Locally, the urban center dominates the extraction and terms of utilization of the resources of its immediate hinterlands. In the broader perspective there is an international system of superordinate and subordinate urban centers, wherein the agents of the dominant cities organize not only the local surpluses of the immediate hinterland, but those of other cities as well (King 1990: 15). In this light, the bias of urban-based policy makers is only natural.

Although dependency interpretations from Frank (1967) onward incorporated the imagery of an international, urban-based hierarchy that orchestrated the accumulation of capital, this model essentially posited a two-tiered system of dominant and subordinate states. Consistent with the interpretation that colonialism had evolved into a neocolonial order that locked states into their former positions of advantage or disadvantage, the dependency model tended to invoke the image of a castelike system, a static world order in which states neither rose nor fell from their fixed rankings. The model was not consistent with the long sweep of history, nor was it consistent with the events of the past several decades in which some states could be seen to have risen or fallen to some intermediate level, vis-à-vis their former position and that of other states. Although dependency appeared to describe accurately the situation and prospects of many nations at the present time, it lacked the dynamism necessary to account for the mobility of states within the international order.

In 1974 Wallerstein introduced the world-system model, and subsequently extensively developed the argument (Wallerstein 1974, 1978, 1979, 1980). Like dependency theory, world-system theory was linked to the Marxist tradition, initially incorporating Frank (1967) and Amin (1976), but following the directive of Fernand Braudel to take the "long view" in understanding patterns of change (So 1990: 169–80). Wallerstein abandoned dependency theory's two-tiered model of international stratification, and posited a third level. In addition to the core (economically dominant) and periphery (underdeveloped and poor) states, there is the intermediate semiperiphery. This tier is occupied by states that have gained upward mobility during periods of international instability, or states that are in decline from former positions of dominance. The model offers a category for the placement of the "little tigers" of the Pacific Rim, such as Taiwan and South Korea, as well as for the downwardly mobile, former imperial powers, like Portugal. Where dependency theory fastened attention on the plight of poor Third World states, world-system theory offers an invitation to begin analysis at any level – core, semiperiphery, periphery – and requires that the entire system be included. The focus is on the whole system, rather than the perspective of the dependent nation alone (Timberlake 1985: 10–11). This appears to be a distinct advantage from the point of view of urban study, because it moves us closer to a global, structural context for the analysis of urban processes, which may be a necessary step in advancing understanding how cities grow and change. This issue is pursued further later in this chapter.

The world-system model preserves the idea that the world economy is integrated through a series of hierarchical exchanges: Inequalities in the power to establish favorable terms of trade among the interacting states provides the basis for exploitation. Dominant states take advantage of the next lower tier or tiers.

In the simplest view, the economic units among which exchanges take place are sovereign states. Recent research (Smith and White 1992) supports in principle Wallerstein's model that divides the national economies of the world into three tiers or blocks, against interpretations that posit a greater number of strata, or a seamless continuum of competing economies. However, it has been argued that in a world system, national boundaries have reduced meaning for the purpose of identifying the territory within which economic activity is contained or focused. It may be more appropriate, if more complicated, to picture exchanges taking place between more or less discrete economic regions, some of which are centered on urban agglomerations. That is, the territories of exchange, conceived as distinct economic regions wherein there is a concentration or focus of activity, are most clearly delineated when they are centered on a particular urban area (Kentor 1985: 29). In general, however, world-system analysis does not particularly feature the role of cities. It does, on the other hand, through an extension of interpretations of historical and explicitly cross-national economic processes, provide a context for the analysis of the expanding and contracting fortunes of cities around the world. As was noted in Chapter 1, convulsive events in Hong Kong or Havana have consequences for real estate values in Manhattan and business competition in Miami. All world centers are linked to a greater or lesser extent in this manner.

The three theories reviewed here focus on structural forces that shape and reshape the world's cities and the experiences of their inhabitants. Modernization theory, with its emphasis on the generative capacity of urban centers, and dependency theory, with its focus on the parasitic nature of urban growth, are bound by their assumptions to remain poles apart in their interpretation of the significance of market-directed urban growth. World-system theory, while siding with the dependency theory interpretation that international linkages are routinely exploitative, holds out the prospect for altered fortunes, at least for some of the world's national economies. The historical record is clear: Economies are socially mobile within the stratified international system of economies, and in the long view some nations move from the periphery to the semiperiphery.

In the current era, this mobility has typically been achieved through the urban-centered expansion of industrial output for export. By implication, some Third World urban growth is productive rather than parasitic, and generative of improvements in the general welfare, i.e., development. World-system theory thus invites further analysis in order to demonstrate what the balance may be between the benefits and liabilities created by urban growth around the world. The crude nature of the comparative data that is at all useful for comparison across nations provides some support for both the generative/diffusionist and parasitic paradigms (Bradshaw 1987; Smith and London 1990).

Examples of the attempt to reconcile the generative and parasitic effects of urbanization are provided in the ambitious works of Armstrong and McGee (1985), and King (1990). The focus of Armstrong and McGee's book, *Theatres of Accumulation* (1985), is the role of the cities of Asia and Latin America in the development process. Their primary concerns are capital accumulation, unbalanced growth, and inequality: Cities are the locus operandi for the profit-seeking machinations of transnationals, and for oligopoly capital. However, the authors balance their emphasis on the economy as the driving force of change with the observation that the major cities are also the point of cultural diffusion for new tastes, consumer habits, and lifestyles. Thus, the processes of concentration (of capital) and diffusion (of cultural innovation) proceed simultaneously, and are complementary rather than contradictory. Large, often primate, cities are arenas in which local growth elites act as investors and brokers; the main beneficiaries are large national companies and international corporations; and the question remains open as to whether the growth and benefits of concentrated economic activity will diffuse to the rest of the nation (41–2). At the same time, there is evidence of convergence in the physical appearance and managerial conventions of the great urban centers, as Third World primate cities mimic the global cities of the industrial capitalist core as the central locations for corporate headquarters, world financial institutions, and administrative and political elites (48).

In this interpretation, one of the central features of inequality emphasized by political economists, the concentration of resources in the growth of Third World urban centers, simply becomes one of the features of Third World trends toward convergence with world-wide ecological patterns. What is diffused from the urban center to the rest of the population are consumer habits. The choice of terms is significant in revealing the paradigmatic shift in emphasis away from the orthodox framework of political economy: "With the modernization of even the remotest areas, certain aspects of the lifestyles and behavior patterns (including the consumerism) of the industrial societies are adopted in market towns and villages even though their production structures may be totally undeveloped" (49).

Anthony King (1990) acknowledges the important contribution of world-systems theory, but says that it has neglected the question of cultural change. The political economy paradigm that has grown up around Wallerstein's work has failed to address the ideational, symbolic, and cultural, or the realm of the "preeconomic" in its overly simplistic, unidirectional, and economistic interpretation of the global process of urban change. King would prefer to pursue the sociological significance of culture within a more anthropological vein, and avoid "Western-centered discourse to give greater attention to civilizational and societal distinctiveness" (9–10). Consistent with such an approach (and following Robertson 1987, 1988), King argues that the global process of urbanization is not unidirectional in terms of its cultural product, that is, it is not a process of Westernization.

Third World urbanization is a process whereby changes in consciousness and habits do not involve a simple global homogenization. Instead, the global force combines with local cultural and historical (including remnant elements of particular imperial, colonial) features, to produce local variations that are a product of the interaction of global and local factors. Although the colonial city is the spearhead of change, such motifs as heightened identity, tradition, and indigenization may be exacerbated by the process of globalization carried on through urban growth. King thus manages to raise the question of urbanism in a new light, indicating that the features of the phenomenon are open to cultural renegotiation. In fact, the symbolic content of the urban form is changed for the core as well as the peripheral states: King points to the example of the Bengal Room in the Victoria Hotel in Vancouver, British Columbia, Canada. The example reflects the interpenetration of style, not its linear diffusion. King says that Third World urbanism, as a matter of urban style, is not a set of conditions and practices transferred from the core to the periphery, but "by moving between the core and the periphery my aim has been to explore and demonstrate the symbiotic, complementary, and essentially interdependent nature of the development of urbanism in the capitalist world economy." A complete analysis of the diffusion of culture between core and periphery would take into consideration the influence of Third World immigrants on the culture of such cities as London, Los Angeles, Miami, Montreal, or New York. The diffusion of the elements of such hybridized urban cultures raises complex questions of the nature and the origins of what it is that is being diffused among the cities of the world. Still, it is well to keep in mind the differential impact of, say, the novelty of Ethiopian or Haitian cuisine, or Andean street musicians plying the informal economy of Western cities, on the one hand, and the pervasiveness of the corporate influence of McDonald's and Coca Cola in Third World cities, on the other.

The work of Armstrong and McGee and of King is intended as a corrective to the overly economistic, structural paradigm of political economy, through the introduction of neomodernization themes that emphasize the synthesis of cultures and the importance of cultural transformation as a major feature of global change. Although the works contain an important message, they appear to reinforce the argument that the cultural transformation that attends the urbanization process is secondary to the consequence of structural transformation. Whether the specific cultural issue is simple convergence toward a Western mode or the need to appreciate the synthetic nature of the global process (as local and indigenous features of the periphery are deepened in place and diffused toward the core), cultural change, even in these works which are determined to make it their focus, appears as a process subordinate to the dominant influence of the progressive globalization of markets and resources.

According to Armstrong and McGee (1985: 49), the chief vector of lifestyle change in the Third World is mass communication and advertising. But what is being diffused here are the appetites and habits that serve the structural core of the for-profit system. Their conclusion (220) places cultural change in its proper perspective: "Modernization" is a strategy for promoting growth through fostering consumer markets for the products of transnationals and national oligopolies:

> The very mechanisms which introduce new technology and larger-scale organization into industry and agriculture deprive the producers of their land, their craft production and their employment, transforming them fully or partially into wage laborers for capitalist production. Similarly, the loans and other financial transfers required for such technology in the modernized sectors create an indebtedness which locks Third World countries into further international system dependency.

The dominant modernization strategy of the past three decades "has been one which benefited a privileged minority, has consolidated existing power structures, has favored metropolitan centers at the expense of the regions and rural areas, *and in part, through the persuasive influence of monopoly media systems, has broken down the obstacles to the further penetration of capitalist production distribution, and consumption"* (emphasis added). The process of diffusion or "modernization" is clearly a component of broader structural changes, and not the other way around.

It is important for urban sociologists to study and understand the nature of cultural change in the wake of urbanization. It is especially important to avoid Western-centric interpretations. Culture change has not been a priority of the political economy paradigm which came to prominence with dependency theory and matured in the form of world-system theory. From the perspective of political economy, the study of culture change and emergent forms of urbanism amounts to the study of responses to more fundamental forces. It seems clear that the study of cultural change must begin with the broader context. As Timherlake (1985: 3) has acknowledged, "the claim is not that world-system processes explain everything." But the image of an international system involving relations of power in pursuit of wealth is the fundamental starting point for understanding globalization, including cultural transformations, and including movements of resistance that arise in response to those transformations.

The reintegration of Third World studies into the mainstream

Within any science there is always a tension between the movement toward specialization and the need to reintegrate subdisciplinary specialties in order to keep track of what has been learned. It makes sense that a reintegration cycle should occur whenever a new paradigm emerges that threatens to dislodge old assumptions. The maturation of the political economy paradigm, through its articulation in world-system theory, appears to be initiating a major shift in contemporary thinking with regard to international trends in urbanization. The world-system concept invites analyses that link urban processes in the core, semi-periphery, and periphery. In doing so, it promises to break down the traditional division of labor that has long existed in urban sociology between those who study Third World urbanization and those who study the city in the advanced economies.

By positing the idea that change in the world occurs in response primarily to the progressive rationalization of the globe in market terms, the world-system model forces us to seek connections between changes taking place in cities throughout the world. It makes possible the image of an international system of cities. However, this does not indicate a renewed search for parallel or equivalent changes in the cities of the underdeveloped and the advanced economies along the lines suggested by modernization theory. The modernization paradigm, with its convergence assumptions, made the search for parallels between the urban process in poor and rich nations hazardous. Modernization theorists were too quick in assuming that superficially similar features implied equivalence, that all societies were on schedule along the road to a common developmental future (Abu-Lughod 1975).

The exploitation assumptions of political economy models, as these models have been applied most frequently in Third World analyses, have different implications with regard to the recognition of common elements of the urban process in poor and rich nations. Here, the prime force is identified as capitalism, and there is no assumption that similar features manifest by cities in poor and rich nations imply that the former are in the process of "catching up." Any implications of convergence are limited, and their consequences are perceived in a much different light than in the case of the modernization paradigm.

Increasingly, urban social scientists are prone to look for connections between economic and spatial processes in distant points on the globe. The connecting force in the seamless arena of action is the expanding international economy, consisting of capital, materials, markets, and labor. The most visible and powerful physical manifestations of the system are the urban nodes of activity that we assume to be worthy of the attention of specialized study. King (1990: 2), who places greater emphasis on the importance of cultural change than some other contemporary urbanologists, urges recognition that the flow of influence and change within the international network of cities is multidirectional. He regards the city as a central construct in the world system and employs the metaphor that, historically, "the world has increasingly become one large, interdependent city: interdependent in that, in major cities of the world (both 'East/West' as well as 'North/South') it is not only people, knowledge, images, and ideas that move between them but also, to varying degrees, capital, labor, and goods."

The metaphor of the world as a single city is instructive although, perhaps, too strong for many of us. More would be willing to entertain the notion that the cities of the world do comprise a single urban system transcendent of national boundaries. National boundaries have less and less meaning as the global economy becomes woven into a single fabric. As national boundaries dissolve – for the purposes of encapsulating economic interests and strategies – the chief physical features of the world map we are left with are the towns, cities, and massive "functional urban regions." Chase-Dunn (1985: 71–2) offers an inviting visualization of a world-city system.

On the global map that he proposes, the only lines that appear would be those that trace the commodity exchanges that take place between urban centers, resulting in something that looks like an airline route map.

Such a map would represent the differential densities of exchange both within and across national boundaries among urban centers. He proposes that the resultant pattern would show:

> Exchanges among the largest cities of the core are dense
> within and across national boundaries, while peripheral cities
> exchange mostly with core cities and very little with one
> another. If we specified this network in terms of the types of
> commodities exchanged we would notice the familiar pattern
> of core-periphery division of labor. Capital intensive goods
> would circulate among core cities and flow to the periphery,
> while labor-intensive raw-materials would flow from the
> periphery to the core. (271)

Such a reconceptualization of space offers the possibility of dramatic innovations in the interpretation of current urbanization patterns, especially those that have drawn the attention of students of Third World urbanization. Although Walters (1985: 67–8) is skeptical about the validity of interpreting patterns within the framework of a single, international urban system, she believes that the frame for urban analysis cannot be assumed to be set by national borders. Her specific concern is to better identify the effective context for understanding urban primacy. "Many studies of urban primacy or other characteristics of urban systems take the nation–state as the unit of analysis, on the assumption that states and urban systems are coterminous." She argues that "there are many cases in which one city system encompasses multiple states, and other cases in which a single state contains multiple city systems" (63–4).

The question of urban primacy has thus become problematic. The size of a city is measured relative to what other cities? Size may be a good proxy for determining the relative importance of an urban center, but within the framework of world-system analysis we are less interested in relative population size than we are interested in such factors as the interplay between technological change and fixed capital; the era in which a particular city emerged and the circumstances under which it achieved whatever level of prominence; or the dynamics of a city's resident units of capital accumulation (corporations) and the local and distant factors affecting the mobility of capital (Chase-Dunn 1985: 290–2). These questions of the context of structure and function are important, and should be included in the analysis of the role of any city. However, there are urban issues that can only be addressed with reference to national policy, such as efforts to control and direct patterns of urban growth. It would therefore appear necessary that for purposes of assessing the effectiveness of policy in bringing urban growth under control, the nation-state must remain the relevant unit of analysis for measuring primacy and evaluating its consequences.

Expanding the framework of urban analysis to its ultimate, global dimensions raises questions of the transferability of concepts and terminology between world regions. For example, overurbanization is a concept most readily applied to regions of rapid urban growth in the Third World. However, world-system analysis, which takes the operation of capital everywhere as its focus, would seem to invite application of the concept to the retrograde circumstances of many cities within core nations. In these instances, characterized by a mismatch between stable or slowly shrinking urban populations and a rapid contraction in the number of available jobs, the overurbanization concept has a startlingly pertinent ring. In this light, overurbanization is not a characteristic of rapidly growing urban populations so much as it is a characteristic of the dynamics of the international economy. It would seem to make little more sense to refer to situations where the transfer of advanced industrial technology to the Third World has a retardant affect on the creation of jobs as overurbanization, without applying the same term to situations where the same technology makes existing urban populations of urban workers redundant. If the term overurbanization is appropriately applied to cities where unemployment holds at high levels despite the transfer of manufacturing jobs from the advanced economies, then certainly the cities in core regions from which the jobs were transferred, with their rising rates of unemployment and downwardly mobile working-class populations, are deserving of the term as well. Of course, with respect to the deindustrializing nations, the concept of "overurbanization" loses some of its clarity. There is no labor-intensive agricultural sector which can be assumed to be standing ready to absorb at a subsistence level a superfluous workforce. Yet, in the deindustrializing city, would-be and former industrial employees make their way into the informal sector, to struggle as unprotected labor outside the regulated economy. The parallel is sufficient to argue for attaching the same label to similarly placed workers throughout the world, and if "overurbanization" seems inadequate in this light, perhaps a new universalism is called for.

The conceptual linking of core and periphery provides the conceptual framework for analyzing the unitary structure of global relations of wealth and power. Concepts like primacy and overurbanization need to be evaluated within the global context. Although the emerging framework is bound to provide new insights, it also potentially undermines useful ways in which concepts have been applied to date. Consider the notion that it may be more useful to discuss primacy as a feature of transnational than national urban systems. This has serious implications for the capacity to address and call national policymakers to task for ignoring primate city patterns in their own state, patterns long recognized as involving a serious form of inequality and neglect of nonmetropolitan regions. "Overurbanization" may have a great deal more intuitive appeal as a concept applied to rapidly urbanizing states than those in which cities are losing population. At the same time, it is necessary to recognize that the restrictive application of terms like overurbanization to Third World regions supports a continued conceptual division of the field.

The informal sector and world urbanization

The movement toward conceptual integration has received its greatest impetus to date from the study of the informal sector. The work of Alejandro Portes and his associates (Portes 1987; Portes, Blitzer, and Curtis 1986; Portes and Sassen-Koob 1987) has been especially important. In the collection on informal economy edited by Castells and Portes (1989), one of the most striking and consistent features is the fully integrated discussion of the informal sector in both core and periphery states. Castells and Portes write that until a few years ago the majority of work on the informal sector was contained in studies of the Third World, and that the prevailing assumption was that the informal sector was a vanishingly small and insignificant part of the advanced economies. This assumption was never valid, and evidence indicates that over the past few decades informal economic strategies have been experiencing a modest to rapid increase in various wealthier nations (Castells and Portes 1989: 18ff).

The informal economy is not merely an aggregate of the activities of the desperate poor trying to eke out a living, though certainly such efforts make up some portion of it. Neither is the informal economy dependent upon large numbers of immigrants who are in some transitional stage of economic assimilation, although the presence of such a population often adds to the bulk of such activity. The definition of informal economic activity has to be broad enough to include the self-employed Latin American street seller, but also, for example, the moonlighting software consultant in Silicon Valley. The definition that Castells and Portes offer is that the informal economy involves income-generating activities that are unregulated by the formal institutions of the state, where other such activities are under regulation (12). The informal economy is in this very broad sense, extralegal, unregulated.

Castells and Portes point out that it is useful to see the presently expanding importance of the informal sector of core states as a response to the restructuring of the international economy. Although the structural foundations of the sector were in place long before the structural crisis of the 1970s, recent changes have been important in its expansion. The reaction of corporate employers to the organization of labor, the number of new regulations imposed by states, the intensity of international competition, and the world recession that has persisted since the mid-1970s have all played a part in dislocating labor. This dislocated labor exists in overlapping subsets that are in part unregulated, unprotected, and underground. As a result, workers in the informal economy tend to share the characteristic of "downgraded labor," labor that receives fewer benefits or lower wages than their counterparts or immediate predecessors (Castells and Portes 1989: 26).

The reasons for the growth of the informal sector in core states underlies the growth of the formal sector in the periphery. In the wealthy economies, the strength of organized labor, the increase in the regulations that govern economic activity, and international competition have produced subcontracting arrangements that filter down to the barrios and Chinatowns of Los Angeles, New York, and other cities as unregulated activity. The same conditions that create underground economies in the industrialized economies also send industrial employment "offshore" to the Third World city as manufacturing jobs in the regulated sector, where wages are sufficiently low and benefits so minimal that such "regulations" are entirely tolerable to capital. The same pressures of "overurbanization" operate in the urban arenas of the core and peripheral states to lower wages: In the Third World, the competition among so many unemployed job-seekers means that those who find work in the regulated sector will count themselves fortunate, whereas workers in the urban centers of the core learn to accept lower wages and reduced benefits, and/or find their way into the informal economy as drivers of "gypsy" cabs or as house painters. Meanwhile, governments in the advanced economies experiment with urban "enterprise zone" policies that mimic the downgrading of labor in the informal sector in the reduction of labor-protection standards.

Within the cities of the Third World, as in the cities of the industrialized nations, the informal sector grows alongside the formal economy. As is the case in wealthier economies, there is a considerable range of wages earned in the informal sector (Peil 1981: 109). Although comparative data is lacking, it appears that the largest numbers of informal workers struggle at or near subsistence (e.g., Moir 1981: 116). There is a natural tendency for lucrative trade and service provision to be soon taken up by legitimate concerns that squeeze small-volume competitors back onto the margins.

The cocaine trade offers an interesting and instructive exception, however. Its illegal nature prevents direct competition by legitimate enterprise, and in this way an entire sector of economic activity is insulated and sustained. Jimenez (1989) observes that the drug trade did not create the informal sector in Bolivia, but it has infused it with life and fundamentally transformed the underground economy. At the same time that it has provided society with a serious challenge to social order, it operates very much like a living success story of economic development as scripted by the modernization theorists.

During the 1970s the stagnant Bolivian economy, which had been dependent on extractive, agricultural, and crafts exports, was given new life by the rapid expansion of the production and processing of cocaine. The world demand for the product coupled with its illegal nature meant that it made sense for the raw material to be processed in the country of origin, rather than exported for processing and profit taking in the consuming nations, as would more likely be the case for legitimate products. Under these circumstances, an internally articulated system for production, processing, and shipment was set up at the national and local level, with profits and wages plowed hack into the national and local economy through consumption and investment activity. Families that produced coca and manufactured cocaine paste, the buyers and intermediaries, those who processed the drug in pure form, the exporters, and the corrupt officials generated a substantial aggregate income, which, in part, remained within the country.

A numerically important category involved in the trade was the families who grew and processed coca. They spent the money they earned on trucks, domestic electrical appliances, land, homes, and education for their children. The consumption of foreign-made goods was conspicuous. The demand for smuggled, foreign-produced goods found satisfaction in La Paz's "little Miami," where street peddlers offered merchandise of every kind. The importance of the thriving informal economy in Bolivian cities is enormous. It employs 48 percent of the working population, whereas the formal private sector employs 17 percent, with the remainder made up by public sector employment (Jimenez 1989: 140–4).

What is wrong with the picture is all too clear. The space left within the world economy for providing structural social mobility for large numbers of Third World entrepreneurs is outside the law; in the case of the international cocaine trade this is apparent enough, but it remains true to a greater or lesser extent for all informal activity around the world. Minimally, the informal economy offers an escape from taxation and licensing. But the informal economy also operates outside of minimum wage provisions, worker health and safety and other working condition stipulations, and it shades into outright criminal activities, from prostitution and illegal gambling through the production, distribution and sale of illegal drugs. Squatter housing is appropriately included in the category of the illegal underground because, by definition, it involves the appropriation of properties for which the occupants have no legal claim.

Among the major issues addressed by Third World urban sociology traditionally, perhaps the informal economy is the one most indicative of the importance and the maturation of political economy under the world-system approach. This is because it illustrates the seamlessness of the structural forces that impact the cities of the world. Today, the restructuring of the world economy displaces large segments of the working class of the industrialized nations while generating a proto-working-class force in Third World cities. On the periphery the pool of would-be industrial workers concentrated in cities grows too rapidly while in the core the pool of displaced workers fails to evaporate. Cities are overpopulated with workers; we say, "overurbanized." As workers find their way into the shadowy realms created or left by the dynamics of capitalism, we say that their employment has become "informal." In Europe, North America, and the Third World urban workers and the unemployed are underhoused and unhoused because either there are not enough jobs or other economic niches, or wage and petty-profits levels do not meet the costs of providing shelter. In rich and poor countries, in obviously differing proportions, individuals and families slip toward the fringe of the available supply of housing, and some are left to shelter themselves, illegally.

The world-system model is a powerful conceptual tool for urban sociology because it opens the door to a comprehensive analysis of structural forces effecting change in cities everywhere. However, like other theories that are global in scope, world-system theory has been faulted for being insensitive to local, region-by-region and city-by-city variations. In the next chapter, we return to the general debate between those who stress general patterns and those who emphasize the importance of understanding local variations in the impact of global conditions. First we examine more closely the experiences of some of those involved in making a living in the informal economy of Third World cities.

MANAGING URBAN LIVES

Third World women in the informal sector

Employment in the informal sector is not restricted to Third World settings: Unprotected and unrecorded work is a feature of the labor market in all nations. Nevertheless, one segment of the world-wide army of unprotected labor that has received a large share of attention is the street

trader and petty entrepreneur of Third World cities. These traders provide services or goods, operating as independent, self-employed petty mer-
chants or tradespeople, or work unrecorded for small entrepreneurs
whose enterprise may rest wholly or partly within the informal sector.
Generalization is hopelessly complicated here because some small-scale
traders are licensed and regulated, making them part of the formal sector,
and some may be part of a "chain" or guild of sellers who are employed
by relatively large concerns. The services provided range from the sale
of lottery tickets or newspapers, automobile repair, crafts production
and sale, the sale of produce grown some distance from the city by the
seller herself, to various forms of activities where the service or goods
are in themselves illegal.

Taken as a whole, the rise of the informal sector has been termed
"revolutionary" in its significance as a vehicle for affording popular participation in expanding economies (De Soto 1987; Chickering and
Salahdine 1991). As noted earlier in this chapter, informal trades that
provide anything from a meager subsistence to a comfortable living for
the individuals engaged in them, together add up to a substantial proportion of the economic activities in a given nation.

De Soto's (1989) *The Other Path,* in which he argues that the informal sector constitutes an irreversible revolutionary force for economic
change in Peru, nevertheless transmits a bleak picture of life in rapidly
growing Peruvian cities. He describes a pervasive and growing disregard
for the law, leading to an increasingly permissive popular view regarding illegal activities. For example, "Everyone from the aristocratic lady
to the humblest man acquires smuggled goods. No one has any scruples
about it; on the contrary, it is viewed as a kind of challenge to individual ingenuity or as revenge against the state" (6). Migrants to the
city, who are quickly made to feel alien and unwelcome have, in
De Soto's view, gravitated easily into illegal trades in order to survive
in a society that rejects their presence. Despite the official and popular
cold shoulder, migrants have over the last four decades come to make
up the bulk of the informal activities that have produced over 40 percent
of all housing in Lima (valued at over eight billion dollars). They swell
the ranks of the 91,000 street vendors and operate over 90 percent of
the city's public transportation fleet (13).

Women make up a special category of informal workers in Third
World cities. Although there is a substantial range of income earned by
urban informal sector workers in every country, women typically tend
to fall toward the lower end of the earning scale. Among the reasons
for this bias, women are disproportionately employed in trades that
reflect their traditional place in the household division of labor, which

translates on the street into such poorly remunerated activities as sell-ing small quantities of agricultural produce and prepared foods. Alter-natively, skills gained in their traditional role within the family and societal attitudes toward women's appropriate roles prepare women for equally unrewarding domestic employment as maids. For those who find employment that is not linked to their traditional domestic roles, their gender is still a liability. The subcontracting option, preferred by multi-national corporations seeking to further lower their Third World labor costs, transfers assembly work to informal local concerns that actively seek to employ women. These employees then fall outside of whatever protection might be offered by existing labor regulations. Women may be employed in their homes or take work home as homework, blurring the already vague distinction between informal work for which they receive meager wages and housework and family work for which they receive even less. (See Ward 1990 for an overview of these issues.)

Given the variety of circumstances of informal employment in Third World cities, no individual experience can serve to typify the uncertain-ties of this way of life. Yet, a case study is often invaluable for trans-mitting an unfamiliar reality and bringing it to life. The following account is provided by Bunster (1985).

Maria is an *ambulante* (peddler) who sells potatoes in the San Juan de Miraflores market in Lima. She is a twenty-eight-year-old single parent, has had to "give one baby away," lost two in their infancy, and struggles to keep her remaining two children with her. As is the case with other mothers like her, street peddling allows her to mind her chil-dren during the day while she sells. The family lives in a single room, which Maria cannot afford, and she is constantly threatened with evic-tion. She keeps her seven-year-old daughter with her at times instead of permitting her to go to school. The child helps with the accounts, making change, a part of the trade with which Maria has difficulty.

Maria hopes for a better life for her daughters than the struggle she has had. Maria was sent from her rural home to Lima to live and work as a maid when she was fourteen. It was her second such position. In both of these jobs she was exploited and sexually abused. Her children are the result of liaisons with different men; one of her five pregnancies was the result of sexual abuse. She has never been legally married, but she was happily coupled for a time as the town wife of a man who was killed in a traffic accident. His rural wife received all the compensation from the accident.

Maria's day starts at 3 a.m. She takes a daily early morning bus ride to the wholesale market, where she buys her merchandise. She keeps her meager capital pinned under her clothing to keep it from the thieves who ply the crowds at the market. She herself will have to fix her scales to cheat her customers in order to make ends meet, to subsist. She simply resells most of the potatoes in the two heavy sacks that she purchases that morning, but she will cook and sell some as snacks outside the cinema as well. Sellers at the market look after and sell each other's wares when some crisis, like a sick child, causes one to absent herself from her post. On a good day, Maria can leave the market at 3 p.m. to go home and care for her house and children, but most nights she goes out again to sell prepared food to the cinema-goers. The typical workday of the Lima *ambulante* is eighteen hours.

There is little prospect for upward mobility through increased or diversified sales. Maria remembers the words of a mentor whose observations were based on thirty years of experience as a street vendor: "Each day you have to struggle, you have to be on your feet running after your customers. When one is a young girl tiredness is not felt because peddling seems like a game, one has a good laugh every now and then and the illusion that everything is going to be fine. When one becomes older and more mature one realizes that there is no hope, that days are all the same." (81). Male street vendors reportedly fare better. Men operate with more capital, claim the best market locations, and are able to expand their businesses (Bunster 1985).

N. Nelson (1988) found the same type of gender stratification among trades in the extensive Mathare Valley settlement adjacent to Nairobi, the settlement itself a monument to the informal sector in terms of the form of much of the housing that occupies the site. There is a division of labor reflected in the types of informal trade men and women engage in. Eighty percent of the women in her study brewed local beer (*buzaa*) and sold it from their homes, many of these women also sold (but did not manufacture) clandestinely distilled gin (*changaa*), and many supplemented their income by selling sex. All of these activities were illegal, and those who engaged in them were subject to police harassment and fines. Although demand was high and business brisk (an ecological factor here is that the Mathare Valley settlement is surrounded by military barracks and single men's housing), the income earned by women's manufacturing and service occupations was modest. However, in comparison to the limited number of other low-overhead, easy-entry occupations where women were concentrated, such as vegetable selling (which also had illegal features), the explicitly illegal, self-employed trades of bootlegging and prostitution were substantially more financially rewarding. Yet, all these activities returned a lower profit than the wider range of trades open to men. Men were employed or self-employed as automobile mechanics, plumbers, electricians, drivers of illegal taxis, thieves and fences, builders and letters of illegal housing, distillers of gin, and in innumerable other ways. Some took higher risks in terms of the amount of capital invested or the amount of fines they faced, but earnings were substantially higher in most characteristically male trades. Men also far outnumbered women as proprietors of the more substantial shops and restaurants in the valley.

Nelson offers the following tentative interpretation of inequality between the sexes, an interpretation which, as she notes, indicates an interaction of cultural and structural factors. The cultural constraint – namely, what is viewed as an appropriately feminine pursuit in Kenyan society – sets the context for the development of the structural reinforcement of the observed inequalities. The limited range of activities traditionally perceived as permissible pursuits for women, largely having to do with domestic and childrearing roles, sharply restricts the number of trades open to them. Their more limited educations, another cultural factor reflecting the differential valorization and investment in sons and daughters, also restricts women's options. The presence of children in itself, and the fact that the typical woman trader was "independent" or without husband, created a liability not faced by male entrepreneurs. By contrast, a man in business for himself typically kept a family in the rural area, where subsistence agriculture and occasional paid agricultural labor performed by his wife relieved him of the overhead of family maintenance. Alternatively, if he had a woman in town, she might, under various domestic conventions, still be seen as responsible for the upkeep of household and offspring. Men were thus freer to channel some of their earnings into the kind of capital investments that allowed them to expand businesses and earnings. It is significant, according to Nelson, that the one more lucrative trade in which women predominated, the sale of raw materials to female brewers, female entrepreneurs had managed to break free of the limiting domestic constraints faced by their clients. First, their contacts and expertise grew out of their previous experience as brewers – the woman's work in Mathare Valley. Second, a surprising proportion of these "big women" traders had never had children (Nelson 1988).

In considering the sources of the inequalities evident in examples of informal sector employment it is important to keep in mind the global dimensions of this pattern. Castells and Portes (1989) maintain that evidence from around the world indicates that it is the more recent entrants to the labor force – immigrants (or rural migrants), women, and the young – who are incorporated at the lowest paid and least protected categories of informal enterprise. Local histories and cultural variations can help us to understand the differences in local manifestations of global patterns, but it is the global hypotheses that orient our attention. Exceptionally, individuals may have the power to resist the options that the global economy presents to them, but how often do they have the opportunity to respond individually or collectively in a way that changes the cards they are dealt? This is the issue of human agency discussed in the next chapter.

5

Agency, structure, and urban sociology

In the past twenty years, urban sociology has been marked by a conceptual volatility that contrasts sharply with the previous several decades of temperate debate between those who found cities to be a more alienating and those who found it a less alienating environment. In the 1970s the old urbanism versus community debate was shoved aside by the arrival of Marxist analysis and the language of political economy. By the mid-1980s the Marxists were in retreat and all structural interpretations of urban change were under attack as overly deterministic. Critics argued that world-system models of political economy and equilibrial models of human ecology were obviously inadequate because the grand theories in which they were embedded failed to explain or predict what was happening in particular cities and neighborhoods. General theories were as useful for predicting the direction of urban change in specific localities as a meteorology textbook would be in predicting local weather – relevant but remote. Instead, local outcomes must be the result of local variables, of specific historical and local cultural circumstances and, moreover, the consequence of deliberate human action, of *agency*.

By the mid-1980s there was a growing emphasis in urban sociology on localism and empiricism, and a de-emphasis on theories that posited inexorable global or societal forces but failed to explain variations in the impact of these forces on similarly situated cities. In the new approach, "Laws of development and the dead weight of structure are replaced by the potential for human action to create and reproduce its own environment. Space is socially created, general processes are modified by space-specific characteristics, and the economy does not determine in the last instance. The reaction is against both the structural Marxists and the apolitical, neoclassical theorists and their quantitative counterparts" (Beauregard 1987: 164). The new agenda for social research is to discover what it is that makes each city unique in its response to global forces, and to understand how it is that some cities are able to resist general regional trends while others typify them. The new approach seeks answers to the questions: What are the local tactics, successful and unsuccessful, for mobilizing resources and applying them to growth?; and How are the benefits and costs of modified growth patterns distributed among local populations?

However, despite the widespread appeal of the new agenda across the spectrum of political viewpoints within urban social science, the defection away from the more structural assumptions that have characterized the study of cities is hardly complete. As we have seen thus far in our discussion of contemporary urban sociology, many hold to the assumption that the most important story of urban growth and change is that unseen structures produce broadly similar consequences. Interpretations that make the built environment the product of excess, profit-seeking capital from the primary circuit; or that see the cities of the Third World as instruments for administering the extraction of profits from those regions; or perceive common processes of decentralization and recentralization in response to technological innovation in the cities of the industrialized countries, all describe structurally determined processes. To the extent that such global patterns can be averted or modified by concerted action, such alteration would appear to be contingent upon deliberation and strategy, or agency. Current debate does not center on the question of which of these views is correct, but on the relative degree to which structure and agency prevail.

The present state of urban social science is one in which the structure versus agency question has been added to the debates between ecologists and Marxists, or between political economists and modernization theorists. According to current criticisms, prevailing social theorists have been guilty of denying the capacity of individuals to resist the power of the urban environment and processes associated with the production of the urban environment to shape human lives. Wirth's (1938) image of "urbanism" or Simmel's ([1905] 1950) interpretation of the impact of the metropolis on "mental life" are part of the culturalist tradition that argues that the urban milieu fundamentally altered the human condition – portrayed as an essentially passive medium. The ecologists built models that sought to impose a rational order on the shape and content of cities according to principles borrowed from the physical sciences. Marxists and political economists found inexorable energies that create the global order and, subsequently, the urban spatial order, in the slavish addiction of capital to profit. All of these schemes cling to the premise crucial to the establishment of science: The universe that they study is ordered according to central and discoverable principles. Urbanologists who believe the urban is an important arena that needs to be understood on its own terms, might be forgiven for deterministic interpretations that posit a powerful, underlying order. But individually and collectively these theoretical schemes have left too much unexplained, and many of the most prominent voices in urban science are calling for more modest application of theory and more vigorous attention to local details that make each set of urban spaces unique.

Structuration theory and the agency hypothesis

One of the major theoretical questions in social science today has to do with the extent to which the future is a fixed product of the advancing structural arrangements of the past and present, and the extent to which the structure of arrangements present and future is mediated by human choice. Opinion is thus divided between structural determinism and idealism, between structure and agency, between established theoretical principles of structured society and postmodern destructuralizing philosophies.

All of the paradigms that have touched on the sociology or political economy of cities are divided by this issue, and so the debate is superimposed over the old arguments between proponents of the various paradigms (Flanagan 1993). Hawley's (1986) highly deterministic ecological model of society can be expressed purely in terms of system needs, exclusive of reference to the human components of the system. Other contemporary ecologists concerned with changes in residential neighborhood incorporate choice as an important determinant (Warf 1990). Van den Berg's (1987) metropolitan convergence theory (see Chapter 2) juxtaposes regional systematic tendencies with consumer (family) choices. The culturalist, or urbanism, theories range from Wirth's (1938) highly deterministic rendering of the human condition to Fischer's (1976) subcultural interpretation where the emphasis is on chosen patterns of sociability. The urban Marxists have been divided between Althusserian structuralism and Lefebvre's more idealist interpretation: Lefebvre's accommodation to independent action has caused his work to gain in popularity within the past decade, while structural Marxists have lost favor and/or abandoned their arguments in favor of more flexible models. Political economists, whose perspective is premised on structuralist principles, are urged to move toward an interpretation that pays more attention to local cultural variations, and to the deliberate behaviors of group and individual actors (Gottdiener and Feagin 1988).

Clearly, the direction of theoretical movement in urban sociology for the past decade has been overwhelmingly away from structural determinist interpretations and in the direction of agency. The movement has theoretical, political, and philosophical underpinnings. Theoretically, it is a corrective to the overly materialist models of those who attempted to identify a real urban effect, and who ended up implying that the imaginations and actions of individuals were imprisoned by features of the physical environment. Politically, the movement may be interpreted as the product of a more conservative era than the late sixties and seventies which gave rise to the most persuasive structural models. These models found few redeeming characteristics in the operation of the international marketplace or the powerful economies and private interests that it most benefitted. Philosophically, structural determinism had for too long denied the efficacy of human thought and action in influencing the direction of change. In all, agency was a theoretical, political, and philosophical idea whose time had come.

The most important figure in advancing the cause of agency and drawing sociologists' attention away from structural interpretations is Anthony Giddens, the formulator of *structuration theory*. If it is possible to put his view simply, it is that neither the individual nor society are given, preformed entities, but are emergent properties formed and reformed through the action of each upon the other. In the best postmodern sense, the qualities of society and the individuals that comprise it continuously interpenetrate and give shape to one another. The structures of society are primarily its resources, rules, and ideas which are the constraining and enabling tools by which we, its agents, act, inform, and reconstitute the structure. It is easy to see how such an interpretation of social life would make Giddens impatient with the way most social scientists concerned with the city have traditionally interpreted the relationship between structure and behavior.

Giddens's (1989: 250–3) work is in part shaped by his reaction to the origin and nature of social science, which he believes mistakenly took on the model of the natural sciences. In their efforts to understand change ("modernity"), Durkheim and others sought universal principles (constants or fixed relationships) in societal structure, leading them to posit the preeminence of societal factors over individuals and the freedom to choose. By "starting with" social structure as the fixed component, and individuals as the adaptive components of the social order, sociology embarked on a path that for too long worked against the recognition that the social structure is actually reproduced by the action of individuals, just as individual action is reinforced and informed by social structure. Neither is prior.

To return to the nature of social science in order to illustrate this point, the natural and social sciences are set apart by the relation of their content to their subject matter:

> Natural science is an interpretive endeavor involving a
> hermeneutic framework. Conversely, explanation remains the
> key objective of social science. The chief . . . distinguishing

feature separating the social and natural sciences is that
while the hermeneutics of natural science concern only
the discourse of scientists themselves, in the case of the
social sciences we always work in the context of a double
hermeneutic. . . . Lay members of society routinely
reincorporate social science concepts and findings back into
the world these were coined to illuminate and explain. . . .
The conceptual innovations and empirical discoveries of
social scientists routinely 'disappear' back into the environment of events they describe, thereby in principle reconstituting it. (Giddens 1989: 251–2)

This "reconstitutive" aspect of social science illustrates Giddens's point
that social structure, as he defines it, is modified continuously by
action. This is the basic premise of structuration theory.

Giddens's exploration of the intersection of structure and agency has
had a particularly powerful impact on urban sociology. At various junctures in his work, Giddens (1981, 1984, 1985) draws attention to cities
and the wider effects of urbanism, and argues that urban sociology
deserves a central place in sociology's effort to comprehend the modern
world. Historically, cities have been the main "power containers" in the
process of industrialization. Cities and their radiating influences have
produced a created environment that provides a much different time–
space context for experience and social relations than that provided by
a nonurban milieu. Although urbanism is everywhere, and not contained
within the vaguely bounded urban settings that characterize contemporary cities, cities still constitute a special arena for study in that they
mediate between the locality and wider, regional processes (Giddens
1989: 281).

Giddens's impact on urban sociology may be summarized in the following way. Modern urban studies have been concerned with structural
issues at the most macrological level. Giddens proposes to substitute for
structural analyses an interactionist approach. He appears to offer a
conceptual bridge between social action and social structure, arguing that
more attention be paid to the former than has traditionally been the case.
This implies that attention should be turned from global theories of the
world system, dependency, and restructuring, toward the local level
where the powerful and the less powerful face choices about how to
live today and plan for tomorrow. These are the agents, great and small,
who, through their individual and collective choices, are reconstituting
society.

In Chapter 3, it was pointed out that there are two levels at which
agency has been explored, the ordinary and the elite. At the level of

ordinary citizens, choice may be expressed privately in patterns of consumption, and publicly in popular, grassroots movements. At the level of elites, choice is expressed privately in patterns of investment, and publicly through policies of the state which are designed to enhance or moderate the exercise of market strategies in a system-preserving fashion. In Chapter 3 the efficacy of popular urban movements was considered. In the following section, we consider an outgrowth of the agency thesis with respect to elite actors, the *growth-machine* concept.

Elite agents: The growth machine

If the economic conditions of particular cities during particular eras were strictly a matter of dynamic global economic structures, then we would expect all cities within a region to experience similar fates, more or less simultaneously. Yet, particular cities resist regional trends. Other cities may suffer decline, for example, in step with a regional shift, but recover more vigorously and quickly than their neighbors. In the United States, Boston, Pittsburgh, and Baltimore rebounded early from the economic decline of the northeast. Manhattan underwent a boom in office tower construction on the heels of its deepest economic crisis. At the end of the 1980s San Francisco and other Bay Area cities experienced a vigorous economic recovery from economic recession, but Oakland did not. It is reasoned that, if local conditions vary, global conditions cannot be the effective cause. Local variations must be traced to local explanations and, in particular, to the strategies employed by local elites.

Logan and Molotch (1987) have adapted the principles of structuration theory to an analysis of coalitions of urban elites who, working together, comprise a growth machine dedicated to enhancing the profitability of the local market for investors. The machine consists primarily of politicians, the management of local media, utilities, universities, museums and theaters, organized labor, self-employed professionals, retailers, professional sports teams, and corporate capitalists. According to Logan and Molotch, corporate capitalists are not given a more prominent place than other elites because, despite their great power, they are little interested in the enhancement of land values in a specific locality. Together, the constituents of the growth machine have the potential to "increase aggregate rents and trap related wealth for those in the right position to benefit" (50). Although growth elites are likely to be divided among themselves on a variety of issues, including specific strategies for fostering growth and the kinds of growth that are most desirable, they are united overall by their common interest in absolute growth and the enhanced profitability of properties. They are "People dreaming, planning, organizing themselves to make money from property." They are the "agents through which accumulation does its work at the local level" (12).

The managerialist emphasis argues that simply to propose a systemic relationship between global trends and local conditions, as structuralists do, is to paint an incomplete and oversimplified picture. Who does what to ensure that the local economy will be a part of regional growth or economic recovery? Structural arguments fail to appreciate that "the relationship between demand and supply in the various processes which constitute the production of the built environment is problematic in many ways." It is only through empirical research that the question of "who does what?" can be answered. Research will reveal the true complexity of joining capital and opportunity to produce profit and growth (Healey and Barrett 1990: 94).

Virtually every city now employs experts to attract investment. Depending on circumstances and specific goals, elites choose from a range of potential strategies to enhance the competitiveness of their locality. From their relative vantage points, public and private interests can sponsor development of transportation or shipping facilities, reduce corporate overhead by promoting sympathetic policies on pollution abatement, revise municipal health protection standards or enforcement procedures for industrial workers, attempt to reduce taxes, or work together in innumerable other ways to promote a particular type of growth. Adjustments in welfare legislation can pressure unemployed people to take low-paying jobs, the police and other agents can be used to hamper union organizing, alcohol and gambling laws can be changed, utility costs for potential investors can be defrayed by increasing the rates for the public at large, federal programs can be pursued more vigorously (Logan and Molotch 1987: 58). The deliberate competition undertaken by local interests to attract business is not new. In the United States local entrepreneurs and city officials have traditionally promoted the growth of their city in the unmistaken belief that their competitors in other towns were doing the same, and that one city's business gain was another city's loss (Flanagan 1990: 61–8). Today, in contrast to the historical picture, competition may have become more sophisticated, and a wider range of specialty targets may exist (research and development, information processing, tourism, in addition to manufacturing), but the economics remain the same: growth means higher rents, professional fees, for example.

Logan and Molotch are by no means proposing a simple, equilibrial argument here. They do not suggest that the benefits of growth, when growth coalitions are successful, fall equitably among local populations. They do draw on ecological theory, but their work is most readily classified as a version of structuration theory (although here they are apparently more indebted to the work of Storper and Walker (1983) than to Giddens). At the same time, they say they are inspired in part by Harvey. The business of growth elites is to enhance the circulation of capital, but capital interests are at odds over optimal strategies. Logan and Molotch accept the division of class interests within society, but shy away from mechanical interpretations that depict urban residents as "labor" and the city merely as a "dismal consequence of the logic of capital accumulation" (10–11). For Logan and Molotch societal conflict, as reflected in the urban arena, is produced by the tension between the exchange value of property (market value through rent or sale) and the use value of property (its practical and symbolic significance as, for example, "home"). The quality of the conflict is complicated by the peculiar nature of land as real property, the diversity of the uses to which it may be put, and the fact that the same property is likely to have both exchange and use value, at times even for the same actor (e.g., the resident homeowner) (Logan and Molotch 1987: chapters 1–4).

The image of the city that the growth elite thesis presents is one of conflict, as one or another powerful group schemes and plans to make money from property, and the vast majority of residents "push against these manipulations, embody human strivings for affection, community, and sheer physical survival. The boundaries of our urban sociology are drawn around the meeting place (geographical and analytical) of these two struggles." In this way, Logan and Molotch appear to have posited a structural opposition that invites a structural analysis. They say that their "focus on parochial actors is not meant to slight the obviously crucial linkages between these local urban phenomena, on the one hand, and cosmopolitan political and economic forces, on the other. But for the sake of manageability, our urban sociology must focus on the local manifestations of those linkages." That is, they recognize that a focus on local processes is appropriate only to the telling of part of the story. Their chief objective in this work is to show that *human activism,* i.e., agency, is a force for change in cities (Logan and Molotch 1987: 11–12). An understanding of the wider forces of capital accumulation, the progressive articulation of the world system, economic restructuring, or other structural processes may be important in order to complete the story of the way urban space is utilized and transformed. But general arguments based on remote causes constitute an incomplete urban sociology because they cannot in themselves account for the variations produced by the same structural processes.

The rationale behind the agency argument and its appeal to urbanologists appears to be not so much about ultimate causes as about local manifestations. That is, global structures may be accepted as the context which present probable outcomes. As such, they are the appropriate subject matter of those concerned with matters of global economy and societal change. The process of urbanization and urban change is part of this global picture. But, because urban science is concerned with understanding local patterns, and local patterns vary within as well as between categories defined by global trends, urban scientists need to return their attention to the locality. If some localities vary in their response to external conditions, all localities must be seen as uniquely constituted in some degree. What makes each locality different is its history, its particular resources, and the strategies pursued by its leaders. In following this logic we move increasingly toward a destructured understanding of urban change, and away from theoretical premises toward an open-minded empiricism for urban studies. This is precisely the direction advocated by the "new urban sociology" (Feagin and Gottdiener 1988) that is so much indebted to structuration theory and the concept of agency.

The limitations of the agency thesis

The current trend that gives agency a more prominent place in social theory is a basic departure from classical sociological perspectives. It focuses on the fact that there is a degree of independence of individual choice from structural constraints. The idea that all behavior is not dictated in its minutest detail by the imbedded structural features of society is not new. There are no theories in sociology that proclaim an absence of choice, just as there are none, including structuration theory, that argue that individuals are perfectly unconstrained by the historical stream into which they step to make history as they choose. Within urban sociology, the major theoretical orientations that we have discussed in this book can be arranged along a continuum from the more structurally determinist to the more idealist (Flanagan 1993). In fact, such a continuum makes for an interesting juxtaposition of theories, with structural Marxism, Hawley's equilibrial ecology, and perhaps Wirth's urbanism falling toward the determinist end, and Fischer's subcultural urbanism and Giddens's structuration theory falling toward the idealist pole.

What makes the issue of choice different in structuration theory is that it becomes the focus of sociological analysis. It is this focus on aspects of behavior (choice) that cannot be explained wholly with reference to conventionally understood societal constraints, constraining factors which make up the traditional subject matter of the discipline, that makes for an awkward sociology. Although structuration theory does not deny the influence of structure in shaping experience and choice, it narrows the definition of structure.

The reconceptualization of structure in Giddens's work makes it difficult to incorporate into the existing body of structural concepts. Giddens (1989: 253) is critical of the conventional usage of the concept of structure "in Anglo-Saxon social science." In his work, "structure" is a framework of understandings that gives meaning to thought and action. Structure is a set of rules and resources that are available to individual actors, cognitive guides that allow people to make sense of their place in the world, to make choices. Giddens believes that individuals can be trusted to make good assessments and informed choices with or without the expert guidance of social science, which, at any rate, feeds back into the popular consciousness. There are a number of debatable points here, but the most fundamental challenge to sociological practice is the narrowed definition of structure. Rules and resources represent only a fragment of the complete range of social features that have been recognized conventionally as components of social structure.

Thompson (1989) calls Giddens's restriction of the discussion of structure "a recipe for confusion." In what sense can the structures that tie urban areas to rural hinterlands be understood in terms of rules? Is it theoretically productive to reduce differential access to education to a discussion of rules and resources? Where Giddens insists that actors usually have a good understanding of the nature of their social involvement, Thompson illustrates his concern over the nature of subjects' "knowing" by raising Marx's question of workers' consciousness:

> To insist that a structural principle *must* be some such rule, or must be capable of being analyzed in terms of rules, is to force on the material a mode of conceptualization which is not appropriate to it. . . . It seems unhelpful and misleading to interpret Marx's account of the structural relations involved in the capitalist system of production in terms of 'sets of rules and resources.' The constitution of labour power as a commodity, the determination of its value as the labour time socially necessary for its production, its exchange on the market under conditions which guarantees that it exchanges at its value and yet simultaneously produces a surplus value and profit: these features of the capitalist system cannot be treated as so many 'rules' that workers follow when they turn up at the factory gates, as if every worker who accepted a job had an implicit (albeit partial) knowledge of Marx's *Capital*.

Thompson's point is that Marx believed he was uncovering the essence of class relations which for everyday participants remain concealed beneath capitalism's phenomenal form. In the traditional sense, and in this case the Marxist sense, the nature of the process is beyond the understanding of the individuals involved in it. In its conventional sense, structure is a far more powerful and pervasive force than Giddens gives it credit: From Giddens's perspective, it is still possible to talk about propertyless members of society as having options, at least within a narrowed range. Thompson (1989: 73) points out that such an individual's options are reduced to one – to sell labor. "It is not difficult to see that the individual who has one option has no options . . . it is senseless to say that he or she 'could have done otherwise.'" In this light, Thompson concludes, "Structure and agency no longer appear to be complementary in terms of a duality, but the antagonistic poles of a dualism, such that structural constraint may so limit the options of the individual that agency is effectively dissolved."

What of the options open to elites, such as those that people Logan and Molotch's growth machine? Surely, agency works better at that level? Although elites may have greater freedom to choose, and to make their choices count, as social theory the growth-machine thesis contains two important flaws. First, the argument is incomplete because it simply proposes that powerful agents strive to serve their own interests without placing those interests in any wider context. Second, a focus on local elites only yields insights into local processes which involves a truncated analysis of systemic relationships that exist on a broader field.

Lake (1990: 180) writes:

> Agents beg for context. . . . The case for an 'interest driven social construction of cities' will always be incomplete if it ignores the prior questions of how and why interests are established. Activists are surely important but only as they have become spectacularly adept at exploiting the potentialities offered by a capitalist structure. A focus on agents and their interests demands elucidation of the structures that provide opportunities for the pursuit and realization of particular kinds of interests through particular ways and means in particular times and places.

A failure to consider the origins of the agents we find in place, competing and maneuvering, begs the questions raised by the structuralist critics of capitalism.

Yet, Logan and Molotch do consider the structural context that gives rise to their agents. They refer to changes in the international political economy that raise new challenges for growth machines, to the "trans-nationalization of production" that has produced a situation where, "To a degree never known before, local interests in place are being shaped by the changing ordering of international spatial relations. This high degree of regional dependence on 'foreign' events has long been true for cities of the Third World; it is now becoming true for the industrial societies as well – even for the United States" (Logan and Molotch 1987: 248–53). In this way, Logan and Molotch do what structuration theorists say all good analysts must do – relate their study to the relevant global factors. Yet, they plead that the nature of their enterprise, as urban social scientists, restricts their ability to pursue their analysis beyond the local area. This, according to Lake (1990: 181–3), is the fatal flaw in their approach. I would add that this also points to a very important difficulty that separates structural analysts from those who find the agency argument more compelling. Lake points out that although Logan and Molotch indicate the necessity of placing the actions of growth elites in their appropriate structural context, they say that they must restrict their analysis to the local manifestations of local–global linkages for the sake of manageability. Lake writes:

> This manageability is gained at a severe cost. It truncates theorization at the point where theorization is most needed: clarification of the intersection between the local and the global, of agency and structure. . . . It imposes an arbitrary, artificial, and theoretically unsupportable truncation at the boundaries of the locality. It once again relies on a reductive empiricism to read off local outcomes from the interaction of local actors.

It is worth emphasizing this important issue, because it would seem to have serious implications for the future of urban sociology. The concept of agency moves us away from global theory, toward an emphasis on localism and empiricism. Can social scientists who define their object of study in terms of locality – the city – be required to maintain a field of vision that does any more than acknowledge that there is a wider political and economic context that impinges on local events, especially when that wider context permits broad variations in outcomes from city to city? After all, the variation in urban fortunes within broadly defined categories of urban places (Sunbelt cities, old industrial centers, Third World capitals) is what led to the current local and empiricist response in the first place. On the other hand, structuralists are understandably concerned that an empirical emphasis on the exceptional characteristics of locality will lead to token, tacked-on, and fragmentary attention to structural factors. In that event, we might expect a flood of case studies that make brief reference to a remote political and economic world system, restructuring, or dependency, and then focus on historical and cultural factors that make the neighborhood or metropolitan region in question a unique case. The trend of thought in urban sociology raises serious methodological questions with implications for maintaining a conceptual balance between the general and the particular.

A final critical point regarding the limitations of the agency argument applies specifically to Giddens's observations that urban study, and the study of the spatial aspects of social life, are central to an understanding of contemporary society. Giddens's view of the role of the city is reminiscent of the position taken much earlier by Max Weber (1905). Weber said that the importance of the city in the advance of history lay more in the past than the present. Similarly, Giddens's point applies more to the advent of industrial capitalism than it does to the present. In the past, the city embodied and expressed the nature of the modern era. The features of the created environment that were formerly contained within more clearly bounded urban places have overspilled those boundaries. "The old city–countryside relation is replaced by a sprawling expansion of a manufactured or a 'created environment'" (Giddens 1984: 184). The importance of the created environment as a shaper of human experience is now society-wide, just as Weber concluded that the city as the shaper of experience had lost its distinctiveness and been replaced by the nation-state.

Giddens thus adds weight to the question of whether it makes sense to set aside the city as a distinct area of sociological study in a world where the characteristics of the created environment have become the characteristics of society itself. Saunders (1989: 232) says this calls into question Giddens's comment on the central importance of urban study for the understanding of the modern social order. First, Giddens doesn't think the city is the important milieu it once was. Second, his conceptualization of the created environment is unclear, and "confuses questions of capitalism and industrialism with those of territoriality and spatial differentiation." Relatedly, there is Giddens's interpretation of the specific nature of the impact of the created environment on experience and behavior: In his view, the environment imparts a quality of "hostility or aversion to the main patterns of conduct involved in modern social and economic life." It is a situation in which the "major cultural values lose their grip upon the day-to-day lives of individuals" (Giddens 1985: 323). These assertions reveal Giddens to be a traditional culturalist in his views on the impact of life in cities or the mass society, with close ties to the visions of Durkheim and Simmel, reviewed in Chapter 1. Saunders (1989: 232) comments that the content of Giddens's view "supports a rather conservative romanticism which assumes without proof or argument" that a routinized existence in a created environment is more alienating than a routinized existence in a "natural" environment.

The content of Giddens's interpretation of urbanism need not put us off. It does no more than remind us that the ghosts of Durkheim, Simmel, and Wirth attend the contemporary practice of urban science along with those of Marx and Weber. At any rate, it is a relatively minor issue that cannot cause us to lose sight of the real challenge Giddens has raised for contemporary sociology, and for urban sociology in particular. The implications are far-reaching: People have a fundamental understanding of their place and the nature of their participation in society; all individuals have some degree of choice in every situation; as a consequence, action cannot be attributed to structural dictates; social science needs to pay special attention to behaviors and outcomes involving choice. Within urban science, this directive has led to a new emphasis on localism and a belief in the efficacy of local elites and the ability of common citizens to influence the direction of change. It has introduced to urban science in particular a tension between those who believe any analysis should follow from theoretical premises based on global structural arrangements and those who believe that more fundamental insights will arise from an open-minded investigation of local histories. Whether this tension is warranted by the structurationist innovation of thought or not is pursued in the next section. One avenue that has been proposed to dissolve the emerging tension between more structural and idealist approaches is to combine them.

Agency, structure, and the prospects of synthesis

Given the nature of the difference that separates the structuralist and agency emphases, and the fact that, increasingly, the difference seems only to involve a matter of degree, it is natural to entertain the prospect of an integrated approach. Agency advocates or managerialists are interested only in subduing the more determinist aspects of structural interpretation, they are not interested in eliminating structural considerations.

Cadwallader (1988), an urban geographer, observes that there currently are actually three levels of urban analysis to be considered in the structure versus agency controversy. He identifies the structuralist approach with Marxism, a reduction which seems to have some purpose, given his particular interpretation of the differences that divide the structuralists from agency theorists. A second, elite or managerial approach is broadly Weberian with respect to its emphasis on the importance of distinguishing analytically between economic and political power bases. A third approach, which Cadwallader identifies as "behavioral," is rooted in the more micrological/phenomenological tradition of urban studies. It views issues of perception and definition in all their complexity from the point of view of individual experience and subjectivity.

By separating the consideration of managerial power from that of the microsociology of individual experience and definition, Cadwallader seems to complicate the agency argument. Cadwallader's differentiation separates the consideration of elite political actors from that of the remainder of the urban population. Research and writing about how people define and communicate reality at the individual level involves a set of methodologies distinct from the macrological analyses of political or economic power. In contrast, the component of the postmodern or agency approach that is concerned with the way individuals "define the situation" makes it difficult to measure and aggregate individual images, and has led to arguments about the fundamental nature of cognitive processing and philosophical debates about subject–object relationships. According to Cadwallader, the proponents of micrological perspectives have been interested only in promoting a fuller understanding among the more macrologically concerned urban sociologists of the complexity of behavioral variables. The implications of this level of human action and reaction in determining the general direction of metropolitan change, therefore, seem modest.

Cadwallader does suggest that the behavioral approach may provide a complement to the managerial approach, for example, with regard to consumer behavior. It might be demonstrated how individual choices in the housing market need to be seen in connection with the operation of mortgage and lending companies and realtors. Again, this offers a modest prospect regarding the impact of popular agency, and should serve to overcome any tendencies toward interpretations of "consumer sovereignty" that otherwise might be implied by the behavioral perspective (Cadwallader 1988: 236–8).

Cadwallader has a clear idea of how the three levels of analysis might be integrated. He would seem to agree with Lake that the study of managers and their institutional affiliations cries out for context. Managerial study should be considered a framework or approach to research questions, not a theory. The study of managers risks degeneration "into a mindless empiricism," and studies of "urban managerialism should be related to more general theories concerning the political economy of cities in capitalist society." Those who approach the study of cities from a Marxist perspective, not at all a dead science for Cadwallader, dismiss the agency thesis because it posits no broader context within which managers are constrained to make their choices (233–5). It nevertheless remains true that "General causes can, through the presence of localized contingencies, produce different outcomes in different places" (245).

Cadwallader's conclusion is that all three levels of analysis – structural, managerial, and behavioral – have their place in an integrated and complete urban sociology. He chooses the issue of housing to illustrate how this might be done. One would begin with Harvey's observation that the built environment is produced by the secondary circuit of capital, supported by Walker's (1981) application of that thesis to suburbanization in particular, and the earlier Castell's (1977) comment that the single-family suburban house is the maximal unit of consumption under capitalism. We could add any number of observations that point to the convenient division of interests within the working class that home ownership represents. However, since capital does nothing on its own, Marxist structural theory needs to be supplemented by institutional analysis that identifies the mechanisms and actors that move capital in the direction of real estate trends. Whether one is attempting to explain suburbanization or gentrification, analysis needs to address the mobilization and channeling of finance capital into emergent, smart investment strategies. Savings and loan associations, banks, mortgage companies make capital available for certain types of construction, which naturally sets up a mainstream of building activity that mobilizes the imaginations and resources of builders and developers, is touted by realtors who operate to protect and promote safe investment areas, while government at all levels does its part to ensure the buoyancy of property markets.

The integrated study of structure and agency at the managerial level still leaves room for consideration of the role of popular choice in shaping the built environment. Although it is true to say that the emergence of a self-conscious middle class with a consumerist ideology was "socially created to a certain extent, through advertising and the availability of mortgage money, it also reflects some latent desire for the characteristics associated with suburban living" (Cadwallader 1988: 241). That is, neither the needs of capitalism, nor the response of the entrepreneurs of the multifaceted real estate industry, alone or in combination, dictated what consumers would do. The logic of choice at the level of the individual does enter the system in an important fashion. With regard to gentrification, Cadwallader (1988: 241–2) is persuaded that this movement reflects a shift in consumer preference which, in turn, reflects a demographic shift in family or household composition variables. Later marriages, fewer children, and dual-career households generated a lifestyle preference for city living: The kinds of household units that prefer inner city living "are not merely produced by the availability of gentrified housing." A full understanding of where and how people live involves an appreciation for the "symbiotic" relationship between production and consumption, and the study of the kinds of mediating institutions that engineer or facilitate the market process. In addition, it is important to keep in mind that choice and behavior are partially constrained by structural opportunities, that each family does not necessarily live as it would choose.

Cadwallader's call for an integrated approach appears reasonable on the surface. In fact, it is not far from the convergent path that both structuralists and structurationists have already proposed or are presently following in their work. As we saw in Chapter 3, structuralists increasingly acknowledge the mediation of the state, or turn their attention to grassroots movements in order to understand the expression of the popular will. At the same time agency theorists express interest in the intersection of structure and choice, though their definition of structure clouds the issue by fundamentally reducing it to a set of negotiated, normative components. On the agency side, the localist emphasis that has emerged so strongly in urban sociology would seem to be permanently at odds with the idea of structural givens. Researchers are urged to acknowledge the influence of the global political economy, but will the detailed empirical availability of local phenomena, and the easy impression that the key to understanding each place is its uniqueness, allow researchers to work back up the analytic chain to consider remote and constant external factors? This is a persistent question posed in the remaining pages.

Sheppard's (1988) critique of Cadwallader's proposal that urban sociologists pursue an eclectic approach is persuasive. Although eclecticism may sound attractive in principle, it can be equivalent to the proverbial effort to combine oil and water (Sheppard's metaphor). The product of the combination of structure and agency orientations may prove useless because of the wide gulf in the background assumptions they express. An emphasis on agency is attractive to proponents of the consumer sovereignty point of view, who assume autonomy of individual action and follow neoclassical interpretations of economics. Structuralists, on the other hand, are persuaded by Marxist assumptions about the material foundations of behavior. In that view, markets are not socially optimal: They are certainly not harmonious social exchange mechanisms (Sheppard 1988: 256–7).

To combine elements of theories that begin with such disparate assumptions raises serious questions about the logical integrity of the resulting science. Is there something sleight of hand about developing theories with just a little Marxism or just a little managerialism? Clark (1988: 253) raises this question, and responds that the flirtation with structuration "has been in some sense a way of avoiding a head-on clash with the major issues including a Marxist approach to capital and labor." Eclecticism is viewed by its critics as an easy way out, a license to choose fragments of theories wherever they seem to offer a plausible interpretation of evidence. It finds plausibility in many arguments, is often ideologically uncommitted, and is therefore open to attack from all sides.

A good example of the advantages and liabilities of eclecticism within the context of current urban theories is provided by Warf (1990). He believes that urban ecology continues to offer important insight into the urban process, especially with regard to local residence patterns. He proposes to revive the ecological approach by grafting it onto the analysis of the division of labor and structuration theory, and placing the whole within the appropriate framework of international historical events as they relate to shifts in the global political economy. The approach leads, he believes, to a new appreciation of the importance of ethnicity and cultural dynamics.

The site of Warf's study is the named neighborhoods of Brooklyn. Warf argues that current, local, ethnic residential patterns need to be understood, in part at least, as the outcomes of a local history of ethnic invasion and succession. The patterns result from episodes of immigration and migration, and economic restructurings that provided certain kinds of work at certain periods, and were related to expansions and contractions in housing supply vis-à-vis demand. The local situation has responded to such distant events as the Irish potato famine, the mechanization of cotton and introduction of the sugar beet in U.S. agriculture, changes in immigration policy, changes in Soviet emigration policy, and the impending reabsorption of Hong Kong by China.

Warf finds conventional Marxism of little use: It is unable to address the importance of ethnicity, family and religion as active forces in the shaping of neighborhoods. He applauds Castells's (1983) defection from Marxism to a generalized social movements approach because it is an acknowledgement that people are active participants in social change. The local conditions of workers do play an important part in the formation of neighborhoods in that the nature of residence reflects prevailing types of work and levels of remuneration. However, changing patterns of occupation do not determine, rather they interact with, the local character of housing and factors of supply, cost, ownership, transportation, and cultural preference. Added to the influence of prevailing conditions of employment and housing demand is the fact that different immigrant ethnic groups bring with them cultural factors that impinge on occupational and residential choices. Choices within groups are also affected by such variables as family structure, gender relations, and the prevalence of racism that each group is subject to. "Residential choices that affect and reflect community formation are both *contingent,* in that no specific outcome is predictable from a given set of initial conditions, and *durable,* in that they profoundly affect the future patterns of development and change that communities take on. Thus, the choices at any given moment are conditioned by preexisting residential patterns" (Warf 1990: 78). The contingent and episodic characteristics of his conclusion are clearly in step with the structuration model.

Warf follows the dictum that the analysis of local patterns be interpreted with reference to changes in national and international policy and economy. He interprets the emergence of local ethnic residential communities in the context of the nature of Brooklyn's changing economic fortunes, as these in turn reflect changes in the international economy. Yet, other variables peculiar to the nation, region, or metropolitan area interact to produce particular outcomes for Greenpoint, Flatbush or Bay Ridge. Although wartime and shipbuilding, or peacetime and idle shipyards, may have an enormous impact on the local economy, the external origins of change might also be as close as the overflow of would-be Manhattanites unable to pay the astronomical rents on that island. The result of this overflow is the gentrification of select neighborhoods, the pattern of invasion and succession described by the Chicago school ecologists, except with the invading and invaded social classes reversed.

Warf (91–2) summarizes what he believes are the three most important principles revealed by his new ecology. First, local conditions are tightly linked to the global economy and political changes worldwide. Second, the production and configuration of residential space is related to the periodic restructuring of the economy and employment. The ensuing pattern is a modification of existing patterns and the foundation upon which future patterns will be built. Third, local variations in culture must be understood to play a role in any interpretation of neighborhood formation and modification. Above all, we learn that "neighborhood formation is always a contingent process, and within each historical junction only one of numerous possibilities actually emerges; within limits, local geography and history could always have been otherwise."

This last conclusion invites a number of responses, all of them relating to the alleged indeterminacy of the social environment. First, with respect to ecology proper, it seems a reiteration, phrased in structurationist terms, of the conclusion arrived at by Harris and Ullman (1945) at the end of classical ecology's quest for the grand pattern: Local urban land use depends on preexisting patterns of adjacent use, it is multinucleated, and it is not possible to predict from city to city where these nuclei will be situated in any absolute sense. Warf's interest is more modest, limited to residential patterns, but follows the same logic of interactive mutual determination. overall, the resultant pattern defies prediction.

Second, Warf's conclusion reveals that his analysis is not so fundamentally ecological as it is fundamentally structurationist. Everything interdepends on everything else but, given the welter of variables and the complexity of their interaction, the outcome might just as well have been otherwise. Such a conclusion is indicative of structuration theory's greatest liability. As Sheppard (1988: 258) points out, the structuration perspective does not appear to be "good theory" precisely because it doesn't permit systematic statements about whether structure or individual action dominates the relationship between the two; hence, "anything goes." The theory is limited to an ex post facto rationalization of events that have already occurred, but is weak in its ability to predict.

A third point raised by Warf's study is that a theoretically open-minded empirical approach to local processes ends up telling the story of local areas. It may tell us that neighborhood building or any other local process is not dictated by global events, but it doesn't give us much insight into locally emergent factors that can be generalized from one local area to another. Warf is alarmingly tentative about the outcome of the mixing of factors in a given area. It is small wonder in such a complex and contingent world that localism and empiricism are to be trusted over general models. However, with due respect to kindred sciences, it may be all right for geography or history to accentuate the unique, but sociology has always been about generalization. The virtues of localism are simply not virtues for the sociologist.

I have dwelt at some length on Warf's study because I believe it is representative of the strengths and weaknesses of eclecticism based on structurationist assumptions. It seems precisely the sort of approach Cadwallader has in mind. Within this methodological framework, Warf's conclusions are correct. This is because he tests no principle except that local events are mutually determined and related to external factors that are more structural in nature. The problem is that the work does not test any particular thesis about the kinds of local effects one may expect from the capitalist political economy of the world system, except that there will be such effects. If Marxism is the wrong argument, because it fails to predict or to allow for local variations in outcome, then what do the local variations in outcome tell us about how we should revise our understanding of the world system?

It does not appear that the response gleaned from structurationists, localism, and the cultural variations argument will do as an answer. In the present cycle of theoretical and methodological development, the path seems to lead away from theory in the hope that a more open-minded empiricism will produce new theoretical developments. Perhaps urban sociology is more prone to the act of faith that study of the particular will yield refined general theory because its concern is with local space (even if the local is sometimes defined in metropolitan or regional terms). Yet, as different as the case studies favored by the new urban sociology are from the abstracted factorial ecologies of the recent past, they are in the broader methodological sense very similar in the faith they place in the ability of progressively sensitized empiricism to reveal insight into the big picture. The hazards here may go beyond a new era of static abstracted empiricism in urban sociology. There is the possibility, at least, that an empirical focus on agency, as a component of a structurationist or nominally eclectic approach, invites a regression of social theory.

If liberal humanism requires that we give actors greater credit for the freedom to choose, then we also give them greater responsibility for the condition in which they find themselves. We may determine to bear in mind that there is actually a balance between choice and structural constraints, as structuration theory proposes, but if our emphasis is on choice, and on local variations in cultures, what will policy makers, professional colleagues, students, and the general public take away from our studies? Here we might consider the very popular work of Oscar Lewis (1966a, 1966b) regarding the nature of poverty.

The appeal of the culture-of-poverty argument swayed government and a generation of students of sociology and illustrates very nicely the "double hermeneutic" referred to by Giddens, whereby the work of social science informs what participants know of the world and their place in it (Waxman 1983: 91–100). It was Lewis's belief that the conditions of poverty were bound to generate habits of mind and behavior that worked against prospects for social mobility and improved life chances. His careful, local case studies of life in the slums of New York and Puerto Rico and among the poor of Mexico lent dramatic support to the idea that the poor were trapped in a subculture that lent meaning to a life of deprivation and uncertainty, while it ensured that the conditions of that life would not change.

How many of the references to Lewis and his subcultural observations that we have heard and read include reference to the fact that in the same works Lewis pointed clearly to structural factors as the ultimate cause of poverty? The famous attitudinal and behavioral characteristics of the culture of poverty were responses, not causes. The poverty he observed was the result of a market system, of capitalism, that demanded a strata of workers kept at the edge of viability, that periodically generated occupational obsolescence for the most marginal, and wreaked havoc through its predictable but uncontrollable fluctuations of boom and bust. Under such conditions, Lewis believed, a subculture would be created that perpetuated poverty. It was through its popularization that this aspect of Lewis's work was selected-out for deserved criticism as a blaming-the-victim argument. But neither the criticism nor the structural qualifications of the original culturalist interpretation can prevail against the popular appeal of the idea that the poor are responsible for their own condition.

The point is this: What will be the "hermeneutic" consequences of a sociology that reduces the relative importance of structural factors in favor of colorful, localized, empirical accounts, with theory added on selectively and lightly? What new images will inform the popular and policy-making imagination? What new facts will we learn about poverty by studying the poor? About racism by studying the ghetto or the barrio, or Bensonhurst or Howard Beach, for that matter? As urban scientists, can we trust ourselves to work upward from the empirical availability of the neighborhood and street corner to the difficult and remote structural factors, and convey these analytic points with the same vividness and appeal as the descriptions of poverty, homelessness, violence, and despair that are readily yielded by the streets?

As others have pointed out, the study of managers or elites is only an intermediate step. The ultimate concern of any science has to be the structural assumptions it makes about the order of its universe of study. Whether or not one must "begin with" structure and work down is a moot point if we are to continue to refer to what we do as science. There is already consensus that the great structural fact of continuity and change in the world is the international economic system. The following section reviews a work that is dedicated to the deconstruction of oversimplified images of complex urban realities. The authors of that work conclude by positing a powerful global structure to interpret the local evidence.

MANAGING URBAN LIVES

The limitations and uses of the dual-city concept

The kinds of changes explored at the end of Chapter 3, changes that have led to the structural exclusion of large elements of the urban population from the formal or mainstream economy, have invited the observation that postindustrialism is producing two broad social strata in large cities. There are those who remain engaged in a rewarding fashion in the new order, and those who are redundant, permanently excluded – the so-called permanent underclass. The largest cities showcase this division, as central districts undergo the final stages of deindustrialization and conversion to financial and corporate service centers. The result has been referred to as the dual city.

Through its various crises and tensions, in the writings of journalists, the pronouncement of government officials, the works of social analysts, even the fictional *Bonfire of the Vanities* by Tom Wolfe, New York has emerged in the 1990s as the globally visible symbol of the dual city. It embodies the hubris of power and wealth, the capacity for global reach, concentrated on the island of Manhattan. But New York, like any city, is an arena, not an entity in control of the wealth stored within it. The wealth and power it contains are not at the disposal of those charged with managing this urban space. The financial resources manifest in the lavish architectural monuments that house corporate headquarters, the salaries and lifestyle of management and the professionals who provide them with services, and in the inflated values of property and residen tial rents, makes the poverty that is concentrated nearby that much more glaring. Although any city might serve the purpose of illustrating the dual city, New York draws our attention because it is the premier post-industrial metropolis.

The applicability of the dual-city model to New York is explored in depth in a collection of essays edited by Mollenkopf and Castells (1991). New York City lost more manufacturing jobs between the 1940s and the present time than many large cities had ever claimed. From 1950 to 1983, the number of people employed in manufacturing in the city declined from 1,041,000 to 442,000, a loss of 599,000 jobs, or nearly 58 percent (compiled from various sources by Fainstein and Fainstein 1988: 163). During the 1980s, Manhattan experienced a dramatic rise in real estate values, a transformation in spatial structure, an increase in financial and managerial positions, and showed ample evidence that a substantial proportion of the population was living very well. The bottom 20 percent of the population suffered a serious decline in income during the 1980s while New York's economy in general was booming. Poverty increased from 19 to 23 percent. There is no question: During the past decade in New York City, the rich got richer while the poor got poorer (Castells and Mollenkopf 1991: 399–401).

This is the kind of change that has generated the dual-city metaphor. However, Castells and Mollenkopf argue that the metaphor is in some ways inaccurate and misleading, especially in its oversimplified image of a city divided into two strata, the affluent and the poor. Castells and Mollenkopf point out that the decline in manufacturing is only one of several dimensions of a dynamic economy the size of New York's: The point they are making is that the city contains a diversity of workers and a broad middle-income stratum.

It is true that New York's underground economy seems to have grown as rapidly as the city's role as a world financial center. It is true also that much informal sector work is poorly remunerated, and here they include reference to the familiar trades: sweatshop manufacture, "gypsy" cabs, residential renovation, off-the-books childcare, and criminal activities. However, even though the workers in the informal sector are unprotected and many of them are poor, informal sector work is not synonymous with poverty. Many minorities and recent immigrants are poor, but the complete picture of stratification dynamics is more complex than a simple comparison of the high- and low-income extremes reveal.

Castells and Mollenkopf (402–3) propose the following regarding the need to conceptually disaggregate the working population:

> It might help us to understand the social dynamics of New York to think of local society as made up of a predominantly male and white professional group; a female clerical working class, characterized by ethnic diversity; a miscellaneous service sector formed by a disproportionately immigrant labor force, both salaried and self-employed; a public sector divided between white ethnic and native black New Yorkers, with an internal hierarchy in terms of gender; a downgraded manu- facturing sector concentrating a high proportion of male and female Latino workers; and a marginal sector outside the formal labor force, with a strong proportion of minority youth (particularly native blacks and Puerto Ricans) and female headed households.

They warn that even this breakdown remains oversimplified.

According to Castells and Mollenkopf the problem with the dual-city message is that it misguides public sentiments within the middle segments of the population, fostering fear and withdrawal rather than the percep- tion of common interests and organization for action. The point is that there *is* a basis for the dual-city perception, but the division must be drawn between the uppermost strata, which is well connected internally and capable of acting in its own interests, and the remaining layers which are fragmented and have so far proven incapable of collective action.

> The dual city is a useful ideological notion because it aims to denounce inequality, exploitation, and oppression in cities. . . . But its underlying assumptions are rarely made explicit, because those who employ it tend to favor social critique over social theory. The political and emotional charge of a dualist approach and the failure to spell-out its assumptions means that it cannot comprehend the complexity of urban social reality, which is certainly not reducible to a simple dichotomy. (404–405)

Castells and Mollenkopf conclude (413) that "Occupational polarization and income inequality become translated into widespread urban dualism (that is, the simultaneous increase of affluence and misery among significant proportions of the population) only when public policy mirrors the naked logic of the market." The empirical evidence of stratification reveals a much more complex picture. However, they do concede that in the sense that W. J. Wilson spoke of the structurally excluded urban underclass, there is something to the dual-city thesis, that "In this sense, New York is a dual city, in which much of its working-age population (and particularly its minority youth) is outside the formal labor market, creating the conditions for entry into the criminal economy, the informal economy, and the assisted economy, all of which are stigmatized and unregulated segments of the local society" (414). There is an ecological dualism as well: Real estate development and gentrification are reinforcing segregation between affluent white and concentrated minority populations. However, here again a simplistic dualistic vision is misguided. Minority areas of the city are themselves stratified, as opposed to the white middle-class prejudice that sees them as homogeneously troubled and poor.

But beyond these local divisions there is a global, systemic, and overriding dualism that is expressed and given shape by New York City. It is the duality of international restructuring of the form and function of urban space, and the struggle of local groups not directly instrumental to that transformation to fight back in their own interests. Local space today is subject to the overwhelming logic of "the unified world economy organized around the ability to communicate and process information." Within the process of the restructuring of space according to the needs of multinational corporations to know and act, local space becomes incidentally important because every organizational entity, no matter how wide its arena of action, needs to be physically anchored somewhere.

This international force of investment, financial, and technological information is a colonizing force, and the members of the professional–managerial class are the new colonists. "The spatial forms and processes characterizing New York during the 1980s nurtured the rise of the new dominant class in its international dimension while fragmenting subordinate classes and fixing them in specific locales, ignorant of the macroprocesses at work beyond the control of the local communities" (416). Castells and Mollenkopf note that the Edward Koch administration recognized and served the interests of the restructuring forces while it is the mission of the David Dinkins administration to recognize the true nature and serve the interests of locality-based elements of the citizens of New York. By implication, these local interests appear to now to have had little power to resist international trends and powerful global actors, in the form of multinational corporations, whose directors are presented in turn with choices dictated by global forces which they do not control. A change of philosophy in local government, even if that locality is New York City, would seem to make little difference in altering the political and economic forces that drive global and local change. In the final analysis, the efficacy of local actors does seem to be an empirical question. But the question is whether and to what degree localities can deflect, manage, or accommodate to wider change. Urban sociology serves the broader field of political economy by addressing that question. It is helpful to be reminded that the city contains a great heterogeneity, as Wirth observed, and that it is not reducible, empirically, to a simple dichotomization of social class. It is also useful to be reminded, in the context of such an empirical correction, of the global forces that produced the dual city hypothesis, and the validity of that proposition.

The uncertain future of urban sociology

There is a genuine question about the validity and future viability of urban sociology. For the short term, we may assume that the institutional momentum of courses, textbooks and the individual careers of social scientists will carry the traditional distinctiveness of the field forward. The issues that have always been at least the shared property of urban sociology will continue to occupy practitioners who call themselves urban sociologists, urban geographers, urban anthropologists, and the like. However, the present debate regarding structure and agency is only the most recent reflection of a fundamental question regarding the future of urban social science. Is the specialization at all necessary or productive to the progress of social science in general?

The question of the legitimacy of a distinct urban social science persists. It has become increasingly difficult to find the outline of the city in the urban landscape of the industrialized nations. The cultural qualities and organizational features (social, political, economic) associated with cities have never been wholly contained within the vague boundaries of the city, suburbs, metropolis, functional urban region, megalopolis, etc. The idea that "urbanism," as opposed to industrialism (Gans 1962), industrial capitalism (Castells 1977), or even "modernity" (Berger, Berger, and Kellner 1973) has been the key sociological variable characterizing the modern age has often been challenged. If space is a key characteristic that helps to mold and explain social organization (Hawley 1984) or behavior (Giddens 1984, 1989), then why arbitrarily set aside from others one arena relevant to its study? Certainly, such a designation has become more vulnerable to criticism as amorphous urban areas have continued to sprawl and merge over the course of the century. As the migration stream to U.S. cities was reversed for a while in the 1970s, both urban and rural sociologists (along with other rural and urban specialists) found themselves studying and talking about the same population trend. The division of labor, like the concepts "rural" and "urban" that have divided scientists of settled space, is obsolete (Gottdiener 1985).

Despite the attention given to the agency question in the past decade or so, one assumes that most who have chosen to study the city are structuralists at heart. Otherwise, they would hardly have chosen the single most imposing physical product of social life as the focus of their attention, and instead would be occupied with the analysis of more manageable arenas of action. The current methodological emphasis on local exceptionalism or variation represents a type of "weak" convergence in the field of urban studies. It is weak because it does not represent theoretical development (Flanagan 1993). It is instead a methodological comment on where and how to look for the impact of structure. By contrast, there is indication of a "strong" convergence of thought among urbanologists with regard to the general pattern localities are said to be coping with, struggling to reshape, resisting. That is, there is a widespread acceptance of the correctness of the political economist's assumption that cities are chiefly the physical manifestation of the concentrated forces of the international economic order. Whether couched in terms of restructuring or deindustrialization or dependency, the dominant interpretation today is that cities represent knots of activity in the operation of the global economy. Like many "obvious" observations, it is easy to underestimate the significance of this one.

The most important implication for urban sociologists is that a given urban arena is one among many fragments of space connected by social, political, economic, and cultural linkages that are only fractionally "contained" within that or any city. The behaviors of managers and common folk alike arise in response to changing markets and political conditions elsewhere. To discover that there are local variations in the effects that global changes in the supply of energy or other raw materials, regional shifts in labor markets, or political events happening in another hemisphere have on local populations is no more than the discovery that cities each have different histories, heritage, and resources for coping. The discovery that there are local variations in the impact of change, and that individual actors and collective citizens' movements are among the variables that must be considered, is a worthwhile point. But, as Sheppard (1988: 258) comments, "To learn that agents affect structures and that structures effect action is . . . no more earth shattering than to learn that human-environment relations are neither determinist nor possibilist but probabilist." The question is, how much sense does it make to focus on telling the local story? We all are familiar with local news media that manage to come up with the local angle on matters of global significance. The usual result is human interest, but not new information that will help us to understand the big story.

It may be overstating the case to pursue the analogy between the local media's pursuit of the local angle, and urban sociology's pursuit of local exceptions or conformations, resistance or acquiescence, to the reverberations of the global economy. But, the locality *is* the empirical domain of the urbanologist. Because all of social reality is comprised of global and local dimensions, and because, at some level these are mutually emergent and systemically interrelated, the thorough empirical work of the locally oriented social scientist is important. The big story remains beyond the local horizon. It is a structural story, and it will be told, not by the urbanologist focused on the local scene, but by the political economists who address the global dimensions of restructuring, the international dimensions of underdevelopment and development, and political change.

At the beginning of the present century, the world in general and social science in particular were awed by the prodigious dimensions of the city. It was the largest structure available to the sweep of the senses. At the end of the century, given the electronic extensions of the human senses and cognitive sweep, the most magnificent structure that we see but do not control is the vortex of political and economic power that continues to organize and reorganize the most distant elements of global space. It would appear that the ultimate instrument for the study of the intersection of space and social processes is political economy itself, and not an arbitrarily designated discipline that selects the city as its subject matter. As urban sociologists, we have had nearly a century to define that subject matter. In that period of time, we have gained some insight into the difficulty of that enterprise, while the urban, itself, has become more complex.

It is now possible to recognize that the definition of a separate domain for urban science is not possible because the city is an arena of action rather than a universe. Features of the arena, itself, help shape the particular nature of local outcomes. National and international events produce real estate values, labor demand, poverty, and homelessness. Factors peculiar to the local arena such as the crush of housing and office-space demand, wage and benefits levels relative to other places, and local philosophies and strategies regarding how best to provide for human welfare, represent local effects. As the study of local effects, urban sociology is a specialized branch of political economy. As such, it may continue to have a legitimate role in social science. Questions of local ecology, managers and their institutional affiliations, and agency in general, would appear to be subsumable research strategies, not rival theories.

A century ago Durkheim addressed the division of labor in society and described, in essentially ecological terms, the way that size and density of population accentuated specialization and structural complexity. The unit of analysis was society, but there were principles of an urban sociology embedded in that argument. The structural principles that he laid out in that argument remain useful for thinking about specialization and social integration, and urban space as a special set of conditions in any general discussion of social organization. Given the new emphases and debates in contemporary urban sociology, one may ask how much of the work that has been done since the 1890s is relevant today. It appears that much of the empirical and conceptual work can be usefully employed.

It is difficult to envision a prominent place in the future of urban sociology for the classical tradition that culminated in Chicago school concepts of ecology and urbanism. The models are too narrowly deterministic, too committed to finding causality within the urban arena as a closed system. The respective market-based equilibrium and mass society models upon which each is based are today almost universally perceived as oversimplifications. However, drastic reformulations of both ecology and urbanism approaches remain viable. Warf's study of Brooklyn provides valuable documentation of the local impact of world events. Fischer's (1975, 1984) subcultural urbanism thesis provides insight into the interaction between population size and personal choice in producing a social environment peculiar to the large city. It would be not at all surprising to find renewed interest in his thesis among the proponents of structurationism.

The tradition of local community studies, and the newer tradition of network research, are not made obsolete by either an emphasis on political economy or human agency. Community studies have demonstrated the importance of mutually reinforcing local definitions of urban space, at the same time that they have demonstrated the impact of external structural factors that have caused local sentiments to coalesce into defended communities. The classic studies by Gans ([1962] 1982), Suttles (1968), and Young and Willmott (1957) all demonstrated the tensions between the interests of local residents and outside institutions. Although he remains firm in his view that the spatial dimensions of society are the direct product of class relations and conflict under capitalism, Harvey (1987: 270–1) acknowledges the relevance of considering the way that members of different urban communities construct reality, interpreting the relationship of themselves and their territory to outside forces. He is certain that these constructions will reflect conditions of economic oppression or sociopolitical domination depending on the social class of residents.

As the result of research and conceptual development in the tradition of urban sociology, we have come to recognize that community takes many forms, that it is bound to involve elements of both neighborhood and network. The forms of solidarity that present themselves in the city immediately draw our attention to worldwide and national political and economic events. The communities themselves point to conditions and tensions in Cuba, Haiti, Hong Kong, the states of the former Soviet Union. The petty street corner marijuana dealer appears immediately as an element of the informal economy, restructured opportunities, a fixture of local community, an element of a subcultural network, the complex biographical product of structure and agency.

The work that has been done in the name of urban sociology provides a viable legacy of observation and concepts that have roughly to do with the spatial context of experience, behavior, and social organization. Whether in the future the collective effort to study the larger units of social space will continue to be called urban sociology, or adopt a less precise and more appropriate label, many of the ideas discussed here will provide a structural foundation for its agents to act upon.

Bibliography

Abu-Lughod, Janet L. 1975. "The Legitimacy of Comparisons in Comparative Urban Studies." *Urban Affairs Quarterly* 11: 13–35.

Abu-Lughod, Janet L. 1991. *Changing Cities: Urban Sociology.* New York: Harper Collins.

Aldrich, Howard, and Albert J. Reiss, Jr. 1976. "Continuities in the Study of Ecological Succession: Changes in the Race Composition of Neighborhoods and Their Businesses." *American Journal of Sociology* 81: 846–66.

Aldrich, Howard, Catherine Zimmer, and David McEvoy. 1989. "Continuities in the Study of Ecological Succession: Asian Businesses in Three English Cities." *Social Forces* 67: 920–44.

Alihan, M. 1938. *Social Ecology: A Critical Analysis.* New York: Columbia University Press.

Althusser, Louis. 1970. *For Marx.* New York: Random House.

Althusser, Louis, and Etienne Balibar. 1970. *Reading Capital.* Translated by Ben Brewster. London: NLB.

Amin, Samir. 1976. *Unequal Development: An Essay on the Social Formation of Peripheral Capitalism.* New York: Monthly Review.

Anderson, Elijah. 1990. *Streetwise: Race, Class, and Change in an Urban Community.* Chicago: University of Chicago Press.

Armstrong, Warwick, and T. G. McGee. 1985. *Theatres of Accumulation: Studies in Asian and Latin American Urbanization.* London: Methuen & Co.

Barnes, J. A. 1954. "Class and Committies in a Norwegian Island Parish." *Human Relations* 7:39–58.

Beauregard, Robert A. 1987. "Rediscovering Space, Reinventing Cities: New Debates in Human Geography." *Urban Affairs Quarterly* 23: 161–8.

Begg, Iain G., and Gordon C. Cameron. 1988. "High Technology Location and the Urban Areas of Great Britain." *Urban Studies* 25: 361–79.

Bensman, David, and Roberta Lynch. 1987. *Rusted Dreams: Hard Times in a Steel Community.* New York: McGraw-Hill.

Berger, Peter, Brigitte Berger, and Hansfried Kellner. 1973. *The Homeless Mind: Modernization and Consciousness.* New York: Random House.

Berry, Brian J. L. 1988. "Symposium [on] Human Ecology: A Theoretical Essay by Amos H. Hawley." *Contemporary Sociology* 17: 137–9.

Bing, León. 1991. *Do or Die.* New York: Harper Collins.

Blau, Peter. 1982. "Structural Sociology and Network Analysis: An Overview." In Peter V. Marsden and Nan Lin (eds.), *Social Structure and Network Analysis,* 273–9. Beverly Hills, Calif.: Sage.

Bluestone, Barry, and Bennett Harrison. 1982. *The Deindustrialization of America: Plant Closings, Community Abandonment, and the Dismantling of Basic Industry.* New York: Basic.

Bonnett, Aubry W. 1984. "Voluntarism Among West Indian Immigrants." In Vernon Boggs, Gerald Handel, and Sylvia Fava (eds.), *The Apple Sliced: Sociological Studies of New York City,* 118–30. Prospect Heights, Ill.: Waveland Press.

Booth, Charles. 1902–3. *Life and Labour of the People in London.* Vols. 1–17. London: Macmillan Press.

Borukhov, Eli, Yona Ginsberg, and Elai Werczberger. 1979. "The Social Ecology of Tel Aviv: A Study in Factor Analysis." *Urban Affairs Quarterly* 15: 183–205.

Boyte, Harry C. 1980. *The Backyard Revolution: Understanding the New Citizen Movement.* Philadelphia: Temple University Press.

Bradshaw, York W. 1987. "Urbanization and Underdevelopment: A Global Study of Urbanization, Global Bias, and Economic Dependency." *American Sociological Review* 52: 224–39.

Bunster, Ximena. 1985. "Maria." In Ximena Bunster and Elsa M. Cheney (eds.), *Sellers and Servants: Working Women in Lima, Peru,* 81–131. New York: Praeger.

Burgess, Ernest W. 1925. "The Growth of the City: An Introduction to a Research Project." In Robert E. Park and Ernest W. Burgess (eds.), *The City,* 47–62. Chicago: University of Chicago Press.

Burns, Leland S. 1986. "Urban Growth and Decline as a Force in Regional Development: Issues and a Research Agenda." In Leo Van den Berg, Leland S. Burns, and Leo H. Klaassen (eds.), *Spatial Cycles,* 253–66. Brookfield, Vt.: Gower Publishing Company.

Burt, Ronald S. 1983. "A Note on Inferences Concerning Network Subgroups." In Ronald S. Burt and Michael J. Minor (eds.), *Applied Network Analysis: A Methodological Introduction,* 283–301. Beverly Hills, Calif.: Sage.

Cadwallader, Martin. 1988. "Urban Geography and Social Theory." *Urban Geography* 9: 227–51.

Campbell, Karen E., and Barrett A. Lee. 1992. "Sources of Personal Neighborhood Networks: Social Integration, Need, or Time." *Social Forces* 70: 1,077–100.

Campbell, Karen E., Peter V. Marsden, and Jean S. Hurlbert. 1986. "Social Resources and Socioeconomic Status." *Social Networks* 8: 97–117.

Canavan, Peter. 1984. "The Gay Community at Jacob Riis Park." In Vernon Boggs, Gerald Handel, and Sylvia Fava (eds.), *The Apple Sliced: Sociological Studies of New York City,* 67–82. Prospect Heights, Ill.: Waveland Press.

Castells, Manuel. 1976a. "Theory and Ideology in Urban Sociology." In C. G. Pickvance (ed.), *Urban Sociology: Critical Essays,* 60–84. New York: St. Martin's.

1976b. "Is There an Urban Sociology?" In C. G. Pickvance (ed.), *Urban Sociology: Critical Essays,* 33–59. New York: St. Martin's.

1977. *The Urban Question: A Marxist Approach.* Translated by Alan Sheridan. London: Edward Arnold.

1983. *The City and the Grassroots.* Berkeley and Los Angeles: University of California Press.

Castells, Manuel, and Alejandro Portes. 1989. "World Underneath: Origins, Dynamics, and Effects of the Informal Economy." In Alejandro Portes, Manuel Castells, and Lauren A. Benton (eds.), *The Informal Economy: Studies in Advanced and Less Developed Countries,* 11–37. Baltimore: Johns Hopkins University Press.

Castells, Manuel, and John Hull Mollenkopf. 1991. *Dual City: Restructuring New York.* New York: Russell Sage Foundation.

Chase-Dunn, Christopher K. 1985. "The System of World Cities, A.D. 800–1975." In Michael Timberlake (ed.), *Urbanization in the World Economy,* 269–92. Orlando, Fla.: Academic Press.

Checkoway, Barry, and Carl V. Patton. 1985. "The Metropolitan Midwestern Perspective." In Barry Checkoway and Carl V. Patton (eds.), *The Metropolitan Midwest: Policy, Problems, and Prospects for Change,* 1–28. Urbana: University of Illinois Press.

Cheshire, Paul, and Dennis Hay. 1986. "The Development of the European System, 1971–1981." In Hans-Jurgen Ewers, John B. Goddard, and Horst Matzerath (eds.), *The Future of the Metropolis: Berlin, Paris, London, New York,* 149–69. Berlin: Walter de Gruyter.

Chickering, A. Lawrence, and Mohamed Salahdine. 1991. "Introduction." In Lawrence A. Chickering and Mohamed Salahdine (eds.), *The Silent Revolution: The Informal Sector in Five Asian and Near-Eastern Countries,* 1–14. San Francisco: International Center for Economic Growth, ICS Press.

Clark, W. A. V. 1988. "Definitive Theories or Alternative Perspectives: Comments on Urban Geography and Social Theory." *Urban Geography* 9: 252–4.

Cohen, Albert K. 1955. *Delinquent Boys.* New York: Free Press.

Connor, J. 1986. "Australian Urban Dynamics." In J. H. P. Paelinck (ed.), *Human Behavior in Geographical Space,* 211–63. Aldershot, Hants, England: Gower Publishing Company.

Cox, Kevin R. 1988. "Urban Social Movements and Neighborhood Conflicts: Mobilization and Structuration." *Urban Geography* 8: 416–28.

Craven, P., and Barry Wellman. 1973. "The Network City." *Social Inquiry* 43: 57–8.

Crenshaw, Edward, and Craig St. John. 1989. "The Organizationally Dependent Community: A Comparative Study of Neighborhood Attachment." *Urban Affairs Quarterly* 24: 412–34.

Crist, Raymond E. 1989. "Export Agriculture and the Expansion of Urban Slum Areas." *American Journal of Economics and Sociology* 48: 143–9.

De Soto, Hernando. 1989. *The Other Path: The Invisible Revolution in the Third World.* New York: Harper & Row.

Duncan, Otis Dudley. 1959. "Human Ecology and Population Studies." In

Philip M. Hauser and Otis Dudley Duncan (eds.), *The Study of Population: An Inventory and Appraisal*, 678–716. Chicago: University of Chicago Press.

Durkheim, Emile. [1893] 1933. *The Division of Labor in Society*. Translated by George Simpson. New York: Free Press.

Eberstein, Isaac W., J. Michael Wrigley, and William J. Serow. 1985. "An Examination of the Utility of Ecological and Economic Base Approaches to Regional Structures." *Social Science Quarterly* 66: 34–49.

Engels, Fredrick. [1845] 1970. "Early Slum Conditions: Manchester in 1844." In A. R. Desai and S. Devadas Pillai (eds.), *Slums and Urbanization*, 24–33. Bombay: Popular Prakashan. Reprint of Fredrick Engels. 1936. *The Condition of the Working Class*. Translated by Florence Kelley Wischnewetsky. London: Unwin Hyman Ltd.

Fainstein, Norman I., and Susan S. Fainstein. 1988. "Governing Regimes and the Political Economy of Development in New York, 1946–1984." In John Hull Mollenkopf (ed.), *Power, Culture, and Place: Essays on New York City*, 161–200. New York: Russell Sage Foundation.

Feagin, Joe R. 1985. "The Social Costs of Houston's Growth: A Sunbelt Boomtown Reexamined." *International Journal of Urban and Regional Studies* 9: 164–85.

1986. "Toward a New Urban Ecology." *Contemporary Sociology* 15: 531–3.

1987. "The Secondary Circuit of Capital: Office Construction in Houston, Texas." *International Journal of Urban and Regional Studies* 11: 172–92.

1990. "Extractive Regions in Developed Countries: A Comparative Analysis of the Oil Capitals, Houston and Aberdeen." *Urban Affairs Quarterly* 25: 591–619.

Fernandez-Kelly, M. Patricia, and Anna M. Garcia. 1989. "Informalization at the Core: Hispanic Women, Homework, and the Advanced Capitalist State." In Alejandro Portes, Manuel Castells, and Lauren A. Benton (eds.), *The Informal Economy: Studies in Advanced and Less Developed Countries*, 247–64. Baltimore: Johns Hopkins University Press.

Fields, Allen B. 1984. "Slinging Weed: The Social Organization of Streetcorner Marijuana Sales." *Urban Life* 13: 247–70.

Firey, Walter. 1945. "Sentiment and Symbolism as Ecological Variables." *American Sociological Review* 10: 140–8.

Fischer, Claude S. 1975. "Toward a Subcultural Theory of Urbanism." *American Journal of Sociology* 80: 1,319–41.

1982. *To Dwell Among Friends: Personal Networks in Town and City*. Chicago: University of Chicago Press.

1984. *The Urban Experience*. Second Edition. New York: Harcourt, Brace, Jovanovich.

Flanagan, William G. 1990. *Urban Sociology: Images and Structure*. Boston: Allyn & Bacon.

1993. "The Structural Roots of Action and the Question of Convergence." Forthcoming in Ray Hutchison (ed.), *Research in Urban Sociology: Volume 3*. Greenwich, Conn.: JAI Press.

Foner, Nancy. 1987. "Introduction: New Immigrants and Changing Patterns in New York City." In Nancy Foner (ed.), *New Immigrants in New York*, 1–33. New York: Columbia University Press.

Frank, Andre Gunder. 1967. *Capitalism and Underdevelopment in Latin America: Historical Studies of Chile and Brazil.* New York: Monthly Review Press.

Frankenberg, Ronald. 1966. *Communities in Britain: Social Life in Town and Country.* Baltimore: Penguin.

Frisbie, W. Parker, and John D. Kasarda. 1988. "Spatial Processes." In Neil J. Smelser (ed.), *Handbook of Sociology*, 629–66. Beverly Hills, Calif.: Sage.

Gale, Dennis E. 1981. "Upward Socioeconomic Transition in Selected OECD Cities." Washington, D.C.: United States Department of Housing and Urban Development.

——— 1984. *Neighborhood Revitalization and the Postindustrial City: A Multinational Perspective.* Lexington, Mass.: Lexington Books.

Galster, George C. 1987. "The Ecology of Racial Discrimination in Housing." *Urban Affairs Quarterly* 23: 84–107.

Gans, Herbert J. 1962. "Urbanism and Suburbanism As Ways of Life: A Reevaluation of Definitions." In Arnold M. Rose (ed.), *Human Behavior and Social Processes: An Interactionist Approach*, 625–48. Boston: Houghton Mifflin.

——— [1962] 1982. *The Urban Villagers.* Updated and expanded edition. New York: Free Press.

——— 1984. "American Urban Theories and Urban Areas: Some Observations of Contemporary Ecological and Marxist Paradigms." In Ivan Szelenyi (ed.), *Cities In Recession: Critical Responses to the Urban Politics of the New Right*, 278–308. Beverly Hills, Calif.: Sage.

Giddens, Anthony. 1981. *A Contemporary Critique of Historical Materialism.* Vol. 1: *Power, Property, and the State.* London: Macmillan Press.

——— 1984. *The Constitution of Society: Outline of the Theory of Structuration.* Cambridge: Polity Press.

——— 1985. *The Nation-State and Violence.* Vol. 2: *A Contemporary Critique of Historical Materialism.* Berkeley and Los Angeles: University of California Press.

——— 1989. "A Reply to My Critics." In David Held and John B. Thompson (eds.), *Social Theory of Modern Societies: Anthony Giddens and His Critics*, 249–310. Cambridge University Press.

Gilbert, Alan. 1992. "The Housing of the Urban Poor." In Alan Gilbert and Josef Gugler (eds.), *Cities, Poverty, and Development: Urbanization in the Third World*, 114–54. Oxford University Press.

Gordon, David M. 1984. "Capitalist Development and the History of American Cities." In William K. Tabb and Larry Sawers (eds.), *Marxism and the Metropolis: New Perspectives in Urban Political Economy*, 21–53. Oxford University Press.

Gottdiener, Mark. 1985. *The Social Production of Urban Space.* Austin: University of Texas Press.

Gottdiener, Mark, and Joe R. Feagin. 1988. "The Paradigm Shift in Urban Sociology." *Urban Affairs Quarterly* 24: 163–87.

Gottman, Jean. 1961. *Megalopolis: The Urbanization of the Northeastern Sea-board of the United States.* New York: The Twentieth Century Fund.

Granovetter, Mark S. 1973. "The Strength of Weak Ties." *American Journal of Sociology* 78: 1,360–80.

1982. "The Strength of Weak Ties: A Network Theory Revisited." In Peter D. Massden and Nan Lin (eds.), *Social Structure and Network Analysis,* 105–30. Beverly Hills, Calif.: Sage.

Greenbaum, Susan D., and Paul E. Greenbaum. 1985. "The Ecology of Social Networks in Four Urban Neighborhoods." *Social Networks* 7: 47–76.

Guest, Avery M., and Barrett A. Lee. 1983. "The Social Organization of Local Areas." *Urban Affairs Quarterly* 19: 217–40.

Gugler, Josef. 1986. "Internal Migration in the Third World." In Michael Paccione (ed.), *Population Geography: Progress and Prospect,* 194–223. London: Croom Helm.

[1982] 1988. "Overurbanization Reconsidered." In Josef Gugler (ed.), *The Urbanization of the Third World,* 74–92. Oxford University Press.

1992a. "The Urban–Rural Interface and Migration." In Alan Gilbert and Josef Gugler (eds.), *Cities, Poverty, and Development: Urbanization in the Third World,* 62–86. Oxford University Press.

1992b. "The Urban Labor Market." In Alan Gilbert and Josef Gugler (eds.), *Cities, Poverty, and Development: Urbanization in the Third World,* 87–113. Oxford University Press.

Gugler, Josef, and William G. Flanagan. 1976. "On the Political Economy of Urbanization in the Third World." *International Journal of Urban and Regional Research* 1: 272–92.

Guldin, Gregory. 1980. "Whose Neighborhood Is This? Ethnicity and Community in Hong Kong." *Urban Anthropology* 9: 243–63.

Guterbock, Thomas. 1990. "The Effect of Snow on Urban Density Patterns." *Environment and Behavior* 22: 358–86.

Hagedorn, John M. 1988. *People and Folks: Gangs, Crime and the Underclass in a Rustbelt City.* Chicago: Lake View Press.

Hall, Peter. 1984. *The World Cities.* Third Edition. New York: St. Martin's.

1986. "National Capitals, World Cities, and the New Division of Labour." In Hans-Jurgen Ewers, John B. Goddard, and Horst Matzerath (eds.), *The Future of the Metropolis: Berlin, Paris, London, New York,* 135–45 Berlin: Walter de Gruyter.

Hall, Peter, and Dennis Hay. 1980. *Growth Centres in the European Urban System.* Berkeley and Los Angeles: University of California Press.

Hankins, F. Martin. 1987. "The Spatial Determinants of Neighborhood Structure: Cleveland, 1930–1980." Paper presented at the Annual Meeting of the American Sociological Association.

Harris, Chauncy D. 1990. "Urban Geography in the United States: My Experience of the Formative Years." *Urban Geography* 11: 403–17.

Harris, Chauncy D., and Edward L. Ullman. 1945. "The Nature of Cities." *The Annals* 242: 7–17.

Harvey, David. 1973. *Social Justice and the City.* Baltimore: Johns Hopkins University Press.

1982. *The Limits to Capital.* Chicago: University of Chicago Press.

1985a. *Consciousness and the Urban Experience.* Baltimore: Johns Hopkins University Press.

1985b. *The Urbanization of Capital.* Baltimore: Johns Hopkins University Press.

1987. "Flexible Accumulation Through Urbanization: Reflections on Post-Modernism in the American City." *Antipode* 19: 260–86.

Hawley, Amos H. 1944. "Ecology and Human Ecology." *Social Forces* 22: 144–51.

1950. *Human Ecology: A Theory of Community Structure.* New York: Ronald.

1981. *Urban Sociology: An Ecological Approach.* Second Edition. New York: Wiley.

1984. "Human Ecological and Marxian Theories." *American Journal of Sociology* 89: 904–17.

1986. *Human Ecology: A Theoretical Essay.* Chicago: University of Chicago Press.

Healey, Patsy, and Susan M. Barrett. 1990. "Structure and Agency in Land and Property Development Processes: Some Ideas for Research." *Urban Studies* 27: 89–104.

Helmes-Hayes, Richard C. 1987. "'A Dualistic Vision': Robert Ezra Park and the Classical Ecological Theory Of Social Inequality." *The Sociological Quarterly* 28: 387–409.

Hicks, Donald A. 1982. "Urban Strengths/Urban Weaknesses." *Society* (March/ April): 11–16.

Hourihan, Kevin. 1978. "Social Areas in Dublin." *Economic and Social Review* 9: 301–18.

Hudson, James R. 1980. "Revitalization of Inner-City Neighborhoods: An Ecological Approach." *Urban Affairs Quarterly* 15: 397–408.

1987. *The Unanticipated City: Loft Conversions in Lower Manhattan.* Amherst: University of Massachusetts Press.

Hummon, David M. 1986. "Urban Views: Popular Perspectives on Urban Life." *Urban Life* 15: 3–36.

Hunter, Albert J., and Gerald D. Suttles. 1972. "The Expanding Community of Limited Liability." In Gerald D. Suttles (ed.), *The Social Construction of Communities,* 44–81. Chicago: University of Chicago Press.

Hurd, Richard. 1924. *Principles of City Land Values.* New York: The Record and Guide.

Ilchman, Warren F., and Norman Thomas Uphoff. 1969. *The Political Economy of Change.* Berkeley and Los Angeles: University of California.

Inkeles, Alex. 1966. "The Modernization of Man." In Myron Weiner (ed.), *Modernization: The Dynamics of Growth,* 138–50. New York: Basic.

Jimenez, Jose Blanes. 1989. "Cocaine, Informality, and the Urban Economy in La Paz, Bolivia." In Alejandro Portes, Manuel Castells, and Lauren A. Benton (eds.), *The Informal Economy: Studies in Advanced and Less Developed Countries,* 135–49. Baltimore: Johns Hopkins University Press.

Jobse, Rein B., and Barrie Needham. 1988. "The Economic Future of the Randstad, Holland." *Urban Studies* 25: 282–96.

Kasarda, John, and Jurgen Friedrichs. 1986. "Economic Transformation, Minorities, and Urban Demographic–Employment Mismatch in the U.S. and West Germany." In Hans-Jurgen Ewers, John B. Goddard, and Horst Matzerath (eds.), *The Future of the Metropolis: Berlin, Paris, London, New York*, 221–49. Berlin: Walter de Gruyter.

Kawashima, Tatsuhiko. 1987. "Is Disurbanization Foreseeable in Japan?" In Leo van den Berg, Leland S. Burns, and Leo H. Klaassen (eds.), *Spatial Cycles*, 100–26. Aldershot, Hants, England: Gower Publishing Company.

Keeble, David. 1986. "The Changing Spatial Structure of Economic Activity and Metropolitan Decline in the United Kingdom." In Hans-Jurgen Ewers, John B. Goddard, and Horst Matzerath (eds.), *The Future of the Metropolis: Berlin, Paris, London, New York*, 171–99. Berlin: Walter de Gruyter.

Kentor, Jeffrey. 1985. "Economic Development and the World Division of Labor." In Michael Timberlake (ed.), *Urbanization in the World Economy*, 25–40. Orlando, Fla.: Academic Press.

King, Anthony D. 1985. "Colonial Cities: Global Pivots of Change," In R. Ross and G. Telkamp (eds.), *Colonial Cities*, 7–32. Dordrecht, Netherlands: Martinus Nijhoff for the Leiden University Press.

　1990. *Urbanism Colonialism, and the World Economy: Cultural and Spatial Foundations of the World Urban System*. London: Routledge & Kegan Paul.

Knight, Richard V. 1986. "The Advanced Industrial Metropolis: A New Type of World City." In Hans-Jurgen Ewers, John B. Goddard, and Horst Matzerath (eds.), *The Future of the Metropolis: Berlin, Paris, London, New York*, 391–436. Berlin: Walter de Gruyter.

Knox, Paul. 1987. *Urban Social Geography: An Introduction*. Second Edition. New York: Wiley.

Kremensek, Slavko. 1983. "On the Fringe of the Town." In Michael Kenny and David I. Kertzer (eds.), *Urban Life in Mediterranean Europe: Anthropological Perspectives*, 282–98. Urbana: University of Illinois Press.

Kwong, Peter. 1987. *The New Chinatown*. New York: Hill & Wang.

LaGory, Mark, and James Nelson. 1978. "An Ecological Analysis of Urban Growth Between 1900 and 1940." *The Sociological Quarterly* 19: 590–603.

Laguerre, Michel S. 1984. *American Odyssey: Haitians in New York City*. Ithaca, N.Y.: Cornell University Press.

Lake, Robert W. 1990. "Urban Fortunes: The Political Economy of Place: A Commentary." *Urban Geography* 11: 179–84.

Law, Robin and Jennifer R. Wolch. 1991. "Homelessness and Economic Restructuring." *Urban Geography* 12: 105–36.

Ledebur, Larry C. 1982. "Fluctuating Fortunes." *Society* (March/April): 20–2.

Lees, Andrew. 1985. *Cities Perceived: Urban Society in European and American Thought, 1820–1940*. New York: Columbia University Press.

Lefebvre, Henri. 1970. *La Révolution urbaine*. Paris: Gallimard.

　1972. *La Pensée marxiste et la ville*. Paris: Casterman.

　1973. *The Survival of Capitalism*. London: Allison & Busby.

1974. *La Production de l'espace.* Paris: Anthropos.

1979. "Space: Social Production and Use Value." In J. Freiberg (ed.), *Critical Sociology: European Perspective.* New York: Irvington Publishers.

Legates, Richard T., and Chester Hartman. 1986. "The Anatomy of Displacement in the United States." In Neil Smith and Peter Williams (eds.), *Gentrification of the City,* 178–200. London: Allen & Unwin.

Leigh, Roger, David North, and Lynn Steinberg. 1986. "Restructuring and Locational Change in London's Electronic Industries." In Hans-Jurgen Ewers, John B. Goddard, and Horst Matzerath (eds.), *The Future of the Metropolis: Berlin, Paris, London, New York,* 251–84. Berlin: Walter de Gruyter.

Lewis, Oscar. 1966a. "The Culture of Poverty." *The Scientific American* 215 (4): 19–25.

1966b. *La Vida: A Puerto Rican Family in the Culture of Poverty.* New York: Random House.

Lipton, Michael. [1977] 1988. "Urban Bias in World Development." In Josef Gugler (ed.), *The Urbanization of the Third World,* 40–51. Oxford University Press.

Lofland, Lyn. [1973] 1985. *A World of Strangers.* Prospect Heights, Ill.: Waveland Press.

Logan, John R., and Reid M. Golden. 1986. "Suburbs and Satellites: Two Decades of Change." *American Sociological Review* 51: 430–7.

Logan, John R., and Harvey L. Molotch. 1987. *Urban Fortunes: The Political Economy of Place.* Berkeley and Los Angeles: University of California Press.

London, Bruce. 1980. *Metropolis and Nation in Thailand: The Political Economy of Uneven Development.* Boulder, Colo.: Westview.

1985. "The City Hinterland Relationship in an International Context: Development as Social Control in Northern Thailand." In Michael Timberlake (ed.), *Urbanization in the World Economy,* 207–30. Orlando, Fla.: Academic Press.

Lowe, Stuart. 1986. *Urban Social Movements: The City After Castells.* London: Macmillan Press.

Lynch, Kevin. 1960. *The Image of the City.* Cambridge, Mass.: MIT Press.

Lyon, Larry. 1987. *The Community in Urban Society.* Chicago: The Dorsey Press.

Marshall, Adriana. 1987. "New Immigrants in New York's Economy." In Nancy Foner (ed.), *New Immigrants in New York,* 79–101. New York: Columbia University Press.

Marston, Sallie A. 1990. "Introduction." *Urban Geography* 11: 176–8.

Marx, Karl. 1967. *Capital.* 3 Vols. New York: International Publishers.

Matthews, Fred H. 1977. *Quest for an American Sociology: Robert E. Park and the Chicago School.* Montreal: McGill Queens University Press.

McKenzie, R. D. 1926. "The Scope of Urban Ecology." In Ernest W. Burgess (ed.), *The Urban Community: Selected Papers from the Proceedings of the American Sociological Society, 1925,* 167–82. Chicago: University of Chicago Press.

1933. *The Metropolitan Community.* New York: McGraw-Hill.

Miller, Walter. 1969. "Lower Class Culture as a Generating Milieu of Gang Delinquency." In Donal R. Cressey and David A. Ward (eds.), *Delinquency, Crime, and Social Progress*, 332–48. New York: Harper & Row.

Mills, C. Wright. 1959. *The Sociological Imagination*. Oxford University Press.

Mitchell, J. Clyde. 1987. "The Components of Strong Ties Among Homeless Women." *Social Networks* 9: 37–47.

Moir, Hazel. 1981. "Occupational Mobility in the Informal Sector in Jakarta." In S. V. Sethuraman (ed.), *The Urban Informal Sector in Developing Countries: Employment Poverty and Environment*, 109–20. Geneva: International Labor Office.

Moore, Joan W. 1991. *Going Down to the Barrio: Homeboys and Homegirls in Change*. Philadelphia: Temple University Press.

Nec, Victor, and Jimy M. Sanders. 1987. "On Testing the Enclave-Economy Hypothesis." *American Sociological Review* 52: 771–3.

Nelson, Kathryn P. 1988. *Gentrification in Distressed Cities: An Assessment of Trends in Intrametropolitan Migration*. Madison: University of Wisconsin Press.

Nelson, Nici. 1988. "How Women and Men Get By: The Sexual Division of Labor in a Nairobi Squatter Settlement." In Josef Gugler (ed.), *The Urbanization of the Third World*, 183–203. Oxford University Press.

Park, Robert E. 1915. "The City: Suggestions for the Investigation of Human Behavior in the City." *American Journal of Sociology* 20: 577–612.

    1926a. "The Urban Community as a Spatial Pattern and a Moral Order." In Ernest W. Burgess (ed.), *The Urban Community: Selected Papers from the Proceedings of the American Sociological Society, 1925*, 3–20. Chicago: University of Chicago Press.

    1926b. "Our Racial Frontier of the Pacific." *Survey* 56: 192–6.

    [1929] 1952. "Sociology, Community, and Society." In Robert E. Park (ed.), *Human Communities: The City and Human Ecology*, 178–209. Glencoe, Ill.: Free Press.

Park, Robert E., and Ernest W. Burgess. 1921. *Introduction to the Science of Sociology*. Chicago: University of Chicago Press.

Parsons, Talcott. 1951. *The Social System*. New York: Free Press.

Peattie, Lisa R. 1975. "'Tertiarization' and Poverty in Latin America." In Wayne A. Cornelius and Felicity M. Trueblood (eds.), *Urbanization and Inequality: The Political Economy of Urban and Rural Development in Latin America*, 109–23. Beverly Hills, Calif.: Sage.

Peil, Margaret. 1981. *Cities and Suburbs: Urban Life in West Africa*. New York: Africana Publishing.

Portes, Alejandro. 1981. "Modes of Structural Incorporation and Present Theories of Immigration." In Mary M. Kritz, Charles B. Kealy, and Sylvano M. Tomasi (eds.), *Global Trends in Migration*, 279–97. Staten Island, N.Y.: CMS Press.

    1985. *Latin Journey: Cuban and Mexican Immigrants in the United States*. Berkeley and Los Angeles: University of California Press.

    1987. "The Social Origins of the Cuban Enclave Economy in Miami." *Sociological Perspectives* 30: 340–72.

Portes, Alejandro, S. Blitzer, and John Curtis. 1986. "The Urban Informal Sector in Paraguay: Its Internal Structure, Characteristics, and Effects." *World Development* 14: 727–41.

Portes, Alejandro, and Lief Jensen. 1987. "What's an Ethnic Enclave? The Case for Conceptual Clarity." *American Sociological Review* 52: 768–71.

Portes, Alejandro, and Saskia Sassen-Koob. 1987. "Making It Underground: Comparative Material on the Informal Sector in Western Market Economies." *American Journal of Sociology* 93: 30–61.

Portz, John. 1990. *The Politics of Plant Closings.* Lawrence: University Press of Kansas.

Prus, Robert. 1987. "Developing Loyalty: Fostering Purchasing Relationships in the Marketplace." *Urban Life* 15: 331–66.

Rees, P. H. 1979. *Residential Patterns in American Cities: 1960.* Research Paper No. 189, Department of Geography, University of Chicago.

Richardson, Harry W. 1984. "National Urban Development Strategies in Developing Countries." In Pradip R. Ghosh (ed.), *Urban Development in the Third World,* 122–48. Westport, Conn.: Greenwood Press.

Robertson, R. 1987. "Globalization Theory and Civilizational Analysis." *Comparative Civilizations Review* 17: 20–30.

1988. "The Sociological Significance of Culture: Some General Considerations." *Theory, Culture, and Society* 5: 3–23.

Rogers, Everett M. 1987. "Progress, Problems, and Progress for Network Research: Investigating Relationships in the Age of Electronic Communication Technologies." *Social Networks* 9: 285–310.

Rostow, Walter W. 1960. *The Stages of Economic Growth: A Non-Communist Manifesto.* Cambridge University Press.

Salahdine, Mohamed. 1991. "The Informal Sector in Morocco: The Failure of Legal Systems?" In Lawrence A. Chickering and Mohamed Salahdine (eds.), *The Silent Revolution: The Informal Sector in Five Asian and Near Eastern Countries,* 15–38. San Francisco: International Center for Economic Growth, ICS Press.

Sanders, Jimy M., and Victor Nee. 1987. "Limits of Ethnic Solidarity in the Enclave Economy." *American Sociological Review* 52: 745–71.

Saunders, Peter. 1981. *Social Theory and the Urban Question.* New York: Holmes & Meyer.

1989. "Space, Urbanism, and the Created Environment." In David Held and John B. Thompson (eds.), *Social Theory and Modern Societies: Anthony Giddens and His Critics,* 215–34. Cambridge University Press.

Savitch, H. V. 1990. "Postindustrialism with a Difference: Global Capitalism in World-Class Cities." In John R. Logan and Todd Swanstrom (eds.), *Beyond the City Limits: Urban Policy and Economic Restructuring in Comparative Perspective,* 150–74. Philadelphia: Temple University Press.

Sawers, Larry. 1984. "New Perspectives on Urban Political Economy." In William R. Tabb and Larry Sawers (eds.), *Marxism and the Metropolis: New Perspectives in Urban Political Economy,* 3–17. Oxford University Press.

Schmandt, Henry J., and George D. Wendell. 1988. "Urban Research 1965–

1987: A Content Analysis of *Urban Affairs Quarterly.*" *Urban Affairs Quarterly* 24: 3–32.

Schwirian, Kent P. 1977. "Internal Structure of the Metropolis." In Kent P. Schwirian et al. (eds.), *Contemporary Topics in Urban Sociology,* 152–215. Morristown, N.J.: General Learning Press.

Schwirian, Kent P., F. Martin Hankins, and Carol A. Ventresca. 1990. "The Residential Decentralization of Social Status Groups in American Metropolitan Communities, 1950–1980." *Social Forces* 68: 1,143–63.

Sethuraman, S. V. 1981. "Summary and Conclusions: Implication for Policy and Action." In S. V. Sethuraman (ed.), *The Urban Informal Sector in Developing Countries: Employment, Poverty, and Environment,* 188–208. Geneva: International Labor Office.

Sheppard, Eric. 1988. "The Search for Flexible Social Theory: Comments on Cadwallader." *Urban Geography* 9: 255–64.

Shevky, Eshref, and Wendell Bell. 1955. *Social Area Analysis: Theory, Illustrative Application and Computational Procedures.* Westport, Conn.: Greenwood Press.

Shevky, Eshref, and Marilyn Williams. 1949. *The Social Area of Los Angeles: Analysis and Typology.* Berkeley and Los Angeles: University of California Press.

Simic, Andrei. 1983. "Urbanization and Modernization in Yugoslavia: Adaptive and Maladaptive Aspects of Traditional Culture." In Michael Kenny and David I. Kertzer (eds.), *Urban Life in Mediterranean Europe: Anthropological Perspectives,* 203–24. Urbana: University of Illinois Press.

Simmel, Georg. [1905] 1950. "The Metropolis and Mental Life." In Kurt H. Wolf (ed.), *The Sociology of Georg Simmel,* 409–24. New York: Free Press.

Slovak, Jeffrey S. 1986. "Attachments in the Nested Community: Evidence from a Case Study." *Urban Affairs Quarterly* 21: 575–97.

Smith, David A., and Bruce London. 1990. "Convergence in World Urbanization: A Quantitative Assessment." *Urban Affairs Quarterly* 25: 574–90.

Smith, David A., and Douglas R. White. 1992. "Structure and Dynamics of the Global Economy: Network Analysis of International Trade 1965–1980." *Social Forces* 70: 857–94.

So, Alvin Y. 1990. *Social Change and Development: Modernization, Dependency, and World-System Theories.* Beverly Hills, Calif.: Sage.

Steffens, Lincoln, 1904. *The Shame of Cities.* Cambridge, Mass.: McClure Phillips.

Storper, Michael, and Richard Walker. 1983. "The Theory of Labor and the Theory of Location." *International Journal of Urban and Regional Research* 7: 1-43.

Suttles, Gerald D. 1968. *The Social Order of the Slum: Ethnicity and Territory in the Inner City.* Chicago: University of Chicago Press.

Szelenyi, Ivan. 1986. "The Last of the Marxist Sociologists?" *Contemporary Sociology* 15: 707–10.

Teaford, Jon C. 1990. *The Rough Road to the Renaissance: Urban Revitalization in America 1940–1985.* Baltimore: Johns Hopkins University Press.

Thompson, John B. 1989. "The Theory of Structuration." In David Held and

John B. Thompson (eds.), *Social Theory of Modern Society: Anthony Giddens and His Critics*, 56–76. Cambridge University Press.

Thrasher, Frederick. [1927] 1963. *The Gang*. Chicago: University of Chicago.

Timberlake, Michael. 1985. "The World System Perspective and Urbanization." In Michael Timberlake (ed.), *Urbanization in the World-Economy*, 3–4. Orlando, Fla.: Academic Press.

Tocqueville, Alexis de. [1835] 1958. *Journeys to England and Ireland*. Translated by G. Lawrence and K. P. Mayer. London.

Todaro, Michael P. [1979] 1984. "Urbanization in Developing Nations: Trends, Prospects, and Policies." In Pradip K. Ghosh (ed.), *Urban Development in the Third World*, 7–26. Westport, Conn.: Greenwood Press.

Tönnies, Ferdinand. (1887) 1940. *Fundamental Concepts of Sociology (Gemeinschaft und Gesellschaft)*. Translated by Charles P. Loomis. New York: American Book Company.

Van den Berg, Leo. 1987. *Urban Systems in a Dynamic Society*. Aldershot, Hants, England: Gower Publishing Company.

Van den Berg, Leo, Roy Drewett, Leo H. Klaassen, Angelo Rossi, and Cornelis H. T. Kijverberg. 1982. *Urban Europe: A Study of Growth and Decline*. Oxford: Pergamon Press.

Vigil, James Diego. 1988. *Barrio Gangs: Street Life and Identity in Southern California*. Austin: University of Texas Press.

Walker, R. 1981. "A Theory of Suburbanization: Capitalism and the Construction of Urban Space in the United States." In M. Dear and A. J. Scott (eds.), *Urbanization and Urban Planning in Capitalist Society*, 383–419. New York: Methuen.

Wallerstein, Immanuel. 1974. *The Modern World System I: Capitalist Agriculture and Origins of the European World-Economy in the Sixteenth Century*. New York: Academic Press.

  1978. "World-System Analysis: Theoretical and Interpretive Issues." In Barbara Hockey Kaplan (ed.), *Social Change in the Capitalist World Economy*, 219–35. Beverly Hills, Calif.: Sage.

  1979. *The Capitalist World Economy*. Cambridge University Press.

  1980. *The Modern World System II: Mercantilism and the Consolidation of the European World-Economy, 1600–1750*. New York: Academic Press.

Walters, Pamela Barnhouse. 1985. "Systems of Cities and Urban Primacy: Problems of Definition and Measurement." In Michael Timberlaker (ed.), *Urbanization in the World-Economy*, 63–85. Orlando, Fla.: Academic Press.

Ward, Kathryn. 1990. "Introduction and Overview." In Kathryn Ward (ed.), *Women Workers and Global Restructuring*, 1–24. Ithaca, N.Y.: Cornell University Press.

Warf, Barney. 1988. "Locality Studies." *Urban Geography* 10: 178–85.

  1990. "The Reconstruction of Social Ecology and Neighborhood Change in Brooklyn." *Environment and Planning D: Society and Space* 8: 73–96.

Waxman, Chaim I. 1983. *The Stigma of Poverty: A Critique of Poverty Theories and Policy*. Second Edition. Elmsford, N.Y.: Pergamon.

Weber, Max. [1905] 1958. *The City*. Translated and edited by Don Martindale and Gertrud Neuwirth. New York: Free Press.

Wellman, Barry, and Barry Leighton. 1979. "Networks, Neighborhoods, and Communities: Approaches to the Study of the Community Question." *Urban Affairs Quarterly* 14: 363–90.

Whyte, William Foote. 1943. *Street Corner Society*. Chicago: University of Chicago Press.

Williams, Peter, and Neil Smith. 1986. "From Renaissance to Restructuring: The Dynamics of Contemporary Urban Development." In Neil Smith and Peter Williams (eds.), *Gentrification of the City*, 204–24. London: Allen & Unwin.

Wilson, Franklin D. 1984. "Urban Ecology: Urbanization and Systems of Cities." *Annual Review of Sociology* 10: 283–307.

Wilson, Kenneth, and Alejandro Portes. 1980. "Immigrant Enclaves: An Analysis of the Labor Market Experience of Cubans in Miami." *American Journal of Sociology* 86: 295–319.

Wilson, Thomas C. 1985. "Urbanism and Tolerance: A Test of Some Hypotheses Drawn from Wirth and Stouffer." *American Sociological Review* 50: 117–23.

    1986. "Community, Population Size, and Social Heterogeneity: An Empirical Test." *American Journal of Sociology* 91: 1,154–69.

    1991. "Urbanism, Migration, and Tolerance: A Reassessment." *American Sociological Review* 56: 117–23.

Wilson, William Julius. 1987. *The Truly Disadvantaged*. Chicago: University of Chicago Press.

Wiseman, Peggy. 1984. *Urban Neighborhoods, Networks, and Families: New Forms for Old Values*. Lexington, Mass.: Heath.

Wirth, Lewis. 1927. *The Ghetto*. Chicago: University of Chicago Press.

    1938. "Urbanism as a Way of Life." *American Journal of Sociology* 4: 1–24.

Wong, Bernard. 1987. "The Chinese: New Immigrants in New York's Chinatown." In Nancy Foner (ed.), *New Immigrants in New York*, 243–71. New York: Columbia University Press.

Young, Michael, and Peter Willmott. 1957. *Family and Kinship in East London*. Baltimore: Penguin.

Zimmer, Basil G. 1988. "Symposium: Human Ecology: A Theoretical Essay by Amos H. Hawley." *Contemporary Sociology* 17: 133–7.

Ziolkowski, Janusz. 1986. "Continuity and Discontinuity in Urban Sociology." *The Polish Sociological Bulletin* 1–2: 5–11.

Zito, Jacqueline M. 1974. "Anonymity and Neighboring in an Urban High-Rise Complex." *Urban Life and Culture* 3: 243–265.

Zukin, Sharon. 1982. *Loft Living: Culture and Capital in Urban Change*. Baltimore: Johns Hopkins University Press.

Index of names

Index of subjects

184

invasion and succession, 48, 50–1, 68, 69, 71, 72, 81
intellectuals and the city, 16–17

Kansas City, 24
Karachi, 109
Key function, 58, 61, 64
Koreatown (New York City), 29

Lima, 132–4
Ljubljana, 34–5
localism, 7, 8–9, 10, 11, 12, 92, 137, 148, 150, 156
London, 2, 18, 76, 77
Los Angeles, 3, 41–3, 96–7, 101
Los Angelesization, 3, 75

Madras, 109
managerialism, 150–2
Manhattanization, 3, 71
Manila, 109
Marxism, 6, 9, 10, 83, 85–7, 90–2, 95, 98, 101–3, 118, 119, 137, 138, 139, 145–7, 151, 153, 154, 156
Mexico City, 109
Miami, 28, 29, 120, 122, 130
Milwaukee, 106, 107
modernization theory, 111, 117, 120, 124

Nairobi, 134
Nashville, 24
neighboring, social relationships, 23–6, 38–9
"new urban sociology," 92, 94, 95, 102, 145, 157
Newark, 25
New York City, 24, 28, 29–33, 70, 74, 158–62

overurbanization, 7, 112–14, 116, 127–9

Paris, 2, 16, 68, 73, 76
Philadelphia, 44, 69, 93

POET, 57
primate city, 113–14, 117, 126–7, 128

Queens (New York City), 30, 32

restructuring, 6, 7, 41, 43, 55, 73, 74, 75, 78–83, 95–7, 104–7, 128, 131, 163, 164
revitalization, *see* gentrification
Rio de Janeiro, 109

San Francisco, 28, 29, 35, 37, 142
São Paulo, 109
Seattle, 25
Seoul, 109, 110
social area analysis, 52, 53
social movements, 4, 11, 98–100, 154
social network, 5, 21, 22, 26–7, 38, 39
street gangs, 8, 40–4, 106–7
structural determinism, 10
structuration, 139–41, 144, 145, 148, 150, 153, 154, 155–7, 165
subcultural theory of urbanism, 20, 36, 37, 145, 148, 165

technology and urban change, 2, 45, 50, 57, 58, 61–5, 66, 67, 71, 77, 78, 82, 96, 105, 116, 123, 126, 127
Tel Aviv, 54

urbanism, 4, 5, 9, 13, 17–18, 20, 34–7, 53, 87, 122, 139, 145, 150

Vancouver, 122

weak ties, strength of, 22, 38
Westernization, 87, 122
Women
  and neighborhood, 24
  Third World traders, 131–6
  Chinese garment workers in the United States, 31–2
world-system theory, 6, 119 *passim*